Defining Beneficial Ownership

Series on International Taxation

VOLUME 93

Series Editors

Introduction & Contents

The Series on International Taxation deals with a wide variety of topics in the global tax arena. The authors include many of the field's leading experts as well as talented newcomers. Their expert views and incisive commentary have proven highly useful to practitioners and academics alike.

Objective

The volumes published in this series are aimed at offering high-quality analytical information and practical solutions to international tax practitioners.

Readership

Practitioners, academics and policy makers in international tax law.

Frequency of Publication

2-3 new volumes published each year.

The titles published in this series are listed at the end of this volume.

Defining Beneficial Ownership

Implications for Preventing Tax Avoidance and Tax Evasion-Related IFFs in Africa

Siddhesh Rao

Wolters Kluwer

Published by:
Kluwer Law International B.V.
PO Box 316
2400 AH Alphen aan den Rijn
The Netherlands
E-mail: lrs-sales@wolterskluwer.com
Website: www.wolterskluwer.com/en/solutions/kluwerlawinternational

Sold and distributed by:
Wolters Kluwer Legal & Regulatory U.S.
920 Links Avenue
Landisville, PA 17538
United States of America
E-mail: customer.service@wolterskluwer.com

ISBN 978-94-035-4559-2

e-Book: ISBN 978-94-035-4569-1
web-PDF: ISBN 978-94-035-4579-0

Dedicated to my mother

About the Author

The author is a post-doctoral researcher at Copenhagen Business School (CBS) with a Ph.D. in international tax law from Institute for Austrian and International Tax law, WU Vienna. His research focuses on the impact of AI on business and tax administration, as well as policy issues related to financial flows and governance. He has also been involved in capacity-building training for government officials and civil society organizations in Eastern Europe and Africa, sharing knowledge and expertise on international tax law and policy. He has taught at various universities and institutions around the world, and co-authored policy reports for UNCTAD and the World Bank. He was a visiting scholar at Meiji University, Tokyo, Japan.

Table of Contents

List of Abbreviations

AEOI	Automatic Exchange of Information
ATAF	African Tax Administration Forum
AUC	African Union Commission
BEPS	Base Erosion and Profit Shifting
BO	Beneficial Ownership
CJEU	Court of Justice of European Union
CMAATM	Convention on Mutual Administrative Assistance in Tax Matters
CRS	Common Reporting Standard
DAC 1	Directive on Administrative Cooperation 1
DAC 2	Directive on Administrative Cooperation 2
DNFBP	Designated Non-Financial Businesses and Professions
EOI	Exchange of Information
EOIR	Exchange of Information on Request
EU	European Union
FATCA	Foreign Account Tax Compliance Act
FATF	Financial Action Task Force
FFIs	Foreign Financial Institution
FSF	Financial Stability Forum
GDP	Gross Domestic Product
ICIJ	International Consortium of Investigative Journalists
IFFs	Illicit Financial Flows
MNEs	Multinational Enterprises
OECD	Organization for Economic Co-operation and Development
SDGs	Sustainable Development Goals
UNCTAD	United Nations Conference on Trade and Development
UNECA	United Nations Economic Commission for Africa

List of Tables

Acknowledgement

The author gratefully acknowledges the support of the Siemens Integrity Initiative and the Carlsberg Foundation through the Rethinking Entrepreneurship in Society project, which enabled further work on this book. Guidance from Prof. Servaas Van Thiel, inspiration from Prof. Michael Lang, advice from Prof. Jeffrey Owens on the tax transparency and corruption project and my supervisor Prof. Georg Kofler were invaluable. The author further acknowledges the support of Prof. Christina Lubinski and Prof. Peter Koerver Schmidt. Without all their support, this book would not have been possible.

CHAPTER 1

Introduction

'Own nothing, but control everything'.

John D. Rockefeller

1.1 BACKGROUND

According to an estimate by the United Nations Conference on Trade and Development (UNCTAD), the African Continent lost 3.7% of its GDP, equivalent to USD 88.6 billion per year, to Illicit Financial Flows (IFFs) between 2013 and 2015.[1] Specifically, Nigeria and South Africa lost USD 42 billion and USD 14.1 billion to IFFs, respectively, in this period.[2] It is estimated that Kenya has lost USD 10.6 billion to IFFs since 1979.[3]

1. UNCTAD, *Economic Development in Africa Report 2020: Tackling Illicit Financial Flows for Sustainable Development in Africa* (United Nations 2020), available at https://unctad.org/system/files/official-document/aldcafrica2020_en.pdf accessed on 13 August 2024; Al Jazeera, *Tax Evasion 'Theft' Robs Africa of $89bn per Year: UN Study* (2020), available at https://www.aljazeera.com/economy/2020/9/28/tax-evasion-theft-rob-africa-of-89-bn-per-year-un-study accessed on 13 August 2024; Deutsche Welle, *Chasing Africa's Tax Dodgers* (2021) available at https://www.dw.com/en/africas-problem-with-tax-avoidance/a-48401574 accessed on 13 August 2024; The Guardian, *Africa Losing Billions from Fraud and Tax Avoidance* (2015) available at https://www.theguardian.com/global-development/2015/feb/02/africa-tax-avoidance-money-laundering-illicit-financial-flows accessed on 13 August 2024; E. van der Does de Willebois et al., *The Puppet Masters: How the Corrupt Use Legal Structures to Hide Stolen Assets and What to Do about It* (World Bank 2011), available at https://star.worldbank.org/sites/star/files/puppetmastersv1.pdf accessed on 13 August 2024; UNCTAD, *Curbing Illicit Financial Flows to Finance Sustainable Development in Africa* (2020), available at https://unctad.org/webflyer/curbing-illicit-financial-flows-finance-sustainable-development-africa accessed on 13 August 2024; UNECA, *Illicit Financial Flows: Report of the High Level Panel on Illicit Financial Flows from Africa*, Addis Ababa, Ethiopia (2015a), available at https://repository.uneca.org/handle/10855/22695 accessed on 21 August 2024.
2. UNCTAD, *Economic Development in Africa Report 2020: Tackling Illicit Financial Flows for Sustainable Development in Africa* (United Nations 2020), available at https://unctad.org/system/files/official-document/aldcafrica2020_en.pdf accessed on 13 August 2024; Vanguard Nigeria,

Preventing IFFs is crucial for securing the necessary public finances for achieving sustainable development goals (SDGs) adopted by the United Nations in 2015. The '2030 Agenda for Sustainable Development' provides a set of seventeen Goals to be achieved by 2030 by developing countries including Goal 16 that aims to promote peace and inclusiveness in society.[4] Subgoal 16.4 focuses on substantially reducing IFFs by 2030.[5] IFFs have been defined in the literature as proceeds from cross-border activities that are illegal including tax evasion in its scope.[6] In addition, tax avoidance

Nigeria Loses $18bn Annually to Illicit Financial Outflows: CISLAC, available at https://www.vanguardngr.com/2021/06/nigeria-loses-18bn-annually-to-illicit-financial-outflows-cislac/ accessed on 13 August 2024.; The ICIR, *Anti-Graft Agencies, CSOs Move to End Illicit Financial Flows in Nigeria,* available at https://www.icirnigeria.org/uk-govt-may-bar-nigerians-accused-of-illicit-financial-flows-money-laundering/ accessed on 13 August 2024; E. van der Does de Willebois et al., *The Puppet Masters: How the Corrupt Use Legal Structures to Hide Stolen Assets and What to Do about It* (World Bank 2011), available at https://star.worldbank.org/sites/star/files/puppetmastersv1.pdf accessed on 13 August 2024; UNCTAD, *Curbing Illicit Financial Flows to Finance Sustainable Development in Africa* (2020), available at https://unctad.org/webflyer/curbing-illicit-financial-flows-finance-sustainable-development-africa accessed on 13 August 2024; UNECA, *Illicit Financial Flows: Report of the High Level Panel on Illicit Financial Flows from Africa,* Addis Ababa, Ethiopia (2015a), available at https://repository.uneca.org/handle/10855/22695 accessed on 21 August 2024; Thisdaylive, *HEDA: Nigeria Loses $18bn to Illicit Financial Flows Annually,* available at https://www.thisdaylive.com/index.php/2021/04/16/heda-nigeria-loses-18bn-to-illicit-financial-flows-annually/ accessed on 13 August 2024.

3. D. Rudich, *Kenya Illicit Finance Risks and Assessment* (The Sentry 2021), available at https://thesentry.org/reports/kenya-illicit-finance/ accessed on 13 August 2024.
4. United Nations, *Sustainable Development Goals,* available at https://www.undp.org/sustainable-development-goals accessed on 13 August 2024; World Bank, *Tackling Illicit Financial Flows: A Toolkit for Policymakers* (2021), available at https://documents.worldbank.org/en/publication/documents-reports/documentdetail/784961468152973030/tackling-illicit-financial-flows-a-toolkit-for-policymakers accessed on 13 August 2024.
5. United Nations, *SDG Goal 16: Promote Peaceful and Inclusive Societies for Sustainable Development, Provide Access to Justice for All and Build Effective, Accountable and Inclusive Institutions at All Levels,* available at https://sdgs.un.org/goals/goal16 accessed on 13 August 2024.
6. B. Schlenther, Addressing Illicit Financial Flows in Africa, *Journal of Financial Crime* 23, no. 4 (2016) https://doi.org/10.1108/jfc-01-2016-0002 accessed 3 September 2025; T.P. Bhusal, Corruption and Illicit Financial Flows in Nepal, *Tribhuvan University Journal* 30, no. 2 (2016) https://doi.org/10.3126/tuj.v30i2.25565 accessed 3 September 2025; M. Thiao, The Effect of Illicit Financial Flows on Government Revenues in the West African Economic and Monetary Union Countries, *Cogent Social Sciences* 7, no. 1 (2021) https://doi.org/10.1080/23311886.2021.1972558 accessed 3 September 2025; N. Akeliwira, Economic and Political Risk Aversions to Illicit Financial Flows: A Rethink of the Portfolio Choice Factors, *Pan African Journal of Governance and Development* 4, no. 1 (2023) https://doi.org/10.46404/panjogov.v4i1.4484 accessed 3 September 2025; H.P.B. Moshi, *Capital Flight and Institutional Frameworks to Promote Transparency,* in S.I. Ajayi and L. Ndikumana (eds), *Capital Flight from Africa: Causes, Effects and Policy Issues,* Oxford: Oxford University Press, Norwegian Agency for Development Cooperation (NORAD) (2014); Global Financial Integrity, *Illicit Financial Flows* (2015), available at https://gfintegrity.org/report/illicit-financial-flows/ accessed on 13 August 2024; World Bank, *Illicit Financial Flows* (2016), available at https://gfintegrity.org/issue/illicit-financial-flows/ accessed on 13 August 2024; UNECA, *Illicit Financial Flows: Report of the High Level Panel on Illicit Financial Flows from Africa,* Addis Ababa, Ethiopia (2015a), available at https://repository.uneca.org/handle/10855/22695 accessed on 21 August 2024; UNCTAD & UNODC, *Conceptual Framework for the Statistical Measurement of Illicit Financial Flows* (2020) available at https://www.unodc.org/documents/data-and-analysis/statistics/IFF/IFF_Conceptual_Framework_for_publication_15Oct.pdf accessed on 13 August 2024.

is also considered IFFs by organizations such as the UNCTAD when assessing IFFs.[7] In order to achieve SDG 16.4, it is essential for African countries to strengthen their enforcement mechanism and introduce policies that curb IFFs.

A key policy for curbing IFFs is implementing a robust definition of beneficial ownership (BO) within the legal framework. It can 'prevent the misuse of legal persons and legal arrangements'.[8] For example, the EU has introduced EU anti-money laundering directive, which aims to combat money laundering (*that includes all forms of IFFs*) and has specific rules for identification of BO; Financial Action Task Force (FATF) completed a full review of its recommendations 24 and 25 with respect to BO of legal persons and legal arrangements which defines BO in a broad manner[9] and the United States has introduced a new law that mandates collecting BO information, including regulations for disclosing the actual beneficial owners of real estate purchased in the US.[10]

This research examines the legal definition of BO of the legal persons and legal arrangements with an aim to prevent IFFs resulting from tax avoidance and evasion in Kenya, Nigeria, and South Africa. These three countries are emerging economies in the African continent and are exposed to significant IFFs. Concerns have been raised about cases of misuse of legal persons and legal arrangements that enable tax avoidance and evasion, corruption and money laundering.[11] This research examines the role of legal

7. Tax avoidance is included in the recently updated statistical Framework for assessing IFFs by UNCTAD, *Economic Development in Africa Report 2020: Tackling Illicit Financial Flows for Sustainable Development in Africa* (United Nations 2020), available at https://unctad.org/system/files/official-document/aldcafrica2020_en.pdf accessed on 13 August 2024.
8. German Federal Government, *G8 Lough Erne German Action Plan*, Germany's Action Plan to prevent the misuse of legal persons and legal arrangements, available at https://www.bundesregierung.de/resource/blob/974430/388980/9bc2bd31db6d650254f566e957385037/g8-lough-erne-deutscher-aktionsplan-data.pdf?download=1 accessed on 23 August 2024.
9. FATF, *FATF Recommendations: International Standards on Combating Money Laundering and the Financing of Terrorism & Proliferation* (FATF 2023), Paris, France, p. 132, available at www.fatf-gafi.org/en/publications/Fatfrecommendations/Fatf-recommendations.html accessed 21 August 2024.
10. Tax Justice Network, *The US Beneficial Ownership Law Has Its Weaknesses, But It's a Seismic Shift*, available at https://taxjustice.net/2021/01/20/the-us-beneficial-ownership-law-has-its-weaknesses-but-its-a-seismic-shift/ accessed on 13 August 2024.
11. M. Walsh-Führing, The Panama Papers: Breaking the Story of How the Rich and Powerful Hide Their Money, *International Affairs* 94, no. 3 (2018) https://doi.org/10.1093/ia/iiy059 accessed 3 September 2025; R. Gordon, Tax Havens and Their Use by United States Taxpayers: An Overview, *Intertax* 9, no. 6/7 (1981) https://doi.org/10.54648/taxi1981050 accessed 3 September 2025; London Summit, *Will Improve Global Tax Transparency*, Anti-Corruption Summit, *London 2016 – Communiqué* (Document submitted by the Government of the United Kingdom, CAC/COSP/IRG/2016/CRP.19, 21 June 2016), at 2-9; J. Christensen, The Hidden Trillions: Secrecy, Corruption, and the Offshore Interface, *Crime Law and Social Change* 57, no. 3 (2012) https://doi.org/10.1007/s10611-011-9347-9 accessed 3 September 2025; FATF, *The Misuse of Corporate Vehicles, Including Trust and Company Service Providers* (FATF 2006), available at https://www.fatf-gafi.org/content/dam/fatf-gafi/reports/Misuse%20of%20Corporate%20Vehicles%20including%20Trusts%20and%20Company%20Services%20Providers.pdf.coredownload.inline.pdf accessed on 13 August 2024; OECD, *Behind the Corporate Veil: Using Corporate Entities for Illicit Purposes* (OECD Publishing 2001), available at https://www.oecd-ilibrary.org/finance-and-investment/behind-the-corporate-veil_9789264195608-en accessed on 13 August 2024; United States Money Laundering Threat Assessment Working Group, *U.S. Money Laundering Threat Assessment* (U.S. Department of the Treasury 2005); United States Government

persons and legal arrangements in concealing BO in Kenya, Nigeria, and South Africa and the legal framework of these countries for BO focusing on the definition of BO in preventing tax-related IFFs.

In recent years, identifying BO has become a top priority for policymakers and international organizations, as it is crucial in the African context due to the loss of tax revenue to IFFs that could be used to finance public expenditure.[12] The aim of this research is to develop a 'good practice' definition of BO and to examine the strengths and weaknesses of the BO concept in the legal framework for preventing tax-related IFFs in Kenya, Nigeria, and South Africa.

This research aims to provide recommendations for policymakers and government officials to develop effective strategies for combating the misuse of legal persons and legal arrangements for preventing tax avoidance and evasion, by strengthening their respective legal frameworks on BO.

1.2 RESEARCH QUESTION

1.2.1 Primary Research Question

This research concerns itself with the following primary research question:

> How can the legal definition of BO of legal persons and arrangements within the legal framework of Kenya, Nigeria, and South Africa be strengthened in order to help prevent tax avoidance and evasion-related IFFs?

Accountability Office, *Report on Company Formations: Minimal Ownership Information is Collected and Available* (GAO 2006), available at https://www.gao.gov/assets/gao-06-376.pdf accessed on 13 August 2024.

12. UNCTAD, *Economic Development in Africa Report 2020: Tackling Illicit Financial Flows for Sustainable Development in Africa* (United Nations 2020), available at https://unctad.org/system/files/official-document/aldcafrica2020_en.pdf accessed on 13 August 2024; P. Gilmour, Lifting the Veil on Beneficial Ownership: Challenges of implementing the UK's registers of beneficial owners, *Journal of Money Laundering Control* 23, no. 4 (2020) https://doi.org/10.1108/jmlc-02-2020-0014 accessed 3 September 2025, available at https://www.emerald.com/insight/content/doi/10.1108/JMLC-02-2020-0014/full/html accessed on 13 August 2024; J. Duri and M. Matasane, Regulation of Beneficial Ownership in South Africa and Zimbabwe, *Journal of Anti-Corruption Law* 1, no. 1 (2023) https://doi.org/10.14426/jacl.v1i1.1315 accessed 3 September 2025; R. Etter-Phoya, E. Danzi and R. Jalipa, Beneficial Ownership Transparency in Africa: The State of Play in 2020, *SSRN Electronic Journal* (2020) https://doi.org/10.2139/ssrn.3640402 accessed 3 September 2025, available at https://papers.ssrn.com/sol3/papers.cfm?abstract_id=3640402 accessed on 13 August 2024; R. Etter-Phoya et al., Beneficial Ownership Transparency in Africa in 2022, *SSRN Electronic Journal* (2023) https://doi.org/10.2139/ssrn.4395017 accessed 3 September 2025, available at https://papers.ssrn.com/sol3/papers.cfm?abstract_id=4395017 accessed on 13 August 2024; N. Akeliwira, Economic and Political Risk Aversions to Illicit Financial Flows: A Rethink of the Portfolio Choice Factors, *Pan African Journal of Governance and Development* 4, no. 1 (2023) https://doi.org/10.46404/panjogov.v4i1.4484 accessed 3 September 2025, available at https://journals.ju.edu.et/index.php/panjogov/article/view/4484/1637 accessed on 13 August 2024.

1.2.2 Sub Research Questions

To address the primary research question, this research would address the following sub-questions:

(a) *What fundamental elements emerge from existing international standards for defining BO?*
(b) *To what extent is the current legal framework for the definition of BO in Kenya, Nigeria and South Africa inconsistent with these elements?*
(c) *What measures could be taken to better align the legal framework for defining BO in Kenya, Nigeria, and South Africa with such principles?*

1.3 METHODOLOGY

This research is based on the primary research conducted under the tax 'transparency and corruption project (2019-2023)'.[13] Focus group calls and three conferences organized under that project resulted in obtaining in-person feedback from participants on their experiences with BO, including country case studies revealing the problems, challenges, and experiences while addressing the issue of BO. Representatives from African countries, civil society organizations, international policy organizations, tax administrations, financial intelligence units and other law enforcement agencies contributed their experiences through case studies and country-specific insights.

The primary objective of this research is to examine the research question from a legal policy discipline with a desk review of the pertinent national and international legislation as well as literature on the legal definition of BO of the legal persons and legal arrangements in Kenya, Nigeria and South Africa. This review will include the relevant laws and regulations on the legal definition of BO of the legal persons and legal arrangements, mutual evaluation reports of the global Forum & FATF, the Tax Justice Network's articles on the legal definition of BO, academic literature from national and international sources, policy briefs of regional civil society organizations and media reports.[14]

This research undertakes a comparative analysis of the legal definition of BO of the legal persons and legal arrangements in Kenya, South Africa, and Nigeria. It is evaluated against the normative framework on BO. This normative framework will be based on the international benchmarks for evaluating the legal definition of BO. The aim of this approach is to identify gaps and provide recommendations to address those gaps in these countries.

---

13. WU Global Tax Policy Center at the Institute for Austrian and International Tax Law, *Tax Transparency and Corruption* (2019-2023), Vienna University of Economics and Business, available at www.wu.ac.at/en/taxlaw/institute/gtpc/current-projects/tax-transparency-and-corruption accessed on 13 August 2024, also *see*: J. Owens and J. Ndubai, *Beneficial Ownership Focus Group, Focus Group Call Summary,* Tax Transparency and Corruption Project (2019-2023), WU Global Tax Policy Centre.
14. Tax Justice Network, *Tax Justice Network Database*, available at https://data.taxjustice.net/home accessed on 13 August 2024.

1.4 STRUCTURE OF THE RESEARCH

To pursue the objectives, the research is divided into six chapters and is structured as follows.

Chapter 1 will outline the research's background, research question, methodology, structure and scope.

Chapter 2 will place the issue into its existing international context. It begins by exploring the size of IFFs as estimated by various international policy organizations such as UNCTAD, World Bank, UNODC, IMF and various civil society organizations such as Tax Justice Network and Oxfam. It fine-tunes these estimates for the reason that there is still no universally accepted definition of IFFs[15] and that the methodologies adopted by these organizations range from estimates based on trade data to estimates based on financial data.[16] It subsequently discusses the different definitions of IFFs that have been used by various international organizations and in the literature. Thereafter, it will relate the term IFFs to the tax area and examine the relationship between tax planning, tax evasion, tax avoidance and aggressive tax planning. In the end, the chapter will set out the reasons why it is necessary to tackle IFFs, in general and more specifically in the African context in the three target countries.

Chapter 3 will explain how transparency is key to tackling tax-related IFFs. For this purpose it will examine the response of governments to tax evasion and avoidance, essentially by pushing the objective of transparency, that is, shining light on all actors involved in IFFs resulting from tax evasion and avoidance, including tax authorities (improving mutual assistance and exchange of information), international financial institutions (ending banking secrecy, FATCA), tax havens (EU and OECD blacklisting), and tax evaders and avoiders themselves (Panama Papers, automatic EOI, prosecution

15. UNCTAD, *Economic Development in Africa Report 2020: Tackling Illicit Financial Flows for Sustainable Development in Africa* (United Nations 2020), available at https://unctad.org/system/files/official-document/aldcafrica2020_en.pdf accessed on 13 August 2024; Global Financial Integrity, *Illicit Financial Flows and Development Indices: 2008-2012* (Global Financial Integrity 2015); World Bank, *The World Bank in Africa* (World Bank 2021), available at https://www.worldbank.org/en/region/afr accessed on 13 August 2024; UNODC, *Estimating Illicit Financial Flows Resulting from Drug Trafficking and Other Transnational Organized Crimes* (UNODC 2011), available at https://www.unodc.org/documents/data-and-analysis/Studies/Illicit_financial_flows_2011_web.pdf accessed on 13 August 2024; IMF, *Regional Economic Outlook: Sub-Saharan Africa* (IMF 2020); Tax Justice Network, *The State of Tax Justice 2020* (Tax Justice Network 2020), available at https://taxjustice.net/wp-content/uploads/2020/11/The_State_of_Tax_Justice_2020_ENGLISH.pdf accessed on 13 August 2024; Oxfam International, *Illicit Financial Flows*, available at https://www.oxfam.org/en/reducing-inequality-what-your-country-doing-tackle-gap-between-rich-and-poor accessed on 13 August 2024; UNECA, *Illicit Financial Flows: Report of the High Level Panel on Illicit Financial Flows from Africa*, Addis Ababa, Ethiopia (2015a), available at https://repository.uneca.org/handle/10855/22695 accessed on 21 August 2024; U.N. Economic Commission for Africa, *Base Erosion and Profit Shifting in Africa: Reforms to Facilitate Improved Taxation of Multinational Enterprises* (U.N. Economic Commission for Africa 2020), available at https://repository.uneca.org/handle/10855/24382 accessed on 21 August 2024.
16. T.P. Bhusal, Corruption and Illicit Financial Flows in Nepal, *Tribhuvan University Journal* 30, no. 2 (2016), 211-224 https://doi.org/10.3126/tuj.v30i2.25565 accessed 3 September 2025, available at https://www.nepjol.info/index.php/TUJ/article/view/25565 accessed on 21 August 2024.

of tax evaders, BEPS, country by country reporting, etc.). In the end, the chapter will set out the reasons why beneficial ownership is a key to tackling misuse of legal persons and legal arrangements.

Chapter 4 will develop a good practice definition of BO against which the national law of the three target countries will be assessed. It will start by reviewing the definition of BO in the area of money laundering (FATF standards), corruption (UN Convention against Corruption and World Bank) and taxation (tax treaties, OECD standards for exchange of financial information in tax matters) and others such as Extractive Industries Transparency Initiative, 2015 G20 principles, Open Ownership and EU 5th AMLD. It will assess the strengths and weaknesses of the definition to extract the positive elements and develop good practices for defining BO.

Chapter 5 will assess and review the current regulatory framework on defining BO in Kenya, Nigeria and South Africa against the normative framework provided in Chapter 4. This chapter will also examine the inconsistencies in the legal framework in these three countries and provide practical advice on possible changes to those legal frameworks.

Chapter 6 will provide a summary of the outcomes and the conclusion, while briefly discussing the impact of the principle of confidentiality, data protection, and taxpayers' rights with a legal framework for BO as a topic for future research.

1.5 DELIMITATIONS

The research does not address other countries where BO could be disguised for tax evasion and avoidance. It also does not imply that all legal persons and legal arrangements are used for illicit purposes, including tax avoidance. Instead, it aims to highlight the misuse of legal persons and arrangements as a tool to disguise BO. The research is limited to Kenya, South Africa and Nigeria as they operate under an English judicial system and are three of the largest economies in Africa. While much of the research on BO to prevent misuse of legal persons and legal arrangements has been focused on the EU,[17] it is essential to note that the African context may differ significantly due to the political environment, extent of corruption and culture. Therefore, adopting the EU approach as the standard against which to measure the legal frameworks for BO in Kenya, South Africa, and Nigeria may not be appropriate in some cases. Additionally, it is challenging to quantify the impact of BO transparency on tax evasion and tax avoidance. The research is limited to the information available in the public domain.

1.6 TERMINOLOGIES

The research uses two terminologies often: BO and BO Transparency. However, there is a distinction between them. The term BO transparency refers to the disclosure of BO

17. The map from the open ownership shows BO Transparency efforts worldwide, and EU countries are most of them all, https://www.openownership.org/en/map/ accessed 3 September 2025.

through public registries.[18] This distinction has been acknowledged by the UNCAC Coalition, which is an international network of civil society organizations. Furthermore, the term BO is often confused with the concept under Articles 10, 11 and 12 of tax treaties. However, both are distinct concepts. The detailed reasons for such distinctions have been elaborated in section 4.4.4.

Furthermore, the terms 'legal persons' and 'legal arrangements' have the same meaning as provided by FATF in its glossary. Legal person refers to 'any entities other than natural persons that can establish a permanent customer relationship with a financial institution or otherwise own property. This can include companies, bodies corporate, foundations, "anstalt," partnerships, or associations and other relevantly similar entities'.[19] 'Legal arrangements refer to express trusts and other similar legal arrangements. Examples of other similar arrangements (for AML/CFT purposes) may include but are not limited to fiducie, certain types of treuhand, fideicomiso and Waqf.'[20]

18. Meaning of BO Transparency by UNCAC coalition, available at https://uncaccoalition.org/learn-more/beneficial-ownership-transparency/ accessed on 13 August 2024.
19. FATF, *FATF Recommendations: International Standards on Combating Money Laundering and the Financing of Terrorism & Proliferation* (FATF 2023), Paris, France, p. 132, available at www.fatf-gafi.org/en/publications/Fatfrecommendations/Fatf-recommendations.html accessed 21 August 2024.
20. *Ibid.*

CHAPTER 2
The Context of the Relationship Between Misuse of Legal Persons and Legal Arrangements and IFFs in Kenya, Nigeria and South Africa

2.1 INTRODUCTION

The previous chapter has explained the key question this research aims to answer, i.e., the role of the legal definition of BO of legal persons and arrangements within the legal framework of Kenya, Nigeria, and South Africa to prevent tax avoidance and evasion related to IFFs. This chapter aims to provide the context of the relationship between misuse of legal persons and legal arrangements and IFFs in the target countries which will be used to demonstrate BO legislation as a solution (Chapter 3). For that purpose, this chapter will review the estimates on the size of IFFs (section 2.2), the definition of IFFs provided in the literature and several international policy organizations (section 2.3), the distinctions between IFFs, tax planning, tax evasion and tax avoidance (section 2.4) and it will highlight why IFFs are a problem (section 2.5).

2.2 ESTIMATES ON THE SIZE OF ILLICIT FINANCIAL FLOWS (IFFs)

To provide context for the research problem, this section highlights the different estimates that have been made over the years regarding the size of IFFs from the African continent and specific African countries. As a note of caution, it should be said that these are rough estimates, because, as we will *see* in the next section, there is no universal definition of IFFs that is used by the different government panels, commissions and international organizations that have addressed the issue.

The 2015 report of the high-level panel on IFFs, led by Thabo Mbeki, mentions that an estimated USD 50 billion is lost in IFFs annually by African countries, and it cites literature that estimated the total amount of IFFs over the period 1960 to 2010 at over USD 1 trillion.[21] Even higher amounts are mentioned in a 2019 report by the African Union Commission, which estimated IFFs from Africa to be USD 50-80 billion per annum, whereas UNCTAD estimated the amount to be USD 88.6 billion per annum.[22] Higher amounts are also mentioned in recent literature, which noted in 2020 that over the past fifty years, African countries have lost more than USD 1.4 trillion to IFFs.[23]

Literature has noted that the total amount lost to IFFs, representing more than 90% of the total GDP of the African Continent and standing at USD 836 billion, is significantly higher than the external debt of USD 770 billion, making the African continent the net debtor to the world.[24] The IFFs significantly burden the African countries compared to the relatively small size of their economies. Countries with natural resources are exposed to significant flight of IFFs. For instance, Kenya is estimated to lose 8.3% of its total GDP, Nigeria is estimated to lose 60% of its financial income annually, and South Africa is estimated to lose one-third of its GDP to IFFs.[25]

21. UNECA, *Illicit Financial Flows: Report of the High Level Panel on Illicit Financial Flows from Africa*, Addis Ababa, Ethiopia (2015a), available at https://repository.uneca.org/handle/10855/22695 accessed on 21 August 2024; African Union, *Agenda 2063: The Africa We Want, African Union Commission*, African Union Commission, 2015, ISBN: 978-92-95104-23-5; J. Duri, Combating Corruption-Related Illicit Financial Flows from Africa: Legal Approaches and Challenges, *African Human Rights Yearbook* 2 (2018), 321-346 https://doi.org/10.29053/2523-1367/2018/v2n1a14 accessed 3 September 2025.
22. African Union Commission (AUC), *Domestic Resource Mobilisation: Fighting Against Corruption and Illicit Financial Flows* (AUC Publishing, Addis Ababa, 2019), available at https://au.int/sites/default/files/documents/37326-doc-k-15353_au_advocacy_brief_brochure_devv3.pdf accessed on 13 August 2024; United Nations Conference on Trade and Development (UNCTAD), *Economic Development in Africa Report 2020: Tackling Illicit Financial Flows for Sustainable Development in Africa* (2020), United Nations, Geneva, Switzerland, available at https://unctad.org/system/files/official-document/aldcafrica2020_en.pdf accessed 3 September 2025; African Union Commission, *Report on Illicit Financial Flows in Africa; Afronomicslaw, Symposium on Illicit Financial Flows (IFF): An Impediment to Africa's Sustainable Development*, available at https://www.afronomicslaw.org/category/analysis/symposium-iff-illicit-financial-flows-impediment-africas-sustainable-0 accessed on 23 August 2024.
23. Landry Signé, Mariama Sow, and Payce Madden, Illicit Financial flows in Africa, Africa Growth Initiative, Policy Brief, Brookings Institute for Africa, March 2020, https://www.brookings.edu/wp-content/uploads/2020/02/Illicit-financial-flows-in-Africa.pdf accessed on 13 August 2024.
24. United Nations Conference on Trade and Development, *Africa Could Gain $89 Billion Annually by Curbing Illicit Financial Flows, U.N. Says*, dated 28 September 2020, available at https://unctad.org/press-material/africa-could-gain-89-billion-annually-curbing-illicit-financial-flows-un-says accessed 3 September 2025; L. Ndikumana and J.K. Boyce, *Capital Flight from Africa: Updated Methodology and New Estimates*, Peri Research Report (2018) available at https://peri.umass.edu/images/CapFlightAfrica-5-28-21.pdf accessed on 13 August 2024, United Nations Economic Commission for Africa (UNECA), *Economic Report on Africa* (2020), available at https://uneca.org/era2020 accessed on 13 August 2024.
25. Africa losing close to Kenya's GDP to illicit financial flows, report, The Star, dated 6 March 2022 https://www.the-star.co.ke/business/kenya/2022-03-06-africa-losing-close-to-kenyas-gdp-to-illicit-financial-flows-report/ accessed 3 September 2025; ICPC decries Nigeria's loss to illicit financial flows, P.M. News, dated 15 November 2020 https://www.vanguardngr.com/2020/11/icpc-decries-nigerias-loss-to-illicit-financial-flows/; UNODC Counters Illicit Financial Flows in Africa, United Nations Office on Drugs and Crime, dated 4 November 2020 https://www.unodc.org/unodc/frontp./2020/November/unodc-counters-illicit-financial-flows-in-africa.html accessed 3 September 2025.

The public finance budgets of African countries pose a unique challenge as most of the debt must be financed through additional taxes or other sources of public finance. In contrast, the funds held in foreign accounts predominantly belong to affluent Africans, surpassing the total public debt. Ndikumana and Boyce have identified a unique phenomenon in that the amount lost through IFFs from African nations exceeds the combined overseas aid and support received from international policy organizations.[26] This indicates that if African countries could halt these illicit outflows, they would no longer require external aid for financial sustenance.

It is crucial to recognize that the estimates indicated above do not include the IFFs arising from tax avoidance as the methodology for estimating IFFs prepared by UNODC only includes 'acts against public revenue provisions' which only covers cases of tax evasion.[27] This suggests that the estimates of IFFs are likely to be even higher in case the numbers from tax avoidance are included in those estimates.

2.3 DEFINITION OF ILLICIT FINANCIAL FLOWS (IFFs)

General

Whereas no universally agreed upon definition of IFFs exists,[28] the World Bank first coined the term in the early 1990s and noted that, while the term had initially been associated with capital flight, it now generally refers to the 'cross-border movement of capital associated with illegal activity or, more explicitly, money that is illegally earned, transferred or used that crosses borders'.[29] This definition has been widely followed by other international actors, which is clear from a policy paper published in 2018 by Maya Forstater, who examines all the existing definitions of IFFs and shows convergence between all the existing definitions.[30]

---

26. UNCTAD, *Economic Development in Africa Report 2020: Tackling Illicit Financial Flows for Sustainable Development in Africa* (United Nations 2020), available at https://unctad.org/system/files/official-document/aldcafrica2020_en.pdf accessed on 13 August 2024.
27. UNCTAD & UNODC, *Conceptual Framework for the Statistical Measurement of Illicit Financial Flows* (2020), available at https://www.unodc.org/documents/data-and-analysis/statistics/IFF/IFF_Conceptual_Framework_for_publication_15Oct.pdf accessed on 13 August 2024.
28. World Bank, *Illicit Financial Flows (IFFs)*, Washington, D.C., USA, available at https://www.worldbank.org/en/topic/financialsector/brief/illicit-financial-flows-iffs accessed on 13 August 2024.
29. The World Bank, *The World Bank Group's Response to Illicit Financial Flows: A Stocktaking*, The World Bank, Washington, D.C., USA, 22 March 2016, at p. 1, para. 1 on Introduction available at https://documents1.worldbank.org/curated/en/502341468179035132/pdf/104568-BR-SecM2016-0112-IDASecM2016-0071-IFC-SecM2016-00423-MIGA-SecM2016-0044-Box394878B-PUBLIC-disclosed-4-5-16.pdf accessed on 13 August 2024; The World Bank, *Illicit Financial Flows*, The World Bank, Washington, D.C., USA, July 2017, available at http://www.worldbank.org/en/topic/financialsector/brief/illicit-financial-flows-iffs accessed on 13 August 2024; J. Duri, Combating Corruption-Related Illicit Financial Flows from Africa: Legal Approaches and Challenges, *African Human Rights Yearbook* 2 (2018), 321-346 https://doi.org/10.29053/2523-1367/2018/v2n1a14 accessed 3 September 2025, available at https://www.ahry.up.ac.za/duri-j accessed on 13 August 2024.
30. M. Forstater, *Illicit Financial Flows, Trade Misinvoicing, and Multinational Tax Avoidance: The Same or Different*? Center for Global Development Policy Paper No. 123 (March 2018), at pp. 5-6,

The table below represents a comprehensive overview of all the existing definitions of IFFs.

Table 2.1 Definition of IFFs (Updated and Adapted from Study on Tax Motivated Illicit Financial Flows, Fostering Change: Tax Motivated Illicit Financial Flows, FCG 2024 Report by the EU Commission)[31]

Year	*Working Definition*	*Source*
2014	'There are various definitions of IFFs, but essentially they are generated by methods, practices and crimes aiming to transfer financial capital out of a country in contravention of national or international laws.'	OECD (2014) IFFs from Developing Countries (p. 16)
2015	'IFFs is defined as any money that is illegally earned, transferred or utilized.'	African Tax Administrators Forum (2015) IFFs and Trade mis invoicing
2015	'Funds crossing borders [that] are illegally earned, transferred, and/or utilized.'	GFI IFFs from Developing Countries: 2004-2013 (2015)
2015	'Money illegally earned, transferred or used.'	High-Level Panel on IFFs from Africa (2015)
2015	'Funds crossing borders that are illegally earned, transferred, and/or utilized.'	Global Financial Integrity (2015)
2016	'IFFs are defined broadly as all cross-border financial transfers, which contravene national or international laws.'	United Nations (2016) Coherent Policies for Combating IFFs

available at https://www.cgdev.org/sites/default/files/illicit-financial-flows-trade-misinvoicing-and-multinational-tax-avoidance.pdf accessed on 13 August 2024; C. Migai, Doctoral thesis, *Illicit Financial Flows, and the Extractive Industries in Africa: A Focus on Transparency and Exchange of Information for Tax Purposes*, at p. 24; Study on Tax Motivated Illicit Financial Flows, *Fostering Change: Tax Motivated Illicit Financial Flows FCG 2024 Report by EU Commission*, at pp. 12-13, available at https://www.eeas.europa.eu/sites/default/files/documents/2024/Study%20on%20Tax.pdf accessed on 13 August 2024.

31. M. Forstater, *Illicit Financial Flows, Trade Misinvoicing, and Multinational Tax Avoidance: The Same or Different*? Center for Global Development Policy Paper No. 123 (March 2018), at pp. 5-6, available at https://www.cgdev.org/sites/default/files/illicit-financial-flows-trade-misinvoicing-and-multinational-tax-avoidance.pdf accessed on 13 August 2024; C. Migai, Doctoral thesis, *Illicit Financial Flows, and the Extractive Industries in Africa: A Focus on Transparency and Exchange of Information for Tax Purposes*, at p. 24; Study on Tax Motivated Illicit Financial Flows, *Fostering Change: Tax Motivated Illicit Financial Flows FCG 2024 Report by EU Commission*, at pp. 12-13, available at https://www.eeas.europa.eu/sites/default/files/documents/2024/Study%20on%20Tax.pdf accessed on 13 August 2024.

Year	*Working Definition*	*Source*
2016	'Generally, refers to cross-border movement of capital associated with illegal activity or more explicitly, money that is illegally earned, transferred or used that crosses borders.'	World Bank (2016) The World Bank Group's response to IFFs: a stocktaking
2016	'There is no agreed definition of the concept of IFFs, but it is generally used to convey three different sources of IFFs: the proceeds of commercial tax evasion, revenues from criminal activities, and public corruption.'	United Nations (2016) World Economic Situation and Prospects 2016
2017	'There are, however, some parameters that members of the Task Force agreed on, namely: i) IFFs constitute money that is illegally earned, transferred or used; and ii) that crosses borders.'	Inter-Agency Task Force on Financing for Development (2017)
2017	'Money illegally earned, transferred, or used that crosses borders.'	World Bank (2017) – IFFs
2020	'IFFs encompass a range of activities that involve the illegal movement of money or capital from one country to another.'	Aziani, A. (2018), IFFs: Conceptual and Operational Issues. In: IFFs. Springer Briefs in Criminology Springer, Cham.
Year unknown	'Illicit [financial] flows include, but are not limited to, cross-border transfers of the proceeds of tax evasion, corruption, trade in contraband goods, and criminal activities such as drug trafficking and counterfeiting.'	United Nations Development Programme (UNDP)
Year unknown	'IFFs are financial flows that are illicit in origin, transfer, or use, reflecting an exchange of value that crosses borders.'	UNODC
2020	'IFFs refer to cross-border transfers of funds that are illegally earned, transferred, or used.'	Irene Musselli and Elisabeth Bürgi Bonanomi, 'IFFs: Concepts and Definition', International Development Policy | Revue internationale de politique de développement [Online], 2020

Year	Working Definition	Source
2020	'The (Oxford) dictionary definition is:' 'forbidden by law, rules or custom. The first three words alone would define "illegal," and this highlights an important feature of any definition IFFs are not necessarily illegal. Flows forbidden by rules or custom may encompass those which are socially and/or morally unacceptable, and not necessarily legally so'.	Estimating IFFs A Critical Guide to the Data, Methodologies, and Findings Alex Cobham and Petr Janský, Oxford University Press

Three main aspects of IFFs emerge from these definitions.[32] A first aspect of IFFs concerns its source. IFFs arise if the act from which the proceeds are generated is illegal, i.e., the source of the income flow is an activity which contravenes legislation, such as tax evasion, criminal activity or corruption.[33] For example, funds generated from drug trafficking, child trafficking, organized crime, the submission of a false return or of falsified information with the aim of evading taxes or customs duties on imports. This 'source' aspect of IFFs is underlined in the above-cited 2016 UN Report on the World Economic Situation and prospects. The question whether IFFs also cover proceeds from activities that are not illegal will be examined in section 2.4.

A second aspect of IFFs concerns the use of the funds, i.e., IFFs arise if the funds are used for illegal activities such as paying for bribery or using funds for the purpose of financing terrorism or criminal activities, which also fall within the scope of IFFs.

A third aspect of IFFs concerns the cross-border transfer, i.e., IFFs arise if the transfer of legally generated funds is made from a country in contravention of the legal framework of that country, for example, a transfer of funds in contravention of foreign exchange and customs legislation. The above-cited OECD definition focuses more on the illegal nature of the transfer, rather than on whether the source through which such funds are generated or if their application to illegal activities falls in that category.[34] This feature of the OECD definition focusing on the illegal nature of the transfer has also been noted by scholars such as Forstater and Migai.[35] As it covers transfers, it

32. For discussion on this *see*: M. Forstater, *Illicit Financial Flows, Trade Misinvoicing, and Multinational Tax Avoidance: The Same or Different?* Center for Global Development Policy Paper No. 123 (March 2018), available at https://www.cgdev.org/sites/default/files/illicit-financial-flows-trade-misinvoicing-and-multinational-tax-avoidance.pdf accessed on 13 August 2024.
33. The World Bank, *The World Bank Group's Response to Illicit Financial Flows: A Stocktaking*, The World Bank, Washington, D.C., USA, 22 March 2016, at p. 1, para. 1 on Introduction available at https://documents1.worldbank.org/curated/en/502341468179035132/pdf/104568-BR-SecM2016-0112-IDASecM2016-0071-IFC-SecM2016-00423-MIGA-SecM2016-0044-Box394878B-PUBLIC-disclosed-4-5-16.pdf accessed 3 September 2025.
34. OECD, *Illicit Financial Flows from Developing Countries* (2014), at p. 16, which states: '*There are various definitions of illicit financial flows, but essentially, they are generated by methods, practices and crimes aiming to transfer financial capital out of a country in contravention of national or international laws*', available at https://www.oecd.org/en/publications/measuring-oecd-responses-to-illicit-financial-flows-from-developing-countries_9789264203501-en.html accessed on 29 August 2024.
35. C. Migai, Doctoral thesis, *Illicit Financial Flows, and the Extractive Industries in Africa: A Focus on Transparency and Exchange of Information for Tax Purposes*, at p. 24.

would also cover in its scope flows from financial activities such as loans or contributions to capital by way of equity, purchases of financial instruments or fixed assets that are in contravention of the law.[36]

Based on the above discussion of the three main criteria of IFFs, i.e., source, use and transfer of cross-border nature – it can be concluded that these criteria are alternative rather than cumulative to be considered IFFs. An activity must only meet one criterion to be classified as IFFs.

From the above definitions of IFFs by various policy actors, it can be discerned that although the precise definitions of IFFs differ, in general, they most often refer in a broad way to all funds that are illegally earned, utilized or transferred across borders. The restrictive definition provided by the OECD, which focuses only on transfer, is outdated as it reflects the situation that existed prior to the global liberalization of capital, when cross-border transfers of money would contravene national foreign exchange legislation. That definition would be insufficient to cover in its scope the funds generated from illicit sources, so that at least a broader definition that covers both source and transfer (as provided by the above-cited UNDP report) would be more adapted to the present-day situation. The author however agrees with the even broader definition as used by most above-cited actors, because this will put countries in a better position to capture all types of IFFs, irrespective of whether the illicit nature stems from the source, the transfer or the use or application of the funds.

2.4 IFFs, TAX PLANNING, TAX EVASION AND TAX AVOIDANCE

From the previous paragraph, it is clear that most actors consider that funds from activities that are illegal, such as crime, corruption or tax evasion, constitute IFFs. This paragraph will address the question to what extent the concept of IFFs should cover not only proceeds from tax evasion activities in the traditional sense, such as submission of false returns or providing falsified information with the aim of evading taxes or customs duties on the imported goods, but also proceeds from tax planning activities that go beyond the acceptable, i.e., aggressive tax planning or tax avoidance activities which, strictly speaking, are legal, but which are undesirable or unethical from a societal point of view.[37]

2.4.1 Tax Planning

Tax planning can be defined as minimizing one's tax liability within the bounds of the law. It is routinely considered perfectly acceptable to structure one's affairs within the

36. M. Forstater, *Illicit Financial Flows, Trade Misinvoicing, and Multinational Tax Avoidance: The Same or Different? CGD Policy Paper* No. 123 (March 2018), at pp. 5-6, available at https://www.cgdev.org/sites/default/files/illicit-financial-flows-trade-misinvoicing-and-multinational-tax-avoidance.pdf accessed on 13 August 2024; UNECA, *A Study on the Global Governance Architecture for Combating Illicit Financial Flows*, Addis Ababa: ECA, April 2018, at p. 2, available at https://repository.uneca.org/handle/10855/24320 accessed on 29 August 2024.
37. Defining Illicit Financial Flows, *CMI, U4 Anti-Corruption Resource Center*, available online at https://www.u4.no/topics/illicit-financial-flows/basics accessed on 29 August 2024.

legal limits. This principle was, for instance, discussed in the case of *Levin v. IRC* (1928), UK, wherein Lord Viscount Summer held that:

> It is trite law that His Majesty's subjects are free, if they can, to make their arrangements so that their cases may fall outside the scope of the taxing Act. They incur no legal penalties, and they, strictly speaking, no moral censure if considering the lines drawn by the legislature for the imposition of taxes makes it their business to walk outside them.[38]

Similarly, in the case of *Duke v. Westminster*, the seminal decision most frequently cited on Tax evasion versus Tax Avoidance, explained tax planning as structuring within the legal boundaries to minimize the tax liability:

> [e]very man is entitled if he can order his affairs so that the tax attaching under the appropriate Act is less than it would be. If he succeeds in ordering them to secure this result, however inappropriate to the Commissioner of Inland Revenue or his fellow taxpayers may be of his ingenuity, he cannot be compelled to pay an increased tax.[39]

Both these decisions demonstrate that a taxpayer can legally structure their tax affairs to limit their tax liability.[40]

2.4.2 Tax Evasion

Tax evasion, however, can be defined as tax minimization activities that include non-compliance with tax law obligations, such as not filing tax returns, not submitting documents, submitting falsified documents, or claiming false deductions. The EU Parliament defines tax evasion as: 'Using illegal practices to avoid paying taxes, for example by not declaring profits or using various ways to avoid paying VAT.'[41]

Tax evasion activities are clearly in contravention of the law and therefore illegal.[42] In contrast to tax evasion, tax planning involves the use of diverse options provided in the tax legislation to minimize the tax burden.

38. UK: *Levene v. Inland Revenue* [1928] UKHL AC 21.
39. UK: *ICR v. Duke of Westminster* [1936] 51 TIR 467.
40. A. Oguttu, *Curbing Offshore Tax Avoidance: The Case of South African Companies and Trusts, University of South Africa*, available at https://uir.unisa.ac.za/handle/10500/1929 accessed on 5 June 2024.
41. European Parliament, *Tax Avoidance versus Tax Evasion: Fiscal Vocabulary Made Easy*.
42. European Commission, *Commission Recommendation of 6.12.2012 on Aggressive Tax Planning*, C(2012) 8806 final, 6 December 2012, available at https://taxation-customs.ec.europa.eu/document/download/995ded83-3321-4935-8b38-db8a2d675e9f_en?filename=c_2012_8806_en.pdf accessed on 5 June 2024; Organization for Economic Cooperation and Development (OECD), *Addressing Base Erosion and Profit Shifting* (2013), at p. 6, available at https://www.oecd.org/en/publications/addressing-base-erosion-and-profit-shifting_9789264192744-en.html accessed on 5 June 2024;, Otto et al., Tax Avoidance, Tax Evasion and Tax Havens, *Arbeit Kammer Wien* (May 2015), at pp. 2-3, available on https://www.arbeiterkammer.at/infopool/wien/Studie_tax_avoidance.pdf accessed on 29 August 2024.

2.4.3 Tax Avoidance

Tax avoidance is traditionally understood as being between the grey area of tax planning and tax evasion. The EU Parliament[43] defines tax avoidance as: *'Using legal instruments in order to pay as little tax as possible, for example by shifting profits to a low-tax country or deducting interest payments for loans with artificially inflated interest rates.'*[44] *(Emphasis added.)*

Examples of tax avoidance include transfer mispricing, tax treaty shopping and hybrid mismatch arrangements. While some countries prosecute the tax avoiders as criminals breaking the law, 'tax avoidance' in principle involves strategies that exploit loopholes in the tax legislation to reduce the tax burden.[45] Often, tax evasion and tax avoidance are confused with one another; however, both have entirely distinct meanings. Some scholars have attempted to make a distinction between tax avoidance and tax evasion based on the type of law applicable in case of non-compliance. For example, Craig Eliff notes that tax avoidance schemes have some standard hallmarks, such as deceit, which may attract criminal law provisions applicable in tax evasion cases.[46] Falsification of facts or documents gravitates more towards tax evasion than avoidance. However, Piccioto presents a different view, arguing that the distinction lies in the penalty law applicable.[47] He argues that if the offence is considered a civil offence, it could be viewed as unlawful tax avoidance. However, if it is viewed as a criminal offence, it could be deemed tax evasion. Cobham from the Tax Justice Network attempts to blur the line between 'Tax evasion' and 'Tax Avoidance' by arguing that non-transparency and loss of revenue needed to finance public budgets are typical in both cases.[48]

A clear line between the concept of 'tax avoidance' and 'tax evasion' should be anchored in law rather than a discussion on the penal consequences or the moral arguments on the loss of revenue to the public treasury which can provide legal certainty – a crucial principle in national and international law.

---

43. European Parliament, *Tax Avoidance Versus Tax Evasion: Fiscal Vocabulary Made Easy.*
44. *Ibid.*
45. D. Meyerowitz, *Meyerowitz on Income Tax*, Cape Town, Taxpayer, 2008, ISBN: 9780981407814, at para. 29.1; K. Huxham and P. Haupt, *Notes on South African Income Tax*, Roggebaai [South Africa], H & H Publications, 2007, ISBN: 9780620378000, at p. 350; section 75 of the South African Income Tax Act 58 of 1962; L. Olivier, Tax Avoidance Options Available to the Commissioner for Inland Revenue, *South African Law Journal* 4 (1997), at 1-3.
46. C. Elliffe, The Thickness of a Prison Wall: When Does Tax Avoidance Become a Criminal Offence? *New Zealand Business Law Quarterly* 17, no. 4 (2011), 441-466, available at https://papers.ssrn.com/sol3/papers.cfm?abstract_id=1992652 accessed on 5 June 2024.
47. S. Piccioto, Illicit Financial Flows and Tax Haven and Offshore Secrecy System, *Tax Justice Network* (2018), at 2, available at https://www.taxjustice.net/2018/02/08/illicit-financial-flows-tax-haven-offshore-secrecy-system/ accessed 3 September 2025.
48. A. Cobham and P. Janský, *Global Distribution of Revenue Loss from Tax Avoidance: Re-estimation and Country Results, WIDER Working Paper Series* wp-2017-55, World Institute for Development Economic Research (UNU-WIDER) (2017), at p. 4, available at https://www.wider.unu.edu/publication/global-distribution-revenue-loss-tax-avoidance accessed on 5 June 2024.

2.4.4 Aggressive Tax Planning

The literature on IFFs lacks a standardized definition of the terms 'tax planning', 'aggressive tax planning' and 'tax avoidance' which can lead to confusion. It is essential to recognize that these categories often overlap, and their classification can be subjective.

The term 'Tax avoidance' has evolved into 'Aggressive Tax Planning'. It is necessary to differentiate the term 'Aggressive Tax Planning' from 'legitimate tax planning'. It refers to cases of tax planning or the use of legal structures by multinational companies and high-income individuals resulting in base erosion and profit shifting (BEPS), whereas 'legitimate tax planning' includes structures adopted by taxpayers that comply with the requirements of the tax law and are entirely legal without any misuse or abuse.

'Aggressive Tax Planning'[49] has been widely criticized and monitored by the OECD. In its 2008 report on the role of tax intermediaries, the OECD defined the term 'Aggressive Tax Planning' as:

> (i) planning that involves a tax position that is tenable but has unintended and unexpected tax revenue consequences and (ii) taking a tax position that is favourable to the taxpayer without openly disclosing that there is uncertainty as to whether significant matters in the tax return accord with the law.[50]

The term 'Aggressive Tax Planning' has also been used in BEPS action plans issued by the OECD in 2013. However, a precise definition has never been established. In its 2012 recommendations addressing aggressive tax planning, the EU Commission characterized it as 'taking advantage of the technicalities of a tax system or mismatches between two or more tax systems to reduce tax liability'.[51]

Countries have also noted the issue and have attempted to define it in their domestic laws. For example, both South Africa and Australia have attempted to define aggressive tax planning while explaining the limits of tax avoidance. The Australian Report on Business Taxation defines any tax planning structure that misuses or abuses the intention of the law as tax avoidance.[52] The South African Revenue Service in 2005 released a discussion paper outlining its position on the tax avoidance structures that

49. *The General report on 2002 IFA Cahiers points out that countries that strictly adhere to private law concept provide more opportunities for tax planning, than countries which adopt purposive approach of interpretation of statutes. On terminology, and national approaches, See*: Form and substance in tax law, International Congress of IFA 2002, Cahiers de droit fiscal international, vol. 87A; Tax treaties and tax avoidance: application of anti-avoidance provisions, International Congress of IFA 2010, Cahiers de droit fiscal international, vol. 95A.
50. Organization for Economic Cooperation and Development (OECD), *Study into the Role of Tax Intermediaries* (OECD Publishing 2008), Paris, France, Glossary, at p. 87, available at https://www.oecd-ilibrary.org/taxation/study-into-the-role-of-tax-intermediaries_9789264041813-en accessed on 5 June 2024.
51. European Commission, Recommendation of 6 December 2012 on Aggressive Tax Planning (2012/772/E.U.) L 338/41, at p. 2, available at https://eur-lex.europa.eu/legal-content/EN/TXT/?uri=celex%3A32012H0772 accessed on 5 June 2024.
52. Australian Government, *Final Report of the Review of Business Taxation: A System Redesigned* (1999), at 6.2(c), available at https://treasury.gov.au/review/review-of-business-taxation accessed on 5 June 2024.

surpass acceptable legal limits.[53] While it is the taxpayer's right to minimize their tax liabilities legally, it is equally important that this right is not abused in a manner that undermines the tax system.[54] Tax evasion and aggressive tax planning are significant issues for many African governments that are striving to secure funds to support their public budgets.[55] They intend to promote tax compliance.[56] However, evidence has

53. South African Revenue Service (SARS), *Discussion Paper on Tax Avoidance and Section 103 of the Income Tax Act, 1962 (Act No. 58 of 1962)* (2005), available at https://www.sars.gov.za/wp-content/uploads/Legal/DiscPapers/LAPD-LPrep-DP-2005-01-Discussion-Paper-Tax-Avoidance-Section-103-of-Income-Tax-Act-1962.pdf?utm_source = rss&utm_medium = rss&utm_campaign = lapd-lprep-dp-2005-01-discussion-paper-tax-avoidance-section-103-of-income-tax-act-1962 accessed on 5 June 2024; L. Steenkamp, Combating Impermissible Tax Avoidance through Efficient Administrative Approaches: What SARS Can Learn from its Canadian Counterpart, *The Comparative and International Law Journal of Southern Africa* 45, no. 2 (July 2012), 227-257, available at https://unisapressjournals.co.za/index.php/CILSA/article/view/11379 accessed on 5 June 2024.
54. Westminster Doctrine, *Oxford*, available at https://www.oxfordreference.com/display/10.1093/oi/authority.20110803121911242 accessed on 5 June 2024; T. Cestnik, *Avoiding Tax Is Okay, but Know the Boundaries, The Globe and Mail*, published 23 May 2019, available at https://www.theglobeandmail.com/investing/personal-finance/taxes/article-avoiding-tax-is-okay-but-know-the-boundaries/ accessed on 5 June 2024; R.W. McGee, The Ethics of Tax Evasion: A Survey of International Business Academics, *SSRN Electronic Journal* (2006) https://doi.org/10.2139/ssrn.803964 accessed 3 September 2025, available at https://papers.ssrn.com/sol3/papers.cfm?abstract_id = 803964 accessed on 5 June 2024.
55. United Nations Conference on Trade and Development (UNCTAD), *Economic Development in Africa Report 2020: Tackling Illicit Financial Flows for Sustainable Development in Africa* (2020), United Nations, Geneva, Switzerland, at p. 182 https://unctad.org/publication/economic-development-africa-report-2020 accessed on 21 August 2024; P. Gilmour, Lifting the Veil on Beneficial Ownership: Challenges of implementing the UK's registers of beneficial owners, *Journal of Money Laundering Control* 23, no. 4 (2020) https://doi.org/10.1108/jmlc-02-2020-0014 accessed 3 September 2025, available at https://www.emerald.com/insight/content/doi/10.1108/JMLC-02-2020-0014/full/html; J. Duri and M. Matasane, Regulation of Beneficial Ownership in South Africa and Zimbabwe, *Journal of Anti-Corruption Law* 1, no. 1 (2023) https://doi.org/10.14426/jacl.v1i1.1315 accessed 3 September 2025; R. Etter-Phoya, E. Danzi and R. Jalipa, Beneficial Ownership Transparency in Africa: The State of Play in 2020, *SSRN Electronic Journal* (2020) https://doi.org/10.2139/ssrn.3640402 accessed 3 September 2025, available at https://papers.ssrn.com/sol3/papers.cfm?abstract_id = 3640402 accessed on 13 August 2024; R. Etter-Phoya et al., Beneficial Ownership Transparency in Africa in 2022, *SSRN Electronic Journal* (2023) https://doi.org/10.2139/ssrn.4395017 accessed 3 September 2025, available at https://papers.ssrn.com/sol3/papers.cfm?abstract_id = 4395017 accessed on 13 August 2024; N. Akeliwira, Economic and Political Risk Aversions to Illicit Financial Flows: A Rethink of the Portfolio Choice Factors, *Pan African Journal of Governance and Development* 4, no. 1 (2023) https://doi.org/10.46404/panjogov.v4i1.4484 accessed 3 September 2025, available at https://journals.ju.edu.et/index.php/panjogov/article/view/4484/1637 accessed on 13 August 2024.
56. W. Abrie and E. Doussy, Tax Compliance Obstacles Encountered by Small and Medium Enterprises in South Africa, *Meditari Accountancy Research* 14, no. 1 (2006), 1-13 https://doi.org/10.1108/10222529200600001 accessed 3 September 2025; A. Adegboye, Taxation, Democracy, and Inequality in Sub-Saharan Africa: Relevant Linkages for Sustainable Development Goals, *Politics & Policy* 51, no. 4 (2023), 696-722 https://doi.org/10.1111/polp.12547 accessed 3 September 2025; M. Bornman and P. Ramutumbu, A Tax Compliance Risk Profile of Guesthouse Owners in Soweto, South Africa, *The Southern African Journal of Entrepreneurship and Small Business Management* 11, no. 1 (2019) https://doi.org/10.4102/sajesbm.v11i1.181 accessed 3 September 2025; E. Maalo, J. Ucieda and J. Mella, Assessing the Information Content of the Auditor General's Report in Voluntary Tax Compliance Decisions in Ghana from the Experts' Perspective, *Studies of Applied Economics* 40, no. 1 (2022) https://doi.org/10.25115/eea.v40i1.7232 accessed 3 September 2025; S. Smulders and G. Naidoo, Addressing the Small Business

shown that some individuals and businesses have engaged in aggressive tax planning practices and a few even in tax evasion. For instance, Panama Paper leaks revealed more than 120 individuals and companies from Nigeria that were using offshore shell companies based in tax havens.[57] Including tax avoidance in the definition of IFFs is crucial to tackling such misuse.

2.4.5 Tax Avoidance and IFFs

Some of the definitions of IFFs cited in Table 2.1 explicitly mention the term tax evasion among the illegal activities that may constitute the source of IFFs, and it is widely accepted that tax evasion gives rise to IFFs because of its illegal nature.[58] However, academic scholars and international policy organizations tracking IFFs are divided on the inclusion of 'tax avoidance' in the scope of IFFs.[59] In its 2018 study, the UN rejects such inclusion on the grounds that tax avoidance means minimizing one's tax liability under the law, which involves using loopholes to structure tax matters so that as little tax as possible is paid.[60] The World Bank, agreeing with that position, states that 'tax avoidance activities, such as legal tax planning and optimization, do not belong to IFFs'.[61]

In contrast, the report of the high-level panel on IFFs from Africa considers that IFFs cover the proceeds from tax avoidance activities on the grounds that tax avoidance goes against 'established rules and norms'.[62] In support of this, Alex Cobham from the Tax Justice Network argues that the term 'Illicit' is distinct from the term 'Illegal'.[63] He uses the Oxford dictionary meaning of the term 'Illicit' to justify his arguments.

Tax Compliance Burden: Evidence from South Africa, *Journal of Economic and Financial Sciences* 6, no. 2 (2013), 263-284 https://doi.org/10.4102/jef.v6i2.260 accessed 3 September 2025.

57. N. Ribadu, *The Impact of Panama Papers on Africa*, at p. 2 https://www.europarl.europa.eu/cmsdata/116489/5%20-%2003%20Ribadu_%20statement.pdf accessed on 21 August 2024.
58. Illicit [financial] flows include, but are not limited to, cross-border transfers of the proceeds of tax evasion, corruption, trade in contraband goods, and criminal activities such as drug trafficking and counterfeiting: Definition of IFF provided by UNDP.
59. United Nations Economic Commission for Africa (UNECA), *Economic Report on Africa* (2017), at p. 35, available at https://www.uneca.org/economic-report-africa-2017 accessed on 21 August 2024.
60. UNECA, *A Study on the Global Governance Architecture for Combating Illicit Financial Flows*, Addis Ababa: ECA, April 2018, at p. 2, available at https://repository.uneca.org/handle/10855/24320 accessed on 29 August 2024, which bases its argument on the case of *ICR v. Duke of Westminster* [1936] 51 TIR 467.
61. The World Bank (2016), *The World Bank Group's Response to Illicit Financial Flows: A Stocktaking*, Washington, D.C. (22 March 2016), at p. 2, para. 2, available at http://documents.worldbank.org/curated/en/502341468179035132/The-World-Bank-Group-s-response-to-illicit-financial-flows-a-stocktaking accessed on 21 August 2024.
62. UNECA, *Illicit Financial Flows: Report of the High Level Panel on Illicit Financial Flows from Africa*, Addis Ababa, Ethiopia (2015a), available at https://repository.uneca.org/handle/10855/22695 accessed on 21 August 2024.
63. A. Cobham, The Significance and Subversion of SDG 16.4: Multinational Tax Avoidance as IFF, *Tax Justice Network* (25 May 2017), available at https://www.un.org/esa/ffd/ffdforum/wp-content/uploads/sites/3/2017/05/ED1-Cobham.pdf accessed on 5 June 2024.

The Oxford Dictionary defines illicit as 'not authorized or allowed; improper, irregular; esp. not sanctioned by law, rule, or custom; unlawful, forbidden'.[64]

Based on its dictionary meaning he concludes that the term illicit has a broader meaning than the meaning of the term 'illegal' and therefore covers tax avoidance in its scope. This argument has been used in Africa by prominent policy organizations, such as the United Nations Economic Commission for Africa (UNECA), the African Union Commission, the African Tax Administration Forum (ATAF) and the African Development Bank, to collectively advocate for inclusion of tax avoidance under the scope of the term IFFs.[65]

There are also other views in the literature which look at the definition of IFFs through a 'developmental approach' rather than a strict legal approach.[66] Pogge and Mehta consider tax avoidance as 'morally wrong' because it has harmful effects on the development of the nation, and therefore, they advocate for it to be considered part of IFFs.[67] In its support, the UN, in its 2019 report, states that 'the harm of base erosion, profit shifting, aggressive tax avoidance and aggressive tax planning due to development, justify considering them illicit flows because they are morally wrong'.[68]

While this 'developmental approach' evaluates the definition of IFFs from an economic necessity point of view, there are also other views in the literature which

64. Oxford English Dictionary, available at https://www.oed.com/dictionary/illicit_adj?tl=true accessed on 5 June 2024.
65. P. Reuters (ed.), *Draining Development? Controlling Flows of Illicit Funds from Developing Countries* (World Bank 2012); *see also* UNCTAD, *Trade and Development Report* (2014); U4, *Combating Illicit Financial Flows: The Role of the International Community*, U4 Expert Answer (2014), available at https://www.u4.no/publications/combating-illicit-financial-flows-the-role-of-the-international-community accessed on 5 June 2024; High-Level Panel on Illicit Financial Flows from Africa (2015); European Parliament, *Report on Tax Avoidance and Tax Evasion as Challenges for Governance, Social Protection and Development in Developing Countries* (2015), available at https://www.europarl.europa.eu/doceo/document/A-8-2015-0184_EN.html accessed on 5 June 2024; C. Aleax and P. Janský, *Background Paper, Illicit Financial Flows: An Overview* (Intergovernmental Group of Experts on Financing for development, 1st session, UNCTAD 2017), available at https://unctad.org/system/files/official-document/tdb_efd1_bp_CJ_en.pdf accessed on 21 August 2024; U.N. Human Rights Council (2016) Final Study on Illicit Financial Flows, Human Rights and the 2030 Agenda for Sustainable Development of the Independent Experts; S. Picciotto, Illicit Financial Flows and the Tax Haven and Offshore Secrecy System, *Tax Justice Network* (2018); ATAF, *The Tax Challenges Arising in Africa from the Digitalisation of the Economy, ATAF Technical Note* – ATAF/CBT/01/19 (2019a); ATAF, *Inclusive Framework Proposals to Address the Tax Challenges Arising in Africa from the Digitalisation of the Economy, ATAF Technical Note* – CBT/02/19 (2019b).
66. EU Commission, *Study on Tax Motivated Illicit Financial Flows*, Fostering Change: Tax Motivated illicit financial flows FCG 2024, p. 15, available at https://www.eeas.europa.eu/sites/default/files/documents/2024/Study%20on%20Tax.pdf accessed on 21 August 2024.
67. Thomas Pogge and Krishen Mehta, *Global Tax Fairness*, Oxford University Press, Oxford, 2016, p. 3.
68. UNECA, *A Study on the Global Governance Architecture for Combating Illicit Financial Flows, Addis Ababa, Ethiopia: ECA* (April 2018a), p.2, available at https://archive.uneca.org/sites/default/files/PublicationFiles/global-governance_eng_rev.pdf accessed on 21 August 2024; UNECA, *Economic Report on Africa 2019: Fiscal Policy for Sustainable Development in Africa*, Addis Ababa, Ethiopia: ECA (2019), p. 125, available at https://repository.uneca.org/handle/10855/41804 accessed on 21 August 2024; and UNECA, *Base Erosion and Profit Shifting in Africa: Reforms to Facilitate Improved Taxation of Multinational Enterprises*, Addis Ababa, Ethiopia: ECA (2018b), https://repository.uneca.org/handle/10855/24382 accessed on 21 August 2024.

adopt a 'political approach' to define IFFs.[69] One such view is given by Cobham from the Tax Justice Network who contends that the 2015 Sustainable Development Goal 16.4 was negotiated with a belief that tax avoidance is part of the definition of IFFs.[70] If tax avoidance is not considered within the scope of the definition of IFFs, then it will lead to a revision of indicators to be met under SDG 16.4, and in particular indicator 17.1 that underscores the need to promote domestic resource mobilization, especially in countries that lack budgetary resources to finance public budgets for collecting tax revenue and other forms of domestic financing.[71] However, Forstater counters this argument by stating that a lack of consensus on the definition of IFFs is a clear indication that tax avoidance was not part of the definition of IFFs while negotiating the SDGs.[72]

For several reasons, the term IFFs should indeed be considered including proceeds from tax avoidance. First, the term 'illicit' indeed goes beyond the term illegal, as illustrated by the dictionary meaning of the term 'Illicit' which not only covers activities that are illegal but also includes those which are against 'customs' such as 'activities which are socially and/or morally unacceptable'.[73] Tax avoidance, though legal, is undesirable and unethical from a societal point of view as it undermines the tax system and deprives countries of much-needed tax revenue which can be used to finance public infrastructure such as schools, roads and hospitals.[74] Second, from an efficiency point of view, a broad definition of IFFs which considers tax avoidance in its scope would provide law enforcement authorities in African countries ability to prosecute and investigate such cases.[75] Therefore, it should be considered

69. Tax Justice Network (2017), *UN Must Defend Target to Curtail Multinational Companies' Tax Abuse,* available: https://www.taxjustice.net/2017/06/23/un-must-defend-target-curtail-multi national-companies-tax-abuse/ accessed on 21 August 2024.
70. A. Cobham and P. Jansky, *Measurement of Illicit Financial Flows: Background Paper Prepared for UNCTAD,* UNODC-UNCTAD Expert Consultation on the SDG Indicator on Illicit Financial Flows, 12-14 December 2017, pp. 1, 5, available at https://www.unodc.org/documents/data-and-analysis/statistics/IFF/Background_paper_B_Measurement_of_Illicit_Financial_Flows_UNCT AD_web.pdf accessed on 21 August 2024.
71. Goal 17: Revitalize the global partnership for sustainable development, United Nations Sustainable Development, United Nations, Department of Economic and Social Affairs, Sustainable Development Goals, A. Cobham, *The Significance and Subversion of SDG 16.4: Multinational Tax Avoidance as IFF,* Tax Justice Network (25 May 2017), p. 4, https://www.un.org/esa/ffd/ ffdforum/wp-content/uploads/sites/3/2017/05/ED1-Cobham.pdf accessed on 21 August 2024.
72. M. Fostater, *Illicit Financial Flows, Trade Misinvoicing, and Multinational Tax Avoidance: The Same or Different?,* CGD Policy Paper No. 123 (March 2018), pp. 7 and 8, https://www.cgdev. org/sites/default/files/illicit-financial-flows-trade-misinvoicing-and-multinational-tax-avoida nce.pdf accessed on 21 August 2024.
73. A. Cobham, *Breaking the Vicious Circles of Illicit Financial Flows, Conflict and Insecurity,* Great Insights magazine 4 February 2016 (2018), https://ecdpm.org/work/prosperity-for-peace-volume-5-issue-1-february-2016/breaking-the-vicious-circles-of-illicit-financial-flows-conflict-and-insecurity accessed on 21 August 2024.
74. Defining Illicit Financial Flows, *CMI, U4 Anti-Corruption Resource Center,* available at https:// www.u4.no/topics/illicit-financial-flows/basics accessed on 29 August 2024.
75. P. Chowla and T. Falcao, *Illicit Financial Flows: Concepts and Scope, Interagency Task Force* (2016), available at https://www.un.org/esa/ffd/wp-content/uploads/2017/02/Illicit-financial -flows-conceptual-paper_FfDO-working-paper.pdf accessed on 21 August 2024. *See also* M. Forstater, *Illicit Financial Flows, Trade Mis invoicing, and Multinational Tax Avoidance: The Same or Different?,* CGD Policy Paper. Washington, D.C.: Center for Global Development (2018),

under the scope of IFFs without any requirement of breach of law. Finally, and with hindsight, The author also agrees with Cobham, because, even though the 2015 SDG 16.4 indicator refers that 'by 2030, significantly reduce illicit financial and arms flows, strengthen the recovery and return of stolen assets and combat all forms of organized crime', and thus not to tax avoidance as part of IFFs, the 2020 Conceptual Framework for the Statistical Measurement of IFFs, which was subsequently adopted by the custodian organizations for SDG 16,[76] explicitly notes that: 'not all IFFs stem from illegal activity. For example, the indicator includes aggressive tax avoidance as an illicit financial flow, as it can be considered detrimental to sustainable development in many countries, even though such activities are generally not illegal'. Similarly, the 2023 UNCTAD Report on tax and customs-related IFFs explicitly refers to aggressive tax avoidance, including transfer mispricing, debt shifting as well as assets and intellectual property shifting.[77]

2.4.6 IFFs, Tax Avoidance and the Use of Legal Vehicles and Arrangements

In the earlier sections, we discussed the scope of IFFs which also includes 'tax avoidance'. It would be worthwhile to also discuss some of the techniques used for 'tax avoidance'. Such techniques include those used by MNEs for profit shifting as well as those used by high-income or high-net-worth individuals for the hiding of income.

The literature has noted numerous tax planning and avoidance strategies available to MNEs for shifting profits across jurisdictions to minimize corporate tax liability.[78] Jánský finds transfer mispricing, utilizing internal debt from entities located in tax havens and shifting profits to jurisdictions with low tax rates as strategies adopted by MNEs for tax avoidance.[79]

pp.7, 9. https://www.cgdev.org/sites/default/files/illicit-financial-flows-trade-misinvoicing-and-multinational-tax-avoidance.pdf accessed on 21 August 2024.

76. UNCTAD & UNODC, *Conceptual Framework for the Statistical Measurement of Illicit Financial Flows* (2020), available at https://www.unodc.org/documents/data-and-analysis/statistics/IFF/IFF_Conceptual_Framework_for_publication_15Oct.pdf accessed on 13 August 2024, The UNODC is the custodian organization for crime related IFF and UNCTAD is the custodian organization for tax- and customs-related IFF, p. 8.
77. UNCTAD, *Statistical Measurement of Tax and Commercial Illicit Financial Flows: Pilot Testing Methodologies for SDG Indicator 16.4.1* (2023), at pp. 8-9 available at https://unctad.org/system/files/official-document/stat2023d1_en.pdf accessed on 21 August 2024.
78. International Monetary Fund (IMF), *Spillovers in International Corporate Taxation, IMF Policy Paper* (IMF, 2014b), Washington, D.C., pp. 25-32, available at https://www.imf.org/external/np/pp/eng/2014/050914.pdf accessed on 21 August 2024.
79. P. Jánský and A. Prats, International Profit-Shifting Out of Developing Countries and the Role of Tax Havens, *Development Policy Review* 33, no. 3 (2015), 271-292, available at https://doi.org/10.1111/dpr.12113 accessed on 21 August 2024, G. Goerdt and W. Eggert, Substitution Across Profit Shifting Methods and the Impact on Thin Capitalization Rules, *International Tax and Public Finance* 29, no. 3 (2021), 581-599 https://doi.org/10.1007/s10797-021-09674-1 accessed on 21 August 2024, J. Garcia-Bernardo and P. Jánský, *Profit Shifting of Multinational Corporations Worldwide* (2021), https://doi.org/10.19088/ictd.2021.005 accessed on 21 August 2024.

One such technique used by MNEs to undertake such strategies is by using shell companies.[80] The OECD defines a shell company as 'that which is formally registered, incorporated, or otherwise legally organized in an economy, but which does not conduct any operations in that economy other than in a pass-through capacity'.[81]

Shell companies are often used to take advantage of anonymity and opacity with the purpose of utilizing them for tax avoidance, money laundering or hiding assets.[82] Hebous and Johannesen,[83] Lejour and van't Riet[84] show the use of shell companies for undertaking transfer mispricing. The FATF also acknowledged the misuse of shell companies for bribery and money laundering.[85] A study in the UK found that, in almost all money laundering schemes perpetrated in the UK, shell companies were used.[86] The OECD has also acknowledged that shell companies are more prone to risk of being used for IFFs than any other legal vehicles. Panama Paper Leaks revealed more than 120 individuals and companies from Nigeria were using offshore shell companies based in tax havens.[87] The African Network of Centers for Investigation which revealed Panama Leak documents related to Africa, noted 'companies in 52 out of 54 African countries' were using such offshore shell companies.[88]

MNEs also use conduit companies that are often used in international tax planning for channelling income such as interest, dividend, royalty or other income to take advantage of the favourable tax rates provided by the double tax treaties or the favourable tax regime existing in the country where the conduit companies are registered. Often, these companies have no substantial economic substance and primarily function as an intermediary. OECD defines a conduit company as an

80. Fraudulent Contracting of Work: Sham Companies (Austria, Estonia and Italy), Euro found 2017, Dublin available on https://www.eurofound.europa.eu/en/publications/2017/fraudulent-contracting-work-sham-companies-austria-estonia-and-italy accessed on 21 August 2024.
81. Chapter 6, Special Entities, *OECD Benchmark Definition of Foreign Direct Investment*, p. 101, available at https://www.oecd-ilibrary.org/special-entities_5km5zb5qf79s.pdf accessed on 21 August 2024.
82. G. Aliprandi, T. Busschots and C. Oliveira, *Mapping the Global Geography of Shell companies* (2023), p. 32, https://www.taxobservatory.eu/publication/mapping-the-global-geography-of-shell-companies/ accessed on 21 August 2024.
83. S. Hebous and N. Johannesen, At Your Service! The Role of Tax Havens in International Trade with Services, *European Economic Review* 135(C) (2021)https://doi.org/10.1016/j.euroecorev.2021.103737 accessed 3 September 2025, available at https://ideas.repec.org/a/eee/eecrev/v135y2021ics0014292121000908.html accessed on 21 August 2024.
84. A. Lejour and M. van't Riet, Disentangling Business- and Tax-Motivated Bilateral Royalty Flows, CPB Discussion Paper (2023), available at https://ideas.repec.org/p/cpb/discus/450.html accessed on 21 August 2024.
85. Financial Action Task Force on Money Laundering, *Report on Non-cooperative Countries and Territories* (14 February 2000), p. 4, https://www.fatf-gafi.org/en/publications/Fatfgeneral/Aboutthenon-cooperativecountriesandterritoriesncctinitiative.html accessed on 21 August 2024.
86. Cabinet Office Performance and Innovation Unit, *Recovering the Proceeds of Crime* (June 2000), available at https://api.parliament.uk/historic-hansard/written-answers/2000/jun/14/criminal-assets accessed on 21 August 2024.
87. N. Ribadu, *The Impact of Panama Papers on Africa*, at p. 2, https://www.europarl.europa.eu/cmsdata/116489/5%20-%2003%20Ribadu_%20statement.pdf accessed on 21 August 2024.
88. *Ibid.*

enterprise 'that obtains or borrows funds, often from unaffiliated enterprises, and remits those funds to its direct investor or another affiliated enterprise'.[89]

There is evidence of use of conduit companies for tax avoidance in Africa.[90] For instance, it was found that a Big Four (one of the four largest global accounting networks in the world: i.e., Deloitte, EY, KPMG, and PwC) was advising on use of a holding company in Mauritius, to reduce withholding tax on dividends in Mozambique to '8% (instead of 20%) and no corporation tax (instead of 32%) through the use of tax treaty and domestic favourable regime in Mauritius'.[91]

The former UN secretary general also called for the stop of the use of conduit companies in Africa for tax avoidance. He stated that: 'The extensive use made by foreign investors of offshore-registered companies operating from jurisdictions with minimal reporting requirements actively facilitates tax evasion. It is all but impossible for Africa's understaffed and poorly resourced revenue authorities to track real profits through the maze of shell companies, holding companies and offshore entities used by investors.'[92]

Literature has also found use of similar techniques for 'tax avoidance' by high-income or high-net-worth individuals.[93] Harrington shows the use of shell companies by high-net-worth individuals for the purposes of hiding assets and tax evasion.[94]

A natural person can control a shell company in various ways such as ownership of companies, through the control of voting rights, the use of nominees, joint ownership of legal vehicles, the use of contracts with the individuals having ownership of assets, controlling the management through appointment and removal of key

89. Chapter 6, Special Entities, *OECD Benchmark Definition of Foreign Direct Investment*, p. 101, available at https://www.oecd-ilibrary.org/special-entities_5km5zb5qf79s.pdf accessed on 21 August 2024.
90. ActionAid, *Deloitte in Africa: Advising Big Businesses on How to Avoid Tax in Some of the World's Poorest Countries*, London (2013), available at https://news.trust.org/item/20131103091909-gqb92/ accessed on 21 August 2024.
91. F. Otto et al., *Tax Avoidance, Tax Evasion and Tax Havens* (May 2015), p. 65, https://www.arbeiterkammer.at/infopool/wien/Studie_tax_avoidance.pdf accessed on 21 August 2024; ActionAid, *Deloitte in Africa: Advising Big Businesses on How to Avoid Tax in Some of the World's Poorest Countries*, London (2013), available at https://news.trust.org/item/20131103091909-gqb92/ accessed on 21 August 2024.
92. K. Annan, *Stop the Plunder of Africa*, New York Times (9 May 2013), available at http://www.nytimes.com/2013/05/10/opinion/global/stop-the-plunder-of-africa.html?_r=0 accessed on 21 August 2024.
93. J.S. Henry, *The Price of Offshore Revisited: New Estimates for Missing Global Private Wealth, Income, Inequality, and Lost Taxes*, Tax Justice Network, London, UK (2012), p. 5, available at https://taxjustice.net/cms/upload/pdf/Price_of_Offshore_Revisited_120722.pdf accessed 21 August 2024; A. Alstadsæter, N. Johannesen and G. Zucman, Tax Evasion and Inequality, *American Economic Review* 109, no. 6 (2019), 2073-2103 https://doi.org/10.1257/aer.20172043 accessed 3 September 2025; M. Fenwick and E. Vermeulen, *Disclosure of Beneficial Ownership after the Panama Papers*, available at https://www.ifc.org/content/dam/ifc/doc/mgrt/focus-14.pdf&ved=2ahUKEwiduITt24iIAxVj3AIHHasdHjsQFnoECBsQAQ&usg=AOvVaw3oQ-lJv7TKmRfgc6FhYqLp accessed 21 August 2024; P. Gilmour, Freeports: Innovative Trading Hubs or Centres for Money Laundering and Tax Evasion? *Journal of Money Laundering Control* 25, no. 1 (2021), 63-71 https://doi.org/10.1108/jmlc-01-2021-0002 accessed 3 September 2025.
94. B. Harrington, Capital Without Borders, Harvard University Press, 2016, available at https://www.hup.harvard.edu/books/9780674244771 accessed 21 August 2024.

decision makers and other methods of controlling the actual ownership of the assets.[95] Multiple layers of legal persons and legal arrangements across different jurisdictions, coupled with inadequate law enforcement and compliance, present significant challenges in identifying the beneficial owners wielding effective control and ownership.[96] This challenge arises due to the need to obtain information from various countries, which results in delayed investigation and prosecution. It also burdens investigative agencies more to obtain crucial information from other countries.

Similarly, trusts have been found to be used for the purposes of tax avoidance.[97] Trust can be used for disguising the ownership of the asset or income with the intent for tax avoidance.[98] The Tax Justice Network estimated that high-net-worth individuals have evaded a sum of USD 21 trillion via offshore trusts.[99] One of the strategies employed by the high-net-worth Individuals for such evasion was using a trust to conceal the disclosure of beneficial owners behind the trust. Trusts are considered an attractive vehicle for tax avoidance as they offer a greater degree of anonymity and weaker regulatory oversight as most jurisdictions still do not require the registration of trusts.

95. Financial Action Task Force (FATF), *Guidance to Beneficial Ownership of Legal Persons (Recommendation 24)* (FATF March 2023), Paris, France; Financial Action Task Force (FATF), available at https://www.fatf-gafi.org/en/publications/Fatfrecommendations/Guidance-Beneficial-Ownership-Legal-Persons.html accessed 21 August 2024.
96. Financial Action Task Force (FATF), *Guidance to Beneficial Ownership of Legal Persons (Recommendation 24)* (FATF March 2023), Paris, France; Financial Action Task Force (FATF), available at https://www.fatf-gafi.org/en/publications/Fatfrecommendations/Guidance-Beneficial-Ownership-Legal-Persons.html accessed 21 August 2024; Global Forum on Transparency and Exchange of Information for Tax Purposes (OECD) and Inter-American Development Bank, *A Beneficial Ownership Implementation Toolkit* (OECD Publishing March 2019), Paris, France, available at https://publications.iadb.org/en/beneficial-ownership-implementation-toolkit accessed 21 August 2024.; Financial Action Task Force (FATF), *The Misuse of Corporate Vehicles, Including Trusts and Company Service Providers* (13 October 2006), available at https://www.fatf-gafi.org/content/dam/fatf-gafi/reports/Misuse%20of%20Corporate%20Vehicles%20including%20Trusts%20and%20Company%20Services%20Providers.pdf.coredownload.inline.pdf accessed on 21 August 2024.
97. Tax Justice Network, *How Do Trusts Work?,* available at https://taxjustice.net/faq/how-do-trusts-work/ accessed 21 August 2024.
98. J. Christensen, The Looting Continues: Tax Havens and Corruption, *Critical Perspectives on International Business* 7, no. 2 (2011), 177-196, available at https://doi.org/10.1108/17422041111128249 accessed 21 August 2024.
99. J.S. Henry, *The Price of Offshore Revisited: New Estimates for Missing Global Private Wealth, Income, Inequality, and Lost Taxes*, Tax Justice Network, London, UK (2012), p. 5, available at https://taxjustice.net/cms/upload/pdf/Price_of_Offshore_Revisited_120722.pdf accessed 21 August 2024; A. Alstadsæter, N. Johannesen and G. Zucman, Tax Evasion and Inequality, *American Economic Review* 109, no. 6 (2019), 2073-2103 https://doi.org/10.1257/aer.20172043 accessed 3 September 2025; M. Fenwick and E. Vermeulen, Disclosure of Beneficial Ownership after the Panama Papers, *SSRN Electronic Journal* (2016) https://doi.org/10.2139/ssrn.2777152 accessed 3 September 2025, available at https://www.ifc.org/content/dam/ifc/doc/mgrt/focus-14.pdf&ved=2ahUKEwiduITt24iIAxVj3AIHHasdHjsQFnoECBsQAQ&usg=AOvVaw3oQ-lJv7TKmRfgc6FhYqLp accessed 21 August 2024; P. Gilmour, Freeports: Innovative Trading Hubs or Centres for Money Laundering and Tax Evasion? *Journal of Money Laundering Control* 25, no. 1 (2021), 63-71 https://doi.org/10.1108/jmlc-01-2021-0002 accessed 3 September 2025; N. Omar, W. Amin and N. Raof, Addressing Offshore Tax Evasion Challenges in the Rising of Digitalization Economy, *Environment-Behaviour Proceedings Journal* 6, no. 18 (2021), 243-248 https://doi.org/10.21834/ebpj.v6i18.3019 accessed 3 September 2025.

Therefore, legal vehicles such as shell companies, conduit companies and legal arrangements such as trusts that offer anonymity, allow avenues for tax avoidance, aggressive tax planning, tax evasion and money laundering through their misuse.[100] The leaks revealed that individuals and MNEs can misuse legal vehicles and legal arrangements for tax avoidance.[101] The anonymity and opacity of legal vehicles also make it challenging for law enforcement agencies such as tax authorities to effectively ensure compliance, as well as to investigate and prosecute non-compliant individuals and entities.

2.5 WHY ILLICIT FINANCIAL FLOWS (IFFs) ARE A PROBLEM

In the previous sections, we discussed the definition of IFFs and the arguments in favour of inclusion of tax avoidance in its scope and how legal vehicles can be misused for the purposes of tax avoidance. In this section, we will discuss why tax avoidance and the resulting IFFs are a problem.

Reuven Avi Yonah argues that employing opaque structures to disguise beneficial ownership to evade taxes or to implement aggressive tax planning schemes hinders the ability of tax authorities to enforce tax compliance, resulting in reduced revenue to finance public budgets and an unfair burden to raise revenue through labour and indirect taxes.[102] It also impedes the tax authority's abilities to investigate and prosecute the actual owners and enforce tax compliance as taxpayers engage in aggressive tax planning strategies or even tax evasion to conceal their identity or BO. It also has another 'corrosive effect'.[103] Kruger and Scholtz state that: 'Most people, at the best of times, dislike paying tax but nothing infuriates them more than the knowledge that others, in like circumstances are honestly and legitimately paying less tax.'[104] It leads to an uneven tax compliance landscape and fosters disrespect towards the tax administration, along with a less serious attitude towards the law.[105] The OECD

100. OECD, *Behind the Corporate Veil, Using Corporate Entities for Illicit Purposes*, p. 25, available at https://www.oecd-ilibrary.org/finance-and-investment/behind-the-corporate-veil_9789264195608-en accessed on 21 August 2024.
101. International Consortium of Investigative Journalists (ICIJ), *Giant Leak of Offshore Financial Records Exposes Global Array of Crime and Corruption* (2016), available at https://www.icij.org/investigations/panama-papers/20160403-panama-papers-global-overview/ accessed on 21 August 2024.
102. R. Avi-Yonah, Globalisation, Tax Competition, and the Fiscal Crisis of the Welfare State, *Harvard Law Review* 113 (2000), 1578 https://doi.org/10.2307/1342445 accessed 3 September 2025.
103. South African Revenue Service (SARS), *Discussion Paper on Tax Avoidance and Section 103 of the Income Tax Act, 1962 (Act No. 58 of 1962)* (2005), available at https://www.sars.gov.za/wp-content/uploads/Legal/DiscPapers/LAPD-LPrep-DP-2005-01-Discussion-Paper-Tax-Avoidance-Section-103-of-Income-Tax-Act-1962.pdf?utm_source = rss&utm_medium = rss&utm_campaign = lapd-lprep-dp-2005-01-discussion-paper-tax-avoidance-section-103-of-income-tax-act-1962 accessed on 5 June 2024.
104. D. Kruger and W. Scholtz, Broomberg on Tax Strategy, 4th ed., Durban: LexisNexis Butterworths, 2003, p. 1.
105. *Ibid.*; H.R. Handler, *Statement on Behalf of the Tax Section, New York State Bar Association, Before the Committee on Finance* (27 April 1999), p. 2, available at https://home.treasury.gov/system/files/131/Report-Corporate-Tax-Shelters-1999.pdf accessed on 21 August 2024.,

also notes this phenomenon in its report on harmful tax competition. It states that tax havens or harmful tax regimes which include tax avoidance 'discourage compliance by all taxpayers'.[106]

Therefore, tax avoidance through IFFs is a moral issue as it pertains to the principle of fairness in tax payments, where some taxpayers pay their fair share of taxes and others do not. To mobilize domestic resources to finance public budgets, countries are required to levy taxes. The situation wherein some taxpayers pay their share of taxes and others do not undermines the morale of tax compliance and leads to additional incidences of tax avoidance. This raises the issue of equality in a tax system.

Apart from the issues of morality and equality, this is also a developmental issue. This is concisely put in a statement by the OECD that says, 'tax avoidance and evasion are economically costly'.[107] Such costs are the outflow of financial resources necessary for funding essential infrastructure projects in the development of Africa. *Ndikumana and Boyce* also express this concern which takes on significant importance as without sufficient funding countries are compelled to seek external aid from international organizations and developed countries, highlighting the importance of retaining these resources within the continent for sustainable growth.[108] Migai points out that IFFs that are comprised of tax avoidance proceeds hinder countries' development by depriving them of the funds to finance public budgets.[109] The OECD also highlights the detrimental impact of IFFs on the development of Africa.[110]

For African countries, literature has noted IFFs to be significant obstacles to their development, depriving them of crucial revenue to finance essential public infrastructure.[111] As discussed in section 1.2, various estimates from international policy

quoted in United States Treasury Department Report on the Problem of Corporate Tax Shelters, U.S. Treasury Department, Washington, D.C., p. 3; United States Treasury Department Report on the Problem of Corporate Tax Shelters, U.S. Treasury Department, Washington, D.C., p. 19.

106. OECD, *Harmful Tax Competition: An Emerging Global Issue* (1998), Paris, para. 30, available at https://www.oecd-ilibrary.org/taxation/harmful-tax-competition_9789264162945-en accessed on 22 August 2024.
107. OECD, *Base Erosion and Profit Shifting (BEPS)*, available at https://www.oecd.org/en/topics/policy-issues/base-erosion-and-profit-shifting-beps.html accessed on 23 August 2024.
108. L. Ndikumana and J.K. Boyce, *Capital Flight from Africa: Updated Methodology and New Estimates* (2018), available at https://peri.umass.edu/images/CapFlightAfrica-5-28-21.pdf accessed on 22 August 2024.
109. C. Migai, *Illicit Financial Flows, and the Extractive Industries in Africa: A Focus on Transparency and Exchange of Information for Tax Purposes*, Doctoral thesis, p. 25.
110. Organization for Economic Cooperation and Development (OECD)/Global Forum, *Tax Transparency in Africa 2021: Africa Initiative Progress Report* (2021), available at https://www.oecd.org/tax/transparency/documents/Tax-Transparency-in-Africa-2021.pdf accessed 21 August 2024.
111. Open Society Foundations, *How Illicit Financial Flows Drain African Economies*, available at https://www.opensocietyfoundations.org/voices/how-illicit-financial-flows-drain-african-economies accessed 21 August 2024. Also Organization for Economic Cooperation and Development (OECD)/Global Forum, *Tax Transparency in Africa 2021: Africa Initiative Progress Report* (2021), available at https://www.oecd.org/tax/transparency/documents/Tax-Transparency-in-Africa-2021.pdf accessed 21 August 2024.

organizations have highlighted the detrimental impact of IFFs on the African Continent.[112] The issue of aggressive tax planning is a pervasive problem confronting numerous countries, mainly in Africa, that are in dire need of funds.[113] A significant amount of IFFs, including tax evasion and other types of IFFs highlighted by various reports yearly, dramatically reduces the funds needed for Africa's development, including critical infrastructure such as education, healthcare, and public transport. The UNCTAD estimates that over USD 89 billion is lost annually across Africa due to corruption, money laundering and tax evasion.[114] In Kenya alone, it is estimated that high-net-worth individuals account for USD 400 million annually in tax evasion.[115] All these estimates indicate significant challenges posed by IFFs in achieving sustainable development goals by undermining the collection of essential funds needed for development in Africa.

2.6 CONCLUDING REMARKS

There is evidence that IFFs result in a significant loss of revenue for African countries that they would otherwise need to finance their public infrastructure. Despite a lack of consensus within the international community regarding the scope of IFFs, discussion in the literature suggests that IFFs are illegal and include tax avoidance in its scope. The primary reason for the prevalence of IFFs is a lack of transparency, which hinders law enforcement agencies from taking appropriate actions. This situation has been exacerbated by bank secrecy and misuse of legal persons and legal arrangements. Coordinated efforts towards enhancing BO legislation can contribute as a solution to prevent misuse of legal persons and legal arrangements. The next chapter will examine coordinated efforts towards enhancing BO legislation that can contribute as a solution to prevent misuse of legal persons and legal arrangements.

112. B. Muchhala, *The Right to Development and Illicit Financial Flows: Realizing the Sustainable Development Goals and Financing for Development, Human Rights Council, Working Group on the Right to Development*, 19th session, Geneva, 23-27 April 2018, available at https://www.ohchr.org/sites/default/files/Documents/Issues/Development/Session19/A_HRC_WG.2_19_CRP_3.docx accessed 21 August 2024.
113. South African Revenue Service, *Discussion Paper on Tax Avoidance*, p. 8, available at https://www.sars.gov.za/wp-content/uploads/Legal/DiscPapers/LAPD-LPrep-DP-2005-01-Discussion-Paper-Tax-Avoidance-Section-103-of-Income-Tax-Act-1962.pdf?utm_source=rss&utm_medium=rss&utm_campaign=lapd-lprep-dp-2005-01-discussion-paper-tax-avoidance-section-103-of-income-tax-act-1962 accessed on 3 September 2025.
114. UNCTAD, *Africa Could Gain $89 Billion Annually by Curbing Illicit Financial Flows* (28 September 2020), available at https://unctad.org/news/africa-could-gain-89-billion-annually-curbing-illicit-financial-flows accessed 21 August 2024; F. Charlier, *Tackling Illicit Financial Flows to Secure Africa's Future, Curb Conflict*, Africa Renewal (February 2021), available at https://www.un.org/africarenewal/magazine/february-2021/tackling-illicit-financial-flows-secure-africas-future-curb-conflict accessed 21 August 2024.
115. Kenya Revenue Authority, *Annual Revenue Performance Report, 2020-2021*, available at https://www.kra.go.ke/news-center/press-release/1299-annual-revenue-performance-fy-2020-2021 accessed on 21 August 2024.

CHAPTER 3

Transparency and Beneficial Ownership Legislation as the Solution to Prevent Misuse of Legal Persons and Legal Arrangements

3.1 INTRODUCTION

From 1980 to 1988, a significant turning point occurred in the economies of countries characterized by the liberalization of trade, the free flow of investments, and the lifting of capital controls.[116] This liberalization has led to a surge in international organized crime and cross-border corruption, increasing IFFs.[117] Such flows are often sent across borders to conceal them initially and then reintegrate them into a legitimate economy – commonly referred to as money laundering. Simultaneously, banking secrecy emerged as a significant concern for policymakers, creating obstacles to criminal prosecution and investigation.[118] This triggered a response from tax authorities along

116. S. Grenfell, Capital Flows and Crises, *Asian-Pacific Economic Literature* 13, no. 2 (1999), 1-15 https://doi.org/10.1111/1467-8411.00059 accessed 3 September 2025; E. Iheanacho, ARLD Approach to Trade Liberalisation and Economic Growth in the Developing Country: Evidence from Nigeria, *African Research Review* 11, no. 2 (2017), 138 https://doi.org/10.4314/afrrev.v11i2.11 accessed 3 September 2025.
117. J. Owens and R. McDonell, *Creating a Better Mechanism to Obtain Beneficial Ownership Information in the International Context*, p. 5, available at https://papers.ssrn.com/sol3/papers.cfm?abstract_id=3161723 accessed on 21 August 2024.
118. J. Christensen, The Hidden Trillions: Secrecy, Corruption, and the Offshore Interface, *Crime Law Soc Change* 57 (2012), 325-343 https://doi.org/10.1007/s10611-011-9347-9 accessed 3 September 2025; R. Halawi, Dirty Money in the Banking Sector, *Journal of Money Laundering Control* 22, no. 3 (2019), 527-542 https://doi.org/10.1108/jmlc-11-2018-0067 accessed 3 September 2025; C. Nguyen, Preventing the Use of Financial Institutions for Money Laundering and the Implications for Financial Privacy, *Journal of Money Laundering Control* 21, no. 1 (2018), 47-58 https://doi.org/10.1108/jmlc-01-2017-0004 accessed 3 September 2025.

different lines, which after a difficult start in the 1990s, accelerated in the new millennium, particularly after the financial crisis of 2008.

This sub-chapter continues to place the research into its context by zooming in on the response of governments to tax evasion and avoidance, essentially by pushing the objective of transparency, that is, shining light on all actors involved in IFFs resulting from tax evasion and avoidance, including tax authorities (improving mutual assistance and exchange of information), international financial institutions (ending banking secrecy, FATCA), tax havens (EU and OECD blacklisting), and tax evaders and avoiders themselves (Panama Papers, automatic EOI, prosecution of tax evaders, BEPS, country by country reporting, etc.).

3.2 EXCHANGE OF INFORMATION AND AN END TO BANKING SECRECY

Literature has noted the '*exchange of information*' (EOI) as a critical policy tool to combat money laundering, tax evasion and other forms of IFFs, as it allows tax authorities access to information that can be used for effective implementation of tax legislation and to balance information asymmetry between the taxpayer and tax authorities.[119] Effective cross-border cooperation between countries results in the use of information received from other countries to assess unpaid taxes and assets. Such cooperation can be facilitated through an EOI network where countries can obtain cross-border information by requesting and providing such information through the legal framework of EOI agreements. A robust network of exchange of information agreements is crucial to ensuring the timely collection of information.

Before we discuss the response of governments to banking secrecy, it is worthwhile to look at the first legal instrument that allowed for the cross-border exchange of tax information,[120] i.e., the 'Convention on Administrative Assistance in Matters of Taxation' drafted by the League of Nations in 1927.[121] It provided for the automatic exchange of information. As neither the US nor the OECD Model expressly provided for the automatic exchange of information under Article 26 of bilateral tax treaties, the

119. M. Keen and J. Ligthart, Incentives and Information Exchange in International Taxation, *International Tax and Public Finance* 13 (2006), 163-180 https://doi.org/10.1007/s10797-006-2316-z accessed 3 September 2025; Global Forum, *Tax Transparency in Africa: Africa Initiative Progress Report 2018* (OECD Publishing 2019a), Paris, pp. 6-7, available at https://www.oecd.org/tax/transparency/documents/africa-initiative-report-2018.pdf accessed 21 August 2024.

120. League of Nations, Art. 1(a) Convention on Administrative Assistance in Matters of Taxation, *Double Taxation and Tax Evasion: Report Presented by the Technical Experts on Double Taxation and Tax Evasion*, 1927.

121. L.U. Cavelti, Automatic Information Exchange Versus the Withholding Tax Regime: Globalization and Increasing Sovereignty Conflicts in International Taxation, *World Tax Journal*, IBFD (June 2013), 177 https://doi.org/10.59403/3a7s4sw accessed 3 September 2025, available at https://www.ibfd.org/shop/journal/automatic-information-exchange-versus-withholding-tax-regime-globalization-and accessed 3 September 2025.

automatic standard for the exchange of information proposed by this instrument was not successful. They allowed for exchange of information only on request.[122]

It is also crucial to examine the development of Article 26 under the OECD Model Convention. It was drafted with a broad scope to permit exchange of all types of information.[123] However, such exchanges were conditional and restricted to the internal laws and administrative practices of states exchanging such information (paragraph 3 of Article 26).[124] Countries used this restriction as an excuse to not exchange banking information. To clarify its intent, in its 2005 update to the OECD Model Tax Convention, the OECD included paragraph 5 to Article 26, which allowed for the exchange of banking information. It stated:

> 5. In no case shall the provisions of paragraph 3 be construed to permit a Contracting State to decline to supply information solely because the information is held by a bank, other financial institution, nominee or person acting in an agency or a fiduciary capacity or because it relates to ownership interests in a person.[125]

However, Austria, Switzerland, Luxembourg, and Belgium expressed reservations about this article in order to exclude this paragraph until 2009, which showed their unwillingness to stop banking secrecy.[126]

In 2000, the OECD founded the Global Forum on Transparency and Exchange of Information for Tax Purposes to spread the implementation of its tax transparency standards[127] and exchange of information internationally.[128] Neve notes that the founding of the Global Forum was the result of dissatisfaction among 'tax haven' countries with 'one-sided views' of the OECD, who felt the need for an inclusive organization.[129]

122. S. Dean, The Incomplete Global Market for Tax Information, *Brooklyn Law School Legal Studies Research Papers*, Research Paper No. 107 (April 2008), 43; U.S. 2006 Model Convention, Art. 26(1) (shall exchange such information as may be relevant); OECD 2005 Model Tax Convention, Art. 26(1) (shall exchange such information as is foreseeably relevant).
123. OECD, *Implementing the Tax Transparency Standards: A Handbook for Assessors and Jurisdictions, Second Edition* (OECD Publishing 2011), para. 1 of Art. 26, p. 95; para. 3 of Art. 26, p. 95; para. 5 of Art. 26, available at https://www.oecd-ilibrary.org/taxation/implementing-the-tax-transparency-standards_9789264110496-en accessed 21 August 2024.
124. OECD, *Implementing the Tax Transparency Standards: A Handbook for Assessors and Jurisdictions, Second Edition* (OECD Publishing 2011), para. 1 of Art. 26, p. 95; para. 3 of Art. 26, p. 95; para. 5 of Art. 26, available at https://www.oecd-ilibrary.org/taxation/implementing-the-tax-transparency-standards_9789264110496-en accessed 21 August 2024; para. 3 of the Art. 26 of OECD Model Tax Convention, p. 95.
125. Paragraph 5 of the Art. 26 of the OECD Model Tax Convention.
126. Organization for Economic Cooperation and Development: Model Tax Convention Updated, Library of Congress, available at https://www.loc.gov/item/global-legal-monitor/2010-07-26/organisation-for-economic-cooperation-and-development-model-tax-convention-updated/ accessed 21 August 2024.
127. M. Somare, *Automatic Exchange of Financial Account Information for Tax Purposes in the Light of Preventive Measures under the 4th Anti-Money Laundering Directive*, Doctoral Thesis, p. 66.
128. OECD, *Automatic Exchange: Common Reporting Standard*, available at https://www.oecd.org/tax/automatic-exchange/common-reporting-standard/ accessed 21 August 2024.
129. L.E.C. Neve, The Peer Review Process of the Global Forum on Transparency and Exchange of Information for Tax Purposes, *Erasmus Law Review* 2 (2017), 89-105, 90 https://doi.org/10.5

In its early years of formation, it focused its efforts on publishing a list of tax havens, which later shifted to enhancing the standards for the exchange of information. This standard for the exchange of information is mainly reflected in the 2002 version of 'Model Agreement on Exchange of Information on Tax Matters' from the OECD and 'Article 26 of the OECD Model Tax Convention'.[130] Both are considered 'minimum standards' and allow for the exchange of 'foreseeably relevant information' on request between contracting states without considering banking secrecy.[131]

This objective of the global forum to set standards for exchange of information internationally is achieved through two exchange standards: 'the Exchange of Information on request (EOIR) and Automatic Exchange of Information (AEOI)'.[132]

Exchange of Information on request means that the tax administration of one jurisdiction shares information with the tax administration of another jurisdiction on request. 'This includes information on the legal and beneficial owners of legal persons and legal arrangements as well as information related to the accounts of the requested person, including relevant banking information.'[133] 'A total of 171 members of the Global Forum have agreed to implement the exchange of information on request.'[134] Several countries have also agreed to peer-review monitoring of the exchange of information on requests to ensure effective implementation. A survey by the OECD revealed that countries recovered USD 1.932 billion based on the information received from the exchange of information.[135]

The EU also attempted to create a policy framework for EOI. The EU savings directive introduced in 2003 and adopted in 2005[136] was a significant early attempt to prevent cross-border tax evasion that essentially provided for the 'automatic exchange of information' on interest payments to 'non-resident beneficial owners' among EU

553/elr.000086 accessed 3 September 2025, available at https://www.elevenjournals.com/tijdschrift/ELR/2017/2/ELR_2017_010_003 accessed 21 August 2024.

130. OECD, *Implementing the Tax Transparency Standards: A Handbook for Assessors and Jurisdictions, Second Edition* (OECD Publishing 2011), available at https://www.oecd-ilibrary.org/taxation/implementing-the-tax-transparency-standards_9789264110496-en accessed 21 August 2024.
131. OECD, *Tax Information Exchange Agreements (TIEAs)*, available at https://www.oecd.org/ accessed 21 August 2024.
132. OECD, *Exchange of Information on Request: Peer Review Process*, available at https://www.oecd.org/tax/transparency/documents/exchange-of-information-on-request-peer-review-process.htm accessed 21 August 2024.
133. FATF, *FATF Recommendations: International Standards on Combating Money Laundering and the Financing of Terrorism & Proliferation*, FATF, Paris, France (2023), p. 132, available at www.fatf-gafi.org/en/publications/Fatfrecommendations/Fatf-recommendations.html accessed 21 August 2024.
134. OECD Global Forum, *Global Forum on Transparency and Exchange of Information for Tax Purposes*, Peer Reviews, available at https://www.oecd-ilibrary.org/taxation/global-forum-on-transparency-and-exchange-of-information-for-tax-purposes-peer-reviews_2219469x accessed 16 July 2024.
135. OECD Global Forum, *Tax Transparency 2015: Report on Progress* (OECD Publishing, 2015) Paris, p. 16, available at https://www.oecd.org/tax/transparency/global-forum-annual-report-2015.pdf accessed on 21 August 2024.
136. European Union, Council Directive 2003/48/EC of 3 June 2003 on taxation of savings income in the form of interest payments, available at https://eur-lex.europa.eu/legal-content/EN/ALL/?uri=celex%3A32003L0048 accessed 21 August 2024.

Member States.[137] It led to increased cooperation among the EU Member Countries to prevent tax evasion.

The literature notes both the positive and negative impacts of the EU savings directive. On a pessimistic tone, Jiminez points out that the 'savings directive did not measure up to the ambitions in view of its serious shortcomings' such as low revenue collections, evasion tactics to move assets to fall outside the scope of the directive, the territorial limitations of the directive, exclusion of legal persons such as companies from its scope and its complexity in application.[138] However, Johannesen through his empirical analysis shows the positive impact of 'a sharp 30–40% reduction in Swiss bank deposits owned by EU residents' caused by the EU savings directive.[139]

While the EU was making its attempts, the world of exchange of information was transformed in 2010, when the US introduced the Foreign Account Tax Compliance Act (FATCA). This legislation obligated US foreign financial institutions (FFIs) to automatically report the account details of US citizens to US tax authorities.[140] Any non-compliance was dealt with by 30% withholding tax on payments to such FFIs from US sources.[141] FATCA showed that 'automatic exchange of information was politically and technologically possible'.[142] Currently, 113 countries are signatories to the FATCA and share information bilaterally with the US.[143] In 2011, the EU introduced Directive on Administrative Cooperation (DAC 1) which established an administrative mechanism for exchange of information among the tax authorities of the EU Member States for preventing tax evasion.[144]

Africa was also not far behind. African members of the Global Forum also acknowledged the critical role of the exchange of information in fostering tax transparency to combat tax evasion and money laundering and to generate and finance the public infrastructure needs of African countries.[145] In 2014, a consensus was reached

137. S. Van Thiel, European Union Action Against Tax Avoidance and Evasion, *CESifo Forum 2/2012*, available at https://www.ifo.de/DocDL/forum2-12-focus2.pdf accessed 21 August 2024.
138. A.M. Jimenez, Loopholes in the EU Savings Tax Directive, *Bulletin for International Taxation*, IBFD, December 2006, available at https://papers.ssrn.com/sol3/papers.cfm?abstract_id=2471813 accessed 21 August 2024.
139. N. Johannesen, Tax Evasion and Swiss Bank Deposits, *Journal of Public Economics* 111 (2014), 61 https://doi.org/10.1016/j.jpubeco.2013.12.003 accessed 3 September 2025.
140. J.F. Kelly, International Tax Regulation by United States Fiat How FATCA Represents Unsound International Tax Policy, *Wisconsin International Law Journal* 34, no. 4 (May 2017).
141. Foreign Account Tax Compliance Act (FATCA), available at https://www.irs.gov/businesses/corporations/foreign-account-tax-compliance-act-fatca accessed 21 August 2024.
142. A. Barreix, J. Roca and F. Velayos, A Brief History of Tax Transparency, *Institutions for Development Sector, Discussion Paper IDB-DP-453*, p. 9, available at https://publications.iadb.org/publications/english/document/A-Brief-History-of-Tax-Transparency.pdf accessed on 21 August 2024.
143. Foreign Account Tax Compliance Act (FATCA), available at https://www.irs.gov/businesses/corporations/foreign-account-tax-compliance-act-fatca accessed 21 August 2024.
144. European Union, Council Directive 2011/16/EU of 15 February 2011 on administrative cooperation in the field of taxation and repealing Directive 77/799/EEC, available at https://eur-lex.europa.eu/legal-content/en/ALL/?uri=celex%3A32011L0016 accessed 21 August 2024.
145. OECD, *Transparency: Africa Initiative*, available at https://www.oecd.org/tax/transparency/what-we-do/technical-assistance/africa-initiative.htm accessed 18 December 2023.

among African Members of the global forum to establish the 'Africa Initiative', a forum that would focus on African needs. It enabled African countries to share good practices and develop policy solutions tailored to their needs.

The Africa Initiative also significantly boosted the exchange of information agreements on the African continent, leading to the expansion of the EOI network through new agreements. Before the existence of the Africa Initiative, the number of agreements for exchanging information between African countries was negligible. As of 2012, African countries have had a bit less than six hundred agreements on exchanging information with other countries.[146] The African Initiative significantly increased the number of agreements among African Countries. The success of the African Initiative can be attributed to the fact that, in 2013, the total number of exchanges of information agreements entered by all African countries was 685.[147] By December 2023, over 3,400 EOI agreements had been established among African countries.[148] In addition to exchanging information on request, ten African countries also implemented an Automatic Exchange of Information (AEOI) and secured positive feedback in their peer review by the global forum on exchanging information on request.[149]

This increase in the network of exchange of information on request, as well as a political climate conducive to the exchange of information between African countries, also led to resource mobilization by African countries in the form of tax collection. In 2014, nine countries[150] on the African continent were able to ascertain USD 233 million from EOIR.[151] In 2021, African countries collected USD 38.9 million through cases identified by EOIR.[152] Tunisia, Kenya, and Uganda collectively traced USD 38.9 million using the EOI framework in 2021.[153] Furthermore, African countries were able to locate USD 1.2 billion with the help of EOI, by way of additional revenues in the form of tax, interest on taxes unpaid, as penalties, which was the result of the investigations launched by the African countries in case of offshore tax evasion cases, as well as programs launched by African countries to motivate tax evaders to pay their taxes through voluntary disclosure programs.[154]

146. *Ibid.*
147. OECD Global Forum, *Tax Transparency in Africa 2018: Africa Initiative Progress Report* (OECD Publishing, 2018) Paris, p. 32, available at https://www.oecd.org/tax/transparency/documents/africa-initiative-report-2018.pdf accessed on 21 August 2024.
148. OECD Global Forum, *Tax Transparency in Africa 2024: Africa Initiative Progress Report* (OECD Publishing, 2024) Paris, p. 19, available at https://www.oecd.org/tax/transparency/documents/tax-transparency-in-africa-2024.htm accessed on 21 August 2024.
149. Sovereign News, *African Countries Are Making Good Strides on Tax Transparency*, available at https://www.sovereigngroup.com/news/news-and-views/african-countries-making-good-strides-on-tax-transparency/ accessed 18 December 2023.
150. OECD Global Forum, *Tax Transparency in Africa 2022: Africa Initiative Progress Report* (OECD Publishing, 2022) Paris, p. 14, available at https://www.oecd.org/tax/transparency/documents/tax-transparency-in-africa-2022.htm accessed on 21 August 2024.
151. *Ibid.*
152. *Ibid.*
153. *Ibid.*
154. *Ibid.*

The need for an extensive EOI treaty network remains prevalent in several African countries, and it is crucial to broaden this network to harness the positive impact of EOI agreements. Broadening the Exchange of Information (EOI) network among nations, encompassing several African countries, will enable access to previously inaccessible cross-border information.

While the evidence showed the positive effects of the EOIR, there were also views that were critical of the exchange of information. In civil society, the Tax Justice Network was a fierce supporter of the automatic exchange of information. 'It became even more vocal after the adoption of the automatic exchange of information in the EU Savings Directive.'[155]

The Tax Justice Network in its 2012 report noted:

> TJN wants automatic information exchange to become the global standard for international cooperation to tackle tax avoidance and evasion. The reason for wishing this is simple: evidence from the USA has shown that when taxpayers know that a source of income will be automatically declared to their tax authority, they are highly likely to be deterred from evading taxes. When the taxpayer knows that the income is not automatically disclosed to the tax authority the deterrent effect falls significantly.[156]

In the literature, Barreix Rocaa and Velayos argued that this critical view of TJN was partially correct. In hindsight, pressure from civil society was vital in developing an automatic exchange of information.[157]

Following the success of FATCA and the pressure from civil society, the G20 in 2013 at Saint Petersburg, made a declaration of its support for the 'automatic exchange of information as the new global standard'.[158] With this political support from the G20, the OECD introduced the CRS, which required countries to automatically exchange information about financial institutions in their jurisdiction and made it a minimum standard for information exchange in 2014.[159] This information is exchanged based on the CRS, globally agreed upon by OECD countries and other major countries, such as India, China, Brazil, South Africa, and Singapore.[160] CRS is considered a new global standard for collecting information on bank account details of account holders. It is established to prevent tax evasion by enhancing the ability of tax administrators to

155. Tax Justice Network, *Tax Us If You Can* (2012), 2nd ed., p. 35, available at www.taxjustice.net/cms/upload/pdf/TUIYC_2012_FINAL.pdf accessed 21 August 2024.
156. *Ibid.*
157. A. Barreix, J. Roca and F. Velayos, A Brief History of Tax Transparency, *Institutions for Development Sector, Discussion Paper IDB-DP-453*, p. 9, available at https://publications.iadb.org/publications/english/document/A-Brief-History-of-Tax-Transparency.pdf accessed on 21 August 2024.
158. G20, *Leaders Declaration 2013*, Russia, p. 13, available at https://www.bundesfinanzministerium.de/Content/EN/Standardartikel/Topics/world/G7-G20/G20-Documents/2013-Russia-Leaders-Declaration.pdf?__blob=publicationFile&v=1 accessed 21 August 2024.
159. OECD, *Standard for Automatic Exchange of Financial Account Information in Tax Matters* (OECD Publishing, 2014), Paris, p. 10, available at https://read.oecd-ilibrary.org/taxation/standard-for-automatic-exchange-of-financial-account-information-for-tax-matters_9789264216525-en#p.1 accessed on 21 August 2024.
160. OECD, *Automatic Exchange of Information*, available at https://www.oecd.org/tax/automatic-exchange/ accessed 18 December 2023.

detect and report tax evasion. A critical distinction between the exchange of information on request and automatic exchange of information is that only the latter is subject to the global forum's peer review process.[161]

The political support from the G20 and the introduction of CRS also had an immediate impact on banking secrecy. Van Thiel points out that only ten countries were in the category of countries that still did not fully implement these 'internationally agreed tax standards',[162] making it impossible to use banking secrecy for tax evasion. As of March 2024, 120 jurisdictions have signed up for CRS, showing its success.[163] After the global financial crisis of 2009, tax transparency standards were not just restricted to financial centres. They were made applicable to all jurisdictions by the global forum.[164]

In the EU, the shift to AEOI as the new standard for exchange of information was formalized through the Directive on Administrative Cooperation (DAC 2) in 2014.[165] It subsequently resulted in the repeal of the Savings Directive.[166]

In the literature, Beer, Coelho, and Sébastien find empirically 'strong evidence suggesting AEOI has been effective in limiting the use of offshore jurisdictions to evade taxes, with deposits therein dropping by an average of 25 per cent after the entering into force of any AEOI agreement'.[167] They also find the EU Savings Directive and CRS to be 'most effective' in comparison to the FATCA.[168] Considering the success of AEOI,

161. OECD, *Exchange of Information on Request: Peer Review Process*, available at https://www.oecd.org/tax/transparency/documents/exchange-of-information-on-request-peer-review-process.htm accessed 18 December 2023.
162. S. Van Thiel, European Union Action Against Tax Avoidance and Evasion, *CESifo Forum* 2/2012, available at https://www.ifo.de/DocDL/forum2-12-focus2.pdf accessed 21 August 2024 By the end of 2010 only ten countries were still in the category: jurisdictions that have committed to the internationally agreed tax standard, but have not yet substantially implemented (Belize, Liberia, Montserrat, Nauru, Niue, Panama, Vanuatu, Costa Rica, Guatemala, Uruguay); OECD, *The Global Forum on Transparency and Exchange of Information for Tax Purposes: A Background Information Brief* (14 October 2010), available at https://web-archive.oecd.org/tax/automatic-exchange/international-framework-for-the-crs/ accessed 21 August 2024.
163. OECD, T*he Global Forum on Transparency and Exchange of Information for Tax Purposes: CRS and CbCr* (14 October 2010), available at https://web-archive.oecd.org/tax/automatic-exchange/international-framework-for-the-crs/ accessed 21 August 2024.
164. M. Somare, *Automatic Exchange of Financial Account Information for Tax Purposes in the Light of Preventive Measures under the 4th Anti Money Laundering Directive*, Doctoral Thesis, p. 66.
165. European Union, Amending Directive 2011/16/EU as regards mandatory automatic exchange of information in the field of taxation, available at https://eur-lex.europa.eu/legal-content/EN/TXT/?uri=celex%3A32014L0107 accessed 21 August 2024.
166. European Parliament, *Repealing the Savings Tax Directive*, available at https://www.europarl.europa.eu/legislative-train/package-tax-transparency-package/file-repealing-the-savings-tax-directive accessed 21 August 2024.
167. S. Beer, M. Coelho, and S. Leduc, Hidden Treasures: The Impact of Automatic Exchange of Information on Cross-Border Tax Evasion, *IMF Working Paper* WP/19/286, p. 27, available at https://www.imf.org/en/Publications/WP/Issues/2019/12/20/Hidden-Treasure-The-Impact-of-Automatic-Exchange-of-Information-on-Cross-Border-Tax-Evasion-48781 accessed 21 August 2024.
168. *Ibid.*

several African countries also indicated their intentions to implement AEOI standards.[169] However, adopting AEOI standards has not been encouraging thus far, as adopting and implementing AEOI can be more challenging than EOIR.[170] Only two countries – Seychelles and South Africa – began implementing the AEOI in 2017.[171] This number has increased to five countries: Ghana, Mauritius, Nigeria, Seychelles, and South Africa.[172] 'Kenya, Morocco, Rwanda, and Tunisia are expected to join this list, increasing the number of African countries implementing the AEOI to nine by 2025.'[173]

In addition to EOIR and AEOI, the Convention on Mutual Administrative Assistance in Tax Matters (CMAATM) was also developed, which provides an international legal framework for the enforcement of tax laws, prevention of tax evasion and avoidance through the exchange of information, mutual assistance in the collection of taxes, and access to documents from other countries necessary for investigation and prosecution.[174] It provides the legal instrument necessary for international cooperation to facilitate joint tax audits and investigations into money laundering and tax evasion cases and ensures the safeguarding of taxpayers' rights regarding the privacy and confidentiality of personal information shared within the framework. African countries have joined the CMAATM, and currently, twenty-two African countries are its signatories.[175] The EOI agreements entered by African countries also comply with CMAATM.[176]

The mere execution of EOI Agreements or the expansion of the network of EOI relationships does not guarantee access to information about tax evasion, money laundering, or corruption. The practical application of the EOI Network relies on the domestic legal and administrative framework for collecting information domestically by the tax administration and other law enforcement agencies and sharing such information between domestic law enforcement agencies and internationally. This requires that law enforcement agencies and tax authorities, especially in African countries, be adequately equipped and trained in information sharing and possess knowledge of existing legal frameworks governing the exchange of information. The objective of fostering an environment of enhanced tax transparency is to utilize

169. OECD Global Forum, *Tax Transparency in Africa 2023: Africa Initiative Progress Report* (OECD Publishing, 2023) Paris, p. 17, available at https://web-archive.oecd.org/temp/2023-07-21/659894-tax-transparency-in-africa-2023.htm accessed on 21 August 2024.
170. *Ibid.*
171. *Ibid.*
172. *Ibid.*
173. *Ibid.*
174. OECD, *The Multilateral Convention on Mutual Administrative Assistance in Tax Matters (Amended by the 2010 Protocol)* (OECD Publishing), Paris, available at https://www.oecd-ilibrary.org/taxation/the-multilateral-convention-on-mutual-administrative-assistance-in-tax-matters_9789264115606-en accessed 21 August 2024.
175. OECD Global Forum, *Tax Transparency in Africa 2022: Africa Initiative Progress Report* (OECD Publishing, 2022) Paris, p. 14, available at https://www.oecd.org/tax/transparency/documents/tax-transparency-in-africa-2022.htm accessed on 21 August 2024.
176. OECD, *Convention on Mutual Administrative Assistance in Tax Matters*, available at https://www.oecd.org/tax/exchange-of-tax-information/convention-on-mutual-administrative-assistance-in-tax-matters.htm accessed 19 June 2023.

available information for tax investigation and recovery, thereby augmenting revenue for the budget.

3.3 TACKLING TAX HAVENS AND HARMFUL TAX COMPETITION

While the exchange of information movement gained speed, there were also other efforts which focused on measures to tackle the use of tax havens and harmful tax competition. Tax havens and preferential tax regimes frequently contribute to the concealment of BO by facilitating tax evasion and avoidance. Both often feature characteristics such as a lack of effective exchange of information, lack of transparency in the regulatory framework, and an absence of a requirement to conduct substantial economic activities for granting tax benefits, making it difficult to identify beneficial owners. Therefore, combating tax havens and harmful tax competition was intrinsically linked to the push for transparency and BO disclosure.

Internationally, a significant turning point occurred when in 1998 the OECD published its first report on 'Harmful Tax Competition: An Emerging Global Issue'.[177] This groundbreaking report focused on the 'tax havens' and 'preferential tax regimes'. It is considered a regime as a 'tax haven' if it has no nominal income taxes and lacks one of three characteristics: effective exchange of information, economic substance, or transparency. It similarly identified 'preferential tax regimes' which focused on effective tax rates instead of nominal tax rates.

Although being considered groundbreaking at that time, Maldonado pointed out the political defeat of a harmful tax competition project.[178] He notes that, as the OECD is a consensus-based organization, the report was unsuccessful, as Switzerland and Luxembourg did not approve it.

The EU was also quick to acknowledge the effects of harmful tax competition. In 1996, the EU Commissioner Mario Monti first mentioned the issue of harmful tax competition and emphasized the need for a comprehensive EU-wide strategy to address it. Monti highlighted in a discussion paper for the Informal Meeting of ECOFIN Ministers that: '*Fiscal degradation occurs through the erosion of the tax base resulting both from tax competition* (the relocation of taxable bases to other countries) and from the development of the underground economy (the relocation of taxable bases towards the black market). The former depends on the differential between effective rates of taxation, the latter on their absolute level.'[179] *(Emphasis added)*

177. OECD, *Harmful Tax Competition: An Emerging Global Issue* (OECD 1998), Paris, para. 30, available at https://www.oecd-ilibrary.org/taxation/harmful-tax-competition_9789264162945-en accessed on 22 August 2024.
178. A. Barreix, J. Roca and F. Velayos, A Brief History of Tax Transparency, *Institutions for Development Sector, Discussion Paper IDB-DP-453*, p. 9, available at https://publications.iadb.org/publications/english/document/A-Brief-History-of-Tax-Transparency.pdf accessed on 21 August 2024.
179. European Commission, Taxation in the European Union: Discussion Paper for the Informal Meeting of the ECOFIN Council, SEC (96) 487 final of 20 March 1996, p. 3, available at https://www.verginet.net/UserFiles/File/Avrupa_Birligi/Taxation/General_Information/taxation_sec(1996)487_en%204%20Ek%203.pdf accessed on 21 August 2024.

Recognizing this need, the ECOFIN[180] adopted the 'Code of Conduct for Business Taxation'[181] which is a '*gentlemen's agreement* between EU Member States to tackle harmful tax competition by means of a collective review process, accompanied by a political commitment to phase out existing harmful tax measures (roll-back) and not to introduce new ones (stand-still)'.[182] Tax regimes in the EU Member States are considered harmful if they affect the decisions of businesses based on 'significantly' lower taxation than the general system. This assessment is based on the criteria such as 'ring fencing, protection of domestic markets, lack of substance i.e. no economic activity or presence, non-transparency as well as not dealing at arm's length'.[183] In 2022, the EU code of conduct was amended to include 'tax features of general application' that allow double non-taxation or multiple utilization of tax benefits.[184]

The EU regime also had an external side under which overseas territories of EU Member States were identified as operating harmful tax regimes under the EU code of conduct and were obliged eventually to abolish their regimes, demonstrating the success of the EU code of conduct.[185]

However, a big political push to tackle tax havens came in the wake of the financial crisis. The G20 at its 2009 summit in Pittsburgh, unequivocally supported the undertaking of preventive measures against tax havens. The communique from the G20 Pittsburgh summit stated: 'We stand ready to use countermeasures against tax havens from March 2010.'[186] The OECD also jointly with the Council of Europe, developed the first 'Multilateral Convention on Mutual Administrative Assistance in Tax Matters' currently participated in by 150 jurisdictions.[187]

The EU Code of Conduct group expanded its external scrutiny of harmful tax regimes from the overseas territories of the Member States to all third countries, and it started blacklisting jurisdictions on the concern of relocation of profits or shifting to

180. Council of the European Union, *The Economic and Financial Affairs Council (ECOFIN)*, available at https://www.consilium.europa.eu/en/council-eu/configurations/ecofin/ accessed 21 August 2024.
181. Council of the European Union, Code of Conduct Group, available at https://www.consilium.europa.eu/en/council-eu/prepara.tory-bodies/code-conduct-group/ accessed 21 August 2024.
182. S. van Thiel, Chapter 23, Harmful Tax Competition, and the Code of Conduct for Business Taxation, in P.J. Wattel et al. (eds), *European Tax Law, Volume I (Full Edition)*, 8th ed., 2022, pp. 801-802.
183. S. van Thiel, Chapter 23, Harmful Tax Competition, and the Code of Conduct for Business Taxation, in P.J. Wattel et al. (eds), *European Tax Law, Volume I (Full Edition)*, 8th ed., 2022, p. 802.
184. Council of the European Union, Code of Conduct Group, available at https://www.consilium.europa.eu/en/council-eu/prepara.tory-bodies/code-conduct-group/ accessed 21 August 2024.
185. European Commission, *Taxation Papers: A History of the Tax Package: The Principles and Issues Underlying the Community Approach* (2006), p. 6, available at https://taxation-customs.ec.europa.eu/document/download/e969dff0-d4f8-4bb2-98f5-eeecd327b31a_en?filename=taxation_paper_10_history_en.pdf accessed on 21 August 2024.
186. G20, *Leaders' Statement, The Pittsburgh Summit*, 24-25 September 2009, available at https://home.treasury.gov/system/files/206/pittsburgh_summit_leaders_statement_250909.pdf accessed on 21 August 2024.
187. OECD, *Convention on Mutual Administrative Assistance in Tax Matters*, available at https://www.oecd.org/en/topics/convention-on-mutual-administrative-assistance-in-tax-matters.html accessed 21 August 2024.

third countries. It was intended to create a level playing field between the EU and third countries.

The code of conduct group was also successful in enhancing transparency through its discussions which resulted in legislative initiatives such as the DAC 1 and DAC 2 which provided for exchange of information, ATAD 1 and ATAD 2 which prevented hybrid mismatches and the EU listing of non-cooperative jurisdictions. The EU also formed the EU Joint Transfer Pricing Forum, which, for the first time, brought transfer pricing to the international tax policy agenda for preventing tax evasion and tax avoidance.[188]

The OECD's and the EU's approaches to combat harmful tax competition have distinct differences. While the OECD approach outlined in the 1998 report primarily focused on the transparency and exchange of information for improving access to BO information, the EU code of conduct for business taxation placed greater emphasis on identifying and eliminating harmful tax regimes within the EU. The approach of the EU's code of conduct indirectly supported BO reforms by undertaking BO as its screening criteria to discourage the future use of structures to disguise BO.[189]

3.4 TACKLING THE PERPETRATORS OF TAX EVASION AND AVOIDANCE AND REVEALING BENEFICIAL OWNERS

Apart from improving the exchange of information and tackling harmful tax competition and tax havens, there have also been other efforts to tackle tax avoidance and tax evasion by individuals. The 2009 global financial crisis brought about austerity measures that required countries to seek additional funds to finance their public budgets. The 2013 offshore leaks, 2014 Lux leaks, 2015 Swiss leaks, 2015 Panama papers, and 2017 Paradise papers brought to attention the misuse of legal persons and legal arrangements for tax evasion and avoidance.[190] The 2013 offshore leaks exposed 130,000 offshore accounts used for tax evasion.[191] The Lux leaks revealed information about the practices of MNEs to reduce tax liabilities.[192] Swiss leaks in 2015 revealed the role of a subsidiary of HSBC bank in assisting its clients in evading taxes.[193] The 2016

188. European Commission, Joint Transfer Pricing Forum, available at https://taxation-customs.ec.europa.eu/taxation/company-taxation/joint-transfer-pricing-forum_en accessed 21 August 2024.
189. Council of the European Union, ECOFIN Council, Criteria 1.4, November 2016 (doc. 14166/16), p. 12, available at https://data.consilium.europa.eu/doc/document/ST-9295-2022-INIT/en/pdf accessed 21 August 2024.
190. A.J. Cockfield, Big Data and Tax Haven Secrecy, *Florida Tax Review* 18, no. 8 (2016), pp. 483, 508-509 https://doi.org/10.5744/ftr.2016.1808 accessed 3 September 2025; M. Esterl, G.R. Simpson and D. Crawford, Stolen Data Spur Tax Probes, *The Wall Street Journal*, 19 February 2008, available at https://www.wsj.com/articles/SB120333229682874855 accessed 21 August 2024.
191. International Consortium of Investigative Journalists (ICIJ), *Offshore Leaks Database*, available at https://offshoreleaks.icij.org/ accessed 21 August 2024.
192. International Consortium of Investigative Journalists (ICIJ), *Luxembourg Leaks*, available at https://www.icij.org/investigations/luxembourg-leaks/ accessed 21 August 2024.
193. International Consortium of Investigative Journalists (ICIJ), *Swiss Leaks*, available at https://www.icij.org/investigations/swiss-leaks/ accessed 21 August 2024.

Panama papers revealed the use of offshore entities by high-net-worth individuals for tax evasion. The 2017 Paradise papers revealed the role of law firms and tax havens being used by wealthy individuals for tax evasion.[194]

The data leaks reemphasized the issue that the lack of information concerning the owners who controlled the legal vehicles and arrangements created the potential for their use in tax avoidance and money laundering domestically and internationally. It was also acknowledged that the opportunity for misuse offered by such vehicles not only facilitates tax avoidance but also acts as a barrier to the sustainable development and growth of the economy and hinders the governance of institutions.[195]

While the issue of misuse of legal persons and legal arrangements was not new, it was brought to the centre stage by these leaks. In the 1990s, while banking secrecy was still an issue, political discourse was moving towards combating money laundering perpetrated by the misuse of financial systems and banking institutions. With this aim in 1989 the FATF, the global organization setting anti-money laundering standards to evaluate the policy framework existing at that time to prevent the misuse of financial and banking institutions, was established.[196] In 1990, it published its first report, containing 'forty recommendations' to combat money laundering.[197] The report emphasized the need to obtain information on beneficial owners by the bank or financial institutions during the opening of bank accounts or the execution of financial transactions.[198] These recommendations were of high significance as, for the first time, an international organization had provided recommendations on identifying BO that would require countries to identify the BO of corporate entities.

The FATF (1990) in its recommendation 13 provided that:

> 'Financial institutions should take reasonable measures to obtain information about the *true identity of the persons* on whose behalf an account is opened or a transaction conducted if there are any doubts as to whether these clients or customers are not acting on their own behalf, in particular, in the case of *domiciliary companies i.e. institutions, corporations, foundations, trusts,* etc. that do not conduct any commercial or manufacturing business or any other form of commercial operation in the country where their registered office is located.' (Emphasis added)[199]

194. International Consortium of Investigative Journalists (ICIJ), *Paradise Papers*, available at https://www.icij.org/investigations/para.dise-papers/ accessed 21 August 2024.
195. Arthur J. Cockfield, Big Data and Tax Haven Secrecy, *Florida Tax Review* 18, no. 8 (2016), p. 514 https://doi.org/10.5744/ftr.2016.1808 accessed 3 September 2025.
196. G7, *1989 Paris Summit, Economic Declaration*, 16 July 1989, para. 53, available at http://www.g8.utoronto.ca/summit/1989paris/communique/index.html accessed 21 August 2024.
197. Financial Action Task Force (FATF), *The Forty Recommendations of the Financial Action Task Force on Money Laundering* (FATF 1990), available at https://www.fatf-gafi.org/media/fatf/documents/recommendations/pdfs/FATF%20Recommendations%201990.pdf accessed 21 August 2024.
198. *Ibid.*
199. *Ibid.*

The UN (1998) also for the first time recognized the role of trusts and other legal vehicles in facilitating money laundering and tax avoidance.[200] The UN noted in its report:

> The principal forms of *abuse of secrecy* have shifted from individual bank accounts to corporate bank accounts and then to *trust and other corporate forms* that can be purchased readily without even the modest initial and ongoing due diligence that is exercised in the banking sector.[201]

And:

> Jurisdictions which offer high levels of secrecy, and a variety of financial mechanisms and institutions providing *anonymity for the beneficial owners* are highly attractive.[202]

The UN report highlighted the importance of identifying BO information to prevent the misuse of trusts, corporate entities, or other forms of institutions that provide anonymity.[203] This UN report recognized for the first time the need to develop a policy framework to tackle the financial secrecy provided by the misuse of legal vehicles and legal arrangements.

The OECD was also not far behind.[204] With the political support of G7, the OECD launched its ambitious project on 'Harmful Tax Competition' to develop 'measures to counter the distorting effects of harmful tax competition on investment and financing decisions and the consequences for national tax bases'.[205]

The OECD published its first report on this project, titled 'Harmful Tax Competition: An Emerging Global Issue'.[206] This groundbreaking report noted tax havens and preferential tax regimes as critical contributors to harmful tax competition based on the absence of transparency in the jurisdiction and the lack of information sharing among

200. J.A. Blum et al., *Financial Havens, Banking Secrecy and Money Laundering*, United Nations Office for Drug Control and Crime Prevention, Global Programme Against Money Laundering (1998), pp. 6, 7, 57, 90-95, available at https://gfintegrity.org/wp-content/uploads/2022/06/UN-FINANCIAL-HAVENS-laundering.pdf accessed 21 August 2024.
201. *Ibid.*
202. J. Owens and R. McDonell, *Creating a Better Mechanism to Obtain Beneficial Ownership Information in the International Context*, p. 5, available at https://papers.ssrn.com/sol3/papers.cfm?abstract_id=3161723 accessed on 21 August 2024. Also *see*, J.A. Blum et al., *Financial Havens, Banking Secrecy and Money Laundering*, United Nations Office for Drug Control and Crime Prevention, Global Programme Against Money Laundering (1998), pp. 6, 7, 57, 90-95, available at https://gfintegrity.org/wp-content/uploads/2022/06/UN-FINANCIAL-HAVENS-laundering.pdf accessed 21 August 2024.
203. *Ibid.*
204. G7, *1996 Lyon Summit, Economic Communique: Making a Success of Globalisation for the Benefit of All*, 21 June 1996, para. 16, available at http://www.g8.utoronto.ca/summit/1996lyon/communique.html accessed 21 August 2024.
205. OECD, *Council at Ministerial Level, Communiqué*, 21-22 May 2006, para. 15(xv), available at https://one.oecd.org/document/PAC/COM/NEWS(2006)13/en/pdf accessed 21 August 2024; J. Owens and R. McDonell, *Creating a Better Mechanism to Obtain Beneficial Ownership Information in the International Context*, p. 5, available at https://papers.ssrn.com/sol3/papers.cfm?abstract_id=3161723 accessed on 21 August 2024.
206. OECD, *Harmful Tax Competition: An Emerging Global Issue* (OECD, 1998) Paris, para. 30, available at https://www.oecd-ilibrary.org/taxation/harmful-tax-competition_9789264162945-en accessed on 22 August 2024.

individuals who benefited from such jurisdictions.[207] In particular, the report identified an extensive double-tax treaty network facilitating treaty shopping by third-country nationals as a hallmark of such jurisdiction.[208]

The critical significance of the report on harmful tax competition was that it allowed countries the option to deny treaty benefits in case the BO criteria were not fulfilled,[209] which was earlier allowed only through the inclusion of recommendations to Article 1 of the OECD model, denying treaty benefits in some instances.[210] The countries that were blacklisted under the project changed their tax system to not be categorized as 'harmful preferential tax regimes' or 'tax havens'.

However, this report could have been more extensive on a few essential and vital issues. First, the standards on tax transparency and exchange of information under the harmful tax competition project were much narrower at that time compared with today.[211] The report also *'did not mention BO* as a crucial piece of information for tax transparency'.[212] Instead, the regime was considered harmful based on the lack of shareholders' registers.[213]

In 2000, the Financial Stability Forum (FSF), an organization that focused on the monetary stability of the global financial system, highlighted the challenges posed by using legal vehicles in the jurisdiction that permits banking secrecy laws.[214] Specifically, the FSF raised concerns about the ease with which legal vehicles such as companies, foundations, trusts, and partnerships can be created in these jurisdictions while allowing secrecy and anonymity.

207. J. Owens and R. McDonell, *Creating a Better Mechanism to Obtain Beneficial Ownership Information in the International Context*, p. 5, available at https://papers.ssrn.com/sol3/papers.cfm?abstract_id=3161723 accessed on 21 August 2024; OECD, *Harmful Tax Competition: An Emerging Global Issue* (OECD, 1998) Paris, para. 52-52, available at https://www.oecd-ilibrary.org/taxation/harmful-tax-competition_9789264162945-en accessed on 22 August 2024.
208. OECD, *Action 6: Preventing the Granting of Treaty Benefits in Inappropriate Circumstances*, OECD/G20 Base Erosion and Profit Shifting Project 2015 (final report), available at https://www.oecd-ilibrary.org/taxation/preventing-the-granting-of-treaty-benefits-in-inappropriate-circumstances-action-6-2015-final-report_9789264241695-en accessed 21 August 2024; J. Owens and R. McDonell, *Creating a Better Mechanism to Obtain Beneficial Ownership Information in the International Context*, p. 5, available at https://papers.ssrn.com/sol3/papers.cfm?abstract_id=3161723 accessed on 21 August 2024.
209. OECD, *Harmful Tax Competition: An Emerging Global Issue* (OECD, 1998) Paris, para. 30, available at https://www.oecd-ilibrary.org/taxation/harmful-tax-competition_9789264162945-en accessed on 22 August 2024.
210. R. Vann, Beneficial Ownership: What Does History (and Maybe Policy) Tell Us, in M. Lang et al. (eds), *Beneficial Ownership: Recent Trends*, IBFD, 2013, p. 295.
211. OECD, *Harmful Tax Competition: An Emerging Global Issue* (OECD, 1998) Paris, para. 67, available at https://www.oecd-ilibrary.org/taxation/harmful-tax-competition_9789264162945-en accessed on 22 August 2024; M. Somare, *Automatic Exchange of Financial Account Information for Tax Purposes in the Light of Preventive Measures under the 4th Anti-Money Laundering Directive*, Doctoral Thesis, p. 65.
212. M. Somare, *Automatic Exchange of Financial Account Information for Tax Purposes in the Light of Preventive Measures under the 4th Anti-Money Laundering Directive*, Doctoral Thesis, p. 65.
213. OECD, *Harmful Tax Competition: An Emerging Global Issue* (OECD, 1998) Paris, para. 67, available at https://www.oecd-ilibrary.org/taxation/harmful-tax-competition_9789264162945-en accessed on 22 August 2024.
214. Financial Stability Forum, *Report of the Working Group on Offshore Centres*, 5 April 2000, available at http://www.fsb.org/wp-content/uploads/r_0004b.pdf accessed 21 August 2024.

The FSF noted in its report:

> The lack of availability of timely information on BO of corporate vehicles (companies, trusts, partnerships and other vehicles with limited liability) established in some OFCs (Offshore financial centers) can thwart efforts against illegal business activities.[215]

Noting these concerns, it is recommended that 'appropriate international body be asked to explore the issue of developing mechanisms to prevent the misuse of corporate vehicles. These mechanisms should assure that supervisors and law enforcement authorities can obtain, on a timely basis, information on BO of corporate vehicles and sharing that information with foreign authorities'.[216]

To implement its recommendation, the FSF asked that the OECD conduct a study to assess the potential misuse of legal vehicles for tax avoidance and money laundering.

This time in history was crucial in developing BO as a policy tool as all the major international policy organizations, i.e., OECD, FATF, UN, and FSF, recognized 'the misuse of legal persons and legal arrangements for tax avoidance and money laundering'.

3.4.1 OECD Report: Behind the Corporate Veil

In response to the FSF's direction, the OECD issued its 2001 report 'Behind the Corporate Veil: Using Corporate Entities for Illicit Purposes'. That report addressed the 'misuse of legal vehicles for money laundering'. That OECD report highlighted that individuals often employ legal vehicles such as trusts and partnerships to conceal their assets and other forms of income from tax authorities.[217]

Part 1 of its report needs special attention, wherein it is noted that:

> Tax authorities in OECD Member countries have also expressed concern that individuals using corporate entities to hide their assets and activities to escape taxes legally due will likely grow.[218]

215. Financial Stability Forum, *Report of the Working Group on Offshore Centres*, 5 April 2000, p. 18, available at http://www.fsb.org/wp-content/uploads/r_0004b.pdf accessed 21 August 2024.
216. Financial Stability Forum, Recommendation 9: Corporate Vehicles and Beneficial Ownership, in *Report of the Working Group on Offshore Centres*, 5 April 2000, p. 4, available at http://www.fsb.org/wp-content/uploads/r_0004b.pdf accessed 21 August 2024.
217. OECD, *Behind the Corporate Veil, Using Corporate Entities for Illicit Purposes*, p. 3, available at https://www.oecd-ilibrary.org/finance-and-investment/behind-the-corporate-veil_9789264195608-en accessed on 21 August 2024.
218. OECD, *Behind the Corporate Veil, Using Corporate Entities for Illicit Purposes*, p. 21, available at https://www.oecd-ilibrary.org/finance-and-investment/behind-the-corporate-veil_9789264195608-en accessed on 21 August 2024; OECD Committee on Fiscal Affairs, *Improving Access to Bank Information for Tax Purposes* (2000), p. 11, available at https://www.oecd-ilibrary.org/taxation/improving-access-to-bank-information-for-tax-purposes_9789264181267-en accessed on 21 August 2024.

It is recommended that countries take measures to prevent the misuse of legal vehicles, such as companies, trusts, partnerships, and foundations.[219] It also advocated for 'the establishment of effective mechanisms to provide BO information to tax authorities and other law enforcement agencies dealing with money laundering. In addition, the report recommended the creation of a legal framework and capabilities to share BO information with national and international law enforcement agencies'.[220]

In 2000, the FATF joined the discourse of BO and conducted an inaugural review of existing rules and regulations to prevent and detect tax evasion and money laundering.[221] This review revealed that shell companies and other legal vehicles that provide anonymity and secrecy have been extensively used for money laundering, including tax evasion.[222]

It especially noted that:

> *Shell corporations and nominees are widely used mechanisms* to launder the proceeds from crime, particularly bribery (e.g. to build up slush funds). The ability for competent authorities to obtain and share information on the *identification of companies and their beneficial owner(s) is therefore essential* for all the relevant authorities responsible for preventing and punishing money laundering.[223]

The review by the FATF highlighted that such vehicles impede law enforcement agencies, including tax authorities, from identifying the actual owners of legal vehicles and accessing relevant information, which creates barriers to the effective enforcement of law compliance.

The review also noted 'difficulties in establishing the BO of some legal persons, including companies issuing bearer shares and of trusts' as an issue of particular concern in its report.[224] It concluded that obtaining BO information of such legal vehicles is crucial for effectively enforcing laws and preventing money laundering, including tax avoidance.[225]

Subsequent reports by various organizations, including the International Trade and Investment Organization and the Society of Trust and Estate Practitioners (STEP),

---

219. OECD, *Behind the Corporate Veil, Using Corporate Entities for Illicit Purposes*, p. 41, available at https://www.oecd-ilibrary.org/finance-and-investment/behind-the-corporate-veil_9789264195608-en accessed on 21 August 2024.
220. OECD, *Behind the Corporate Veil, Using Corporate Entities for Illicit Purposes*, pp. 7-8, available at https://www.oecd-ilibrary.org/finance-and-investment/behind-the-corporate-veil_9789264195608-en accessed on 21 August 2024.
221. Financial Action Task Force (FATF), *Review to Identify Non-Cooperative Countries or Territories: Increasing the Worldwide Effectiveness of Anti-money Laundering Measures* (22 June 2000), p. 20, available at https://www.fatf-gafi.org/content/dam/fatf-gafi/annual-reports/1999%202000%20NCCT%20ENG.pdf accessed on 21 August 2024.
222. *Ibid.*
223. *Ibid.*
224. Financial Action Task Force (FATF), *Review to identify Non-Cooperative Countries or Territories: Increasing the Worldwide Effectiveness of Anti-money Laundering Measures* (22 June 2000), p. 11, available at https://www.fatf-gafi.org/content/dam/fatf-gafi/annual-reports/1999%202000%20NCCT%20ENG.pdf accessed on 21 August 2024.
225. Financial Action Task Force (FATF), *Review to identify Non-Cooperative Countries or Territories: Increasing the Worldwide Effectiveness of Anti-money Laundering Measures* (22 June 2000), available at https://www.fatf-gafi.org/content/dam/fatf-gafi/annual-reports/1999%202000%20NCCT%20ENG.pdf accessed on 21 August 2024.

FATF (2006), and the Caribbean FATF (2010), highlighted the critical role of BO in tackling tax evasion and money laundering.[226]

In 2015, the OECD launched its ambitious base erosion and profit shifting (BEPS) project to counter the practices employed by MNEs to shift profits. The BEPS Action Plan addressed aggressive tax planning (Actions 2 to 5, 12), abuse of double tax treaties (Actions 6, 7 and 14), misuse of transfer pricing (Actions 8, 9, 10, and 13), and an MLI to implement the action plans (Action 15).[227] It also included initiatives such as country-by-country reporting by multinational companies to create enhanced transparency.

In 2018, the FATF, working with the Egmont Group of Financial Intelligence Units, an informal group of FIUs from various countries, conducted a study investigating how BO has been disguised and misused. The joint study revealed that the current BO regulatory framework is ineffective due to the improper implementation of existing standards rather than any deficiencies in the standards themselves.[228] It further highlighted that the ineffective implementation of existing standards results from gaps in the collection and timely dissemination of accurate and current BO information to law enforcement agencies, risk assessment, deterrence (sanctions and penalties), and cross-border sharing of information for enhanced cooperation. In 2024, the FATF updated its recommendations for anti-money laundering.

Not only the OECD, the FATF, and the UNODC but also the UN which adopted the sustainable development goals in 2015 to be achieved by 2030, include the concept of BO that has been integral to SDGs 16 and 17.[229]

SDG Goal 16, Target 16.4 aims by 2030 to 'significantly reduce illicit financial and arms flows, strengthen the recovery and return of stolen assets and combat all forms of organized crime'.[230] SDG 16.4 explicitly mandates the implementation of policy measures to recover stolen and illegally transferred assets and strategies to combat money laundering and corruption.[231] In addition, SDG 17.1 underscores the need to promote domestic resource mobilization, especially in countries that lack budgetary resources to finance public budgets for collecting tax revenue and other forms of

226. FATF, *The Misuse of Corporate Vehicles, Including Trust and Company Service Providers* (FATF 2006) available at https://www.fatf-gafi.org/content/dam/fatf-gafi/reports/Misuse%20of%20Corporate%20Vehicles%20including%20Trusts%20and%20Company%20Services%20Providers.pdf.coredownload.inline.pdf accessed on 13 August 2024.
227. OECD, *Base Erosion and Profit Shifting (BEPS)*, available at https://www.oecd.org/en/topics/base-erosion-and-profit-shifting-beps.html accessed 21 August 2024.
228. FATF – Egmont Group, *Concealment of Beneficial Ownership*, Paris, France (FATF 2018), p. 76, available at https://www.fatf-gafi.org/en/publications/Methodsandtrends/Concealment-beneficial-ownership.html accessed 21 August 2024.
229. United Nations, Department of Economic and Social Affairs, *Sustainable Development Goals*, available at https://sdgs.un.org/ accessed 21 August 2024.
230. UNODC, *SDG 16: Promote Peaceful and Inclusive Societies for Sustainable Development, Provide Access to Justice for All and Build Effective, Accountable and Inclusive Institutions at All Levels*, available at https://www.unodc.org/romena/en/SDG/sdg-16_-promote-peaceful-inclusive-societies-for-sustainable-development--provide-access-to-justice-for-all-and-build-effective--accountable-and-inclusive-institutions-at-all-levels.html accessed 21 August 2024.
231. *Ibid.*

domestic financing.[232] 'It advocates for the transparency of BO information and making it accessible to the public. It recognizes the importance of BO legislation in combatting tax evasion, money laundering and corruption.' In its framework for monitoring the progress towards these goals, the UN noted that using legal persons and legal arrangements to conceal the identity of beneficial owners can facilitate tax evasion, money laundering and corruption, making it difficult for law enforcement agencies to investigate and detect such cases.[233] It recognized the importance of identifying BO as a crucial step to curb the IFFs from Africa to other countries, which are harmful to the sustainable development of the African continent and its fight against corruption.

In addition to SDGs, the UN also acknowledged the importance of policy institutions (the FATF, the Global Forum and the Tax Justice Network) that play a key role in the work on BO.[234]

Acknowledging the BO as a solution to prevent misuse of legal persons and legal arrangements, the G7 also issued principles focusing on the BO of legal persons and legal arrangements, such as trusts, to promote transparency in their creation, existence, and dissolution. These principles later adopted by the G20 are high-level principles on BO.[235]

Several countries are also introducing legislation requiring legal persons and arrangements to disclose BO.[236] The African Union has also acknowledged this imperative, prioritizing the battle against tax evasion and all forms of IFFs as fundamental to its long-term vision.[237] Other organizations, such as open ownership and open data initiatives, have also undertaken initiatives that promote BO legislation. These organizations serve as advocates for the work on BO. Further, the FACTI panel of the UN also works on promoting BO legislation.[238]

232. UNODC, *SDG 17: Revitalize the Global Partnership for Sustainable Development; United Nations Sustainable Development Goals*, available at https://www.unodc.org/unodc/en/about-unodc/sustainable-development-goals/sdg17_-partnerships.html accessed 21 August 2024.
233. Sustainable Development Solutions Network (SDSN), *Indicators and a Monitoring Framework, Launching a Data Revolution for the Sustainable Development Goals*, available at https://sdgs.un.org/publications/indicators-and-monitoring-framework-sustainable-development-goals-17958 accessed 18 August 2020; Transparency International, *Reforming Global Standards on Beneficial Ownership Transparency* (4 March 2022).
234. African Union, *Report of the High-Level Panel on IFFs from Africa: The Importance of Transparency is Evident in Ongoing Approaches to Tackle IFFs*, Addis Ababa, Ethiopia, available at https://au.int/sites/default/files/documents/40545-doc-IFFs_REPORT.pdf accessed 21 August 2024.
235. G20, *High-Level Principles on Beneficial Ownership Transparency*, Australia (2014), available at https://www.ag.gov.au/integrity/publications/g20-high-level-principles-beneficial-ownership-transparency accessed 21 August 2024.
236. Sophie Lemaitre, *Beneficial Ownership Disclosure at the U.N. General Assembly Against Corruption*, CMI – Anti-Corruption Resource Centre (June 2021), available at https://medium.com/u4-anti-corruption-resource-centre/beneficial-ownership-disclosure-at-ungass-2021-d1b3439f8f36 accessed 21 August 2024.
237. African Union, *Agenda 2063: The Africa We Want*, available at https://au.int/en/agenda2063/overview accessed 21 August 2024.
238. Financial Accountability, *Transparency, and Integrity (FACTI) Panel, Issue Note: Beneficial Ownership Information, United Nations; Transparency International*, The FACTI Panel is Showing a Path to a Better Future. Will Governments Take It? (25 September 2020), available at https://www.transparency.org/en/blog/illicit-financial-flows-facti-panel-path-forward-will-governments-act accessed 21 August 2024.

The historical development of tax transparency has been triggered by banking secrecy and acknowledgements of the misuse of legal persons and legal arrangements by several international policy organizations. To prevent misuse of legal persons and legal arrangements, it is essential to develop a policy framework that combats such misuse. Substantial evidence suggests a strong correlation between BO legislation and initiatives aimed at curbing IFFs, which is particularly crucial in the African context.[239] The key takeaway from these discussions is that the lack of or ineffective BO legislation is a key obstacle in efforts to prevent money laundering and tax avoidance. Disclosing BO information of legal persons and legal arrangements is essential for tax transparency as it helps prevent tax avoidance and addresses other issues connected to IFFs, such as money laundering, tax evasion and corruption. The issue of disguising the BO could be avoided if all the countries had legislative frameworks to collect information on BO, along with an exchange of information agreement to share such information with other countries.[240] There is a growing international consensus that BO legislation is critical in preventing money laundering and tax evasion.[241] Several studies undertaken by international policy organizations have highlighted the misuse of legal persons and legal arrangements for tax avoidance and money laundering. Historical developments show that the OECD and the FATF consider BO legislation to be a critical issue. However, it is also important to note that the anti-money laundering framework of the FATF and Global Standards set by the OECD are soft laws. Their effectiveness depends on their successful implementation in domestic legislation.[242]

The OECD, the FATF, the UNODC and other international organizations have already taken initiatives to address the risk associated with the non-transparency of BO of legal persons and legal arrangements. Implementing initiatives aimed at fostering transparency by preventing the misuse of vehicles can contribute to creating a competitive environment that promotes economic growth and sustainable development. It facilitates ease of doing business and attracts investment into the country.[243] Further, such initiatives assist in reducing corruption to a minimum, enabling law enforcement agencies and tax authorities to enforce the laws they are tasked with effectively and to investigate, prosecute and recover proceeds of IFFs, including tax

239. OECD, *Africa Tax Transparency Report 2022: An African Agenda on Tax Transparency* (OECD Publishing) Paris, p. 17, available at https://www.oecd.org/tax/transparency/documents/tax-transparency-in-africa-2022.htm accessed 21 August 2024.
240. Financial Action Task Force (FATF), *Guidance to Beneficial Ownership of Legal Persons (Recommendation 24)*, Paris, France (FATF March 2023); Financial Action Task Force (FATF), available at https://www.fatf-gafi.org/en/publications/Fatfrecommendations/Guidance-Beneficial-Ownership-Legal-Persons.html accessed 21 August 2024.
241. Department for Business Innovation and Skills, HMRC, *Beneficial Ownership Transparency: Enhancing the Transparency of Beneficial Ownership Information of Foreign Companies Undertaking Certain Economic Activities in the U.K.* (March 2016), available at https://assets.publishing.service.gov.uk/government/uploads/system/uploads/attachment_data/file/512333/bis-16-161-beneficial-ownership-transparency.pdf accessed 21 August 2024.
242. M. Somare, *Automatic Exchange of Financial Account Information for Tax Purposes in the Light of Preventive Measures under the 4th Anti-Money Laundering Directive*, Doctoral thesis, p. 81.
243. UK Government, *Policy Paper: G8 Action Plan Principles to Prevent the Misuse of Companies and Legal Arrangements*, available at https://www.gov.uk/government/publications/g8-action-plan-principles-to-prevent-the-misuse-of-companies-and-legal-arrangements accessed 21 August 2024.

avoidance.[244] The information on BO is crucial to creating a transparent and trustworthy financial system that assists law enforcement agencies in their investigation and prosecutions.

As global cooperation moves towards a new era of international cooperation, with the UN Tax Committee eager to play a pivotal role in international tax discourse, this shift presents an opportunity for African countries to enhance their political influence.[245] This leverage can be used to encourage other countries to exchange tax information and information on BO. African countries must develop the necessary abilities to effectively utilize information related to BO. This includes the ability to receive such information from foreign countries and effectively utilize it through proper training of officials managing the data.

3.5 CONCLUDING REMARKS

Liberalization of cross-border capital movements in the early 1990s resulted in an increase in tax avoidance and evasion because it allowed individuals to hide income and wealth in foreign entities or bank accounts and companies to move income into tax-efficient entities in tax havens. This triggered a response from tax authorities along different lines, which accelerated in the new millennium after a difficult start in the 1990s, particularly after the financial crisis of 2008. This chapter discussed the efforts of governments to combat tax evasion and avoidance by increasing transparency, *inter alia*, by improving the exchange of information between tax authorities and ending banking secrecy, tackling harmful tax competition and the use of tax havens and going after the tax evaders and avoiders themselves (*prosecution of tax evaders, BO transparency*).

It was illustrated here that the EOI under bilateral tax treaties based on the OECD model clause had not been helpful, *inter alia*, because several countries had maintained a reservation on the model article (CH, BE, LUX). It provided for EOI only on request and allowed for the refusal to provide info to be possible on different grounds including based on banking secrecy. Gradually, and in particular after the 2008 financial crisis, EOI standards improved with the introduction of AEOI in the 2005 EU savings tax directive, the 2010 FATCA, the withdrawal of the CH, BE, and Lux reservation to Article 26, the adoption of CRS globally, DAC 1 and DAC 2 (2016) in the EU.

This chapter noted that the use of tax havens was tackled under the OECD and EU efforts to combat harmful tax competition, which resulted in the establishment of the OECD Global Tax Forum and EU blacklists of non-cooperative jurisdictions from 2015 onwards.

---

244. Lough Erne G8 Leaders' Communiqué, available at https://www.gov.uk/government/uploads/system/uploads/attachment_data/file/207771/Lough_Erne_2013_G8_Leaders_Communique.pdf accessed 21 August 2024.
245. United Nations, *Promotion of Inclusive and Effective International Tax Cooperation at the United Nations*, Seventy Eighth Session, Item 17(h) of the Provisional Agenda, available at https://financing.desa.un.org/document/promotion-inclusive-and-effective-international-tax-cooperation-united-nations-a78235 accessed 21 August 2024.

Finally, this chapter concludes that these efforts placed a strong emphasis on promoting legislation requiring the identification of beneficial owners behind the legal person and legal arrangements in opaque tax havens.

CHAPTER 4

Normative Framework for the Definition of Beneficial Ownership

4.1 INTRODUCTION

The earlier chapter emphasized the importance of transparency in general, and BO legislation in particular, in the efforts to reduce IFFs resulting from tax evasion and avoidance, including IFFs resulting from the use of legal persons and legal arrangements to disguise the identities of their BO. This chapter aims to develop a good practice definition of BO against which the national laws of the three target countries can be evaluated, and practical advice can be formulated on how they can strengthen their domestic legal frameworks in this respect (Chapter 5). For that purpose, this chapter will review the definitions of BO as developed in the context of money laundering (section 4.2), corruption (section 4.3), and taxation (section 4.4), and assess their strengths and weaknesses to be better able to distil the elements that should appear in a model definition of BO (section 4.5).

4.2 THE BENEFICIAL OWNERSHIP DEFINITION IN COMBATING MONEY LAUNDERING: THE FINANCIAL ACTION TASK FORCE (FATF)

4.2.1 Background

The FATF is an intergovernmental organization established to set standards for combating money laundering. In 1990, the FATF published its first report containing recommendations for combating money laundering.[246] The report emphasized the need to obtain BO information while opening bank accounts or undertaking financial transactions by financial institutions.[247]

In 2012, the first set of forty recommendations was issued to counter money laundering, with subsequent updates in 2019 and 2023.[248] Unlike other international bodies, the FATF does not prescribe specific laws or regulations for its member countries. Instead, it provides a framework for member countries. This allows various approaches through which member countries can meet the objectives of its recommendations.

The forty recommendations contain essential measures that countries should have in place to identify risks; 'develop policies and domestic coordination, pursue money laundering, terrorist financing, and the financing of proliferation, apply preventive measures for the financial sector and other designated sectors, establish powers and responsibilities for the competent authorities e.g. investigative, law enforcement, and supervisory authorities and other institutional measures, enhance the transparency and availability of BO information of legal persons and arrangements and facilitate international cooperation'.[249]

'The FATF Standards comprise the recommendations and their Interpretive Notes, together with the applicable definitions in the glossary.'[250] The FATF also produces guidance, best practice papers, and other advice to aid countries in implementing FATF standards.

Compliance is assessed through mutual evaluation processes[251] and the assessment processes of the International Monetary Fund and the World Bank, which are based on FATF's standard assessment methodology.

For the purpose of this research, the most relevant FATF recommendations are numbers 24 and 25, which set out rules for countries on legislation of BO and BO transparency of legal persons and legal arrangements and the related recommendations 10 and 22, which set out rules for complying with the obligations of financial

246. Financial Action Task Force (FATF), *The Forty Recommendations of the Financial Action Task Force on Money Laundering* (FATF 1990), available at https://www.fatf-gafi.org/media/fatf/documents/recommendations/pdfs/FATF%20Recommendations%201990.pdf accessed 21 August 2024.
247. Financial Action Task Force (FATF), *The Forty Recommendations of the Financial Action Task Force on Money Laundering* (FATF 1990), p. 2, available at https://www.fatf-gafi.org/media/fatf/documents/recommendations/pdfs/FATF%20Recommendations%201990.pdf accessed 21 August 2024.
248. FATF, *FATF Recommendations: International Standards on Combating Money Laundering and the Financing of Terrorism & Proliferation* (FATF 2023), Paris, France, available at www.fatf-gafi.org/en/publications/Fatfrecommendations/Fatf-recommendations.html accessed 21 August 2024.
249. FATF, *FATF Recommendations: International Standards on Combating Money Laundering and the Financing of Terrorism & Proliferation* (FATF 2023), Paris, France, p. 132, available at www.fatf-gafi.org/en/publications/Fatfrecommendations/Fatf-recommendations.html accessed 21 August 2024.
250. *Ibid.*
251. FATF, *Mutual Evaluations*, available at https://www.fatf-gafi.org/en/topics/mutual-evaluations.html accessed 21 August 2024.

institutions and designated non-financial businesses and professions to identify BO as part of their 'customer due diligence'.[252]

Recommendation 24[253] 'deals with the BO of legal persons and states that countries should assess the risks of the misuse of legal persons for money laundering and terrorist financing and prevent such misuse. To implement this recommendation, countries are required to ensure that there is adequate, accurate, and up-to-date information on the BO and control of legal persons that can be obtained or accessed rapidly and efficiently by competent authorities (and financial institutions) through either a register of BO or an alternative mechanism'. They must also prevent misuse of bearer shares and nominee shareholders or directors. Recommendation 25 includes similar provisions for legal arrangements.[254]

Through its Interpretative Notes to recommendation 24,[255] FATF advocates for a multipronged approach to gathering information because it recognizes the shortcomings of a single approach and finds multipronged approaches that are more effective in countries using them.[256] The use of various data sources, in addition to existing ones, supports the transparency of BO information. This assists in providing law enforcement agencies with access to information in a prompt and accurate manner for

252. FATF, *FATF Recommendations: International Standards on Combating Money Laundering and the Financing of Terrorism & Proliferation* (FATF 2023), Paris, France, p. 132, available at www.fatf-gafi.org/en/publications/Fatfrecommendations/Fatf-recommendations.html accessed 21 August 2024.
253. '24. Transparency and beneficial ownership of legal persons – Countries should assess the risks of misuse of legal persons for money laundering or terrorist financing and take measures to prevent their misuse. Countries should ensure adequate, accurate and up-to-date information on the beneficial ownership and control of legal persons that can be obtained or accessed rapidly and efficiently by competent authorities, through either a register of beneficial ownership or an alternative mechanism. Countries should not permit legal persons to issue new bearer shares or bearer share warrants and take measures to prevent the misuse of existing bearer shares and bearer share warrants. Countries should take effective measures to ensure that nominee shareholders and directors are not misused for money laundering or terrorist financing. Countries should consider facilitating access to beneficial ownership and control information by financial institutions and DNFBPs undertaking the requirements in Recommendations 10 and 22.'
254. '25. Transparency and beneficial ownership of legal arrangements – Countries should assess the risks of the misuse of legal arrangements for money laundering or terrorist financing and take measures to prevent their misuse. In, countries should ensure that there is adequate, accurate and up-to-date information on express trusts and other similar legal arrangements including information on the settlor(s), trustee(s), and beneficiary(ies), that can be obtained or accessed efficiently and promptly by competent authorities. Countries should consider facilitating access to beneficial ownership and control information by financial institutions and DNFBPs undertaking the requirements in Recommendations 10 and 22.'
255. FATF, *FATF Recommendations: International Standards on Combating Money Laundering and the Financing of Terrorism & Proliferation* (FATF 2023), Paris, France, pp. 94, 97-98, available at www.fatf-gafi.org/en/publications/Fatfrecommendations/Fatf-recommendations.html accessed 21 August 2024.
256. FATF, *FATF Recommendations: International Standards on Combating Money Laundering and the Financing of Terrorism & Proliferation* (FATF 2023), Paris, France, pp. 94, 97-98, available at www.fatf-gafi.org/en/publications/Fatfrecommendations/Fatf-recommendations.html accessed 21 August 2024.

cross-verification and investigation. This is beneficial in cases of divergence between different data sources or doubt over the accuracy of the data on BO.[257]

'In addition to recommendations 24 and 25, FATF recommendations 10 and 22 deal with BO information and mandate that countries allow financial institutions and designated non-financial businesses and professions (DNFPB) access to BO information.'[258] Three approaches were provided to fulfil this obligation. The first approach obliges companies to maintain a register of BO and identify and update the BO information of the company's shareholders. The second approach requires companies to take all reasonable steps to identify and update the correct beneficial information of the real owners of the company. This approach provides flexibility, as it obliges the identification of the actual beneficial owners of the company under reasonable circumstances. The third approach relies on information collected from existing sources, such as financial institutions and DNFPBs under recommendations 10 and 22, as well as information collected by law enforcement agencies and companies listed on stock exchanges.

The FATF does not mandate a hierarchy of approaches for countries that implement BO recommendations. The FATF acknowledges that countries have different legal, economic, and cultural environments.[259] Therefore, it recognizes that a more than one-size-fits-all approach to implementing BO transparency is needed.[260] It recommends that countries formulate policies to implement BO transparency by considering the risk assessment of their domestic environments.[261] The FATF advocates for a multipronged approach that employs a combination of methods to implement recommendations.[262]

4.2.1.1 Methodology to Assess the Implementation of FATF Recommendations

In 2013, the FATF finalized a methodology for evaluating the implementation of its recommendations by jurisdictions.[263] This methodology focused on two key aspects: effectiveness and technical compliance.[264] The effectiveness of the assessment examines whether a country has taken reasonable steps to address the risks posed by the non-availability of information, and whether it has a legal and administrative framework capable of addressing such risks. The FATF bases its findings on the methodology

257. *Ibid.*
258. Financial Action Task Force (FATF*), Guidance to Beneficial Ownership of Legal Persons (Recommendation 24)* (FATF March 2023), Paris, France; Financial Action Task Force (FATF), available at https://www.fatf-gafi.org/en/publications/Fatfrecommendations/Guidance-Beneficial-Ownership-Legal-Persons.html accessed 21 August 2024.
259. *Ibid.*
260. *Ibid.*
261. *Ibid.*
262. FATF, *Public Statement on Revisions to R.24*, available at https://www.fatf-gafi.org/en/publications/Fatfrecommendations/R24-statement-march-2022.html accessed 21 August 2024.
263. FATF, *Revisions to Recommendation 24 and Its Interpretive Note-Public Consultation*, available at https://www.fatf-gafi.org/en/publications/Fatfrecommendations/Public-consultation-r24.html accessed 21 August 2024.
264. FATF, *Outcomes FATF Plenary* (March 2022), available at https://www.fatf-gafi.org/en/publications/Fatfgeneral/Outcomes-fatf-plenary-march-2022.html accessed 21 August 2024.

to assess the implementation of its recommendations on eleven critical points referred to as immediate outcomes (IOs).[265]

The methodology also examines the country's technical compliance with the recommendations to ensure that the countries have adequate legal and regulatory frameworks that comply with the FATF's recommendations. Its methodology to assess recommendation 24 related to transparency and BO of legal persons provides the key areas crucial for assessing effectiveness and technical compliance.[266] Immediate outcome 5 of the methodologies lists the criteria that must be met to implement recommendation 24 effectively. To assess the implementation of recommendations, countries are examined to determine if they have implemented a mechanism to prevent the misuse of legal persons to prevent tax evasion, money laundering, and the transfer of proceeds from terrorist activities.

This assessment is based on three critical criteria. 'First, a country must establish legal and regulatory frameworks to prohibit the misuse of legal persons and legal arrangements for tax evasion, money laundering, and terrorist financing.' Second, a framework for adequate transparency of legal persons and legal arrangements exists to allow the detection and investigation of misuse by law enforcement agencies. Third, a

265. FATF, *Methodology for Assessing Compliance with the FATF Recommendations and the Effectiveness of AML/CFT Systems* (FATF updated June 2023), Paris, France, p. 16, available at https://www.fatf-gafi.org/en/publications/Mutualevaluations/Fatf-methodology.html accessed 21 August 2024:

   1 Money laundering and terrorist financing risks are understood and, where appropriate, actions coordinated domestically to combat money laundering and the financing of terrorism and proliferation.
   2 International cooperation delivers appropriate information, financial intelligence, and evidence, and facilitates action against criminals and their assets.
   3 Supervisors appropriately supervise, monitor and regulate financial institutions, DNFBPs and VASPs for compliance with AML/CFT requirements commensurate with their risks.
   4 Financial institutions, DNFBPs and VASPs adequately apply AML/CFT preventive measures commensurate with their risks, and report suspicious transactions.
   5 Legal persons and arrangements are prevented from misuse for money laundering or terrorist financing, and information on their beneficial ownership is available to competent authorities without impediments.
   6 Financial intelligence and all other relevant information are appropriately used by competent authorities for money laundering and terrorist financing investigations.
   7 Money laundering offences and activities are investigated, and offenders are prosecuted and subject to effective, proportionate and dissuasive sanctions.
   8 Proceeds and instrumentalities of crime are confiscated.
   9 Terrorist financing offences and activities are investigated and persons who finance terrorism are prosecuted and subject to effective, proportionate, and dissuasive sanctions.
   10 Terrorists, terrorist organizations and terrorist financiers are prevented from raising, moving and using funds, and from abusing the NPO sector.
   11 Persons and entities involved in the proliferation of weapons of mass destruction are prevented from raising, moving and using funds, consistent with the relevant UNSCRs.

266. Financial Action Task Force (FATF), *Guidance to Beneficial Ownership of Legal Persons (Recommendation 24)* (FATF March 2023), Paris, France; Financial Action Task Force (FATF), available at https://www.fatf-gafi.org/en/publications/Fatfrecommendations/Guidance-Beneficial-Ownership-Legal-Persons.html accessed 21 August 2024.

sufficient communication channel must exist for prompt sharing of up-to-date and complete data.

4.2.2 Definition of Beneficial Ownership under FATF Standards

The FATF provides the most widely recognized definition of beneficial ownership – a starting point for discussing this concept.[267] The definition enshrined in the FATF Glossary provides separate definitions for legal persons and legal arrangements.

In case of legal persons, it defines those as:

> In the context of legal persons, beneficial owner refers to the natural person(s) who ultimately owns or controls a customer and/or the natural person on whose behalf a transaction is being conducted. It also includes those natural persons who exercise ultimate effective control over a legal person or arrangement. Only a natural person can be an ultimate beneficial owner, and more than one natural person can be the ultimate beneficial owner of a given legal person.[268]

4.2.2.1 Natural Person

The first key element of this definition is that, according to the FATF definition, a beneficial owner is always a natural person.[269] Therefore, any person other than a natural person is outside the scope of the definition of a beneficial owner, which excludes the possibility of a legal person such as a company, partnership, or legal arrangement such as trusts being considered beneficial owners. In its interpretative note to recommendation 24, it states that legal ownership and beneficial ownership under the FATF definition are two distinct concepts.[270] In footnote 83 to its recommendation 24, it emphasizes that '*the ultimate beneficial owner is always one or more natural persons*'.[271] Further use of 'ultimately *owns or controls*' makes this meaning

267. FATF, *Beneficial Ownership,* available at https://www.fatf-gafi.org/en/topics/beneficial-ownership.html accessed 21 August 2024.
268. FATF, *FATF Recommendations: International Standards on Combating Money Laundering and the Financing of Terrorism & Proliferation* (FATF 2023), Paris, France, p. 132, available at www.fatf-gafi.org/en/publications/Fatfrecommendations/Fatf-recommendations.html accessed 21 August 2024.
269. Financial Action Task Force, *Guidance Transparency of Beneficial Ownership* (2014) available at https://www.fatf-gafi.org/content/dam/fatf-gafi/guidance/Guidance-transparency-beneficial-ownership.pdf accessed 21 August 2024, Open Ownership, *Beneficial Ownership in Law: Definitions and Thresholds,* available at https://www.openownership.org/en/publications/beneficial-ownership-in-law-definitions-and-thresholds/defining-beneficial-ownership/ accessed 21 August 2024.
270. Financial Action Task Force (FATF), *Guidance to Beneficial Ownership of Legal Persons (Recommendation 24)* (FATF March 2023), Paris, France; Financial Action Task Force (FATF), available at https://www.fatf-gafi.org/en/publications/Fatfrecommendations/Guidance-Beneficial-Ownership-Legal-Persons.html accessed 21 August 2024.
271. *Ibid.*

clear, as a legal entity or legal arrangement can never ultimately own or control. A natural person would always exercise ownership and control.[272]

4.2.2.2 'Ultimately Owns or Controls/Ultimate Effective Control'

The second element is that the FATF defines a beneficial owner as a natural person who 'ultimately owns or controls a customer and/or natural person' *or who exercises* 'ultimate effective control of a given legal person or arrangement'.[273]

It clarifies the meaning of the term 'ultimately owns or controls' or 'ultimate effective control' as 'situations in which ownership/control is exercised through a chain of ownership or by means of control other than direct control'.[274] This clarification states that the term refers to either indirect ownership or indirect control.

In addition to clarification, the methodology for assessing compliance with recommendations[275] as well as interpretative notes to recommendation 10 sets out the obligation of the financial institutions and DNFBS to provide how control is to be identified for identification of BO.[276] It provides a cascading approach for such identification.

For legal persons, it states that:

(a) the identity of the natural person(s) (if any) who ultimately has a controlling ownership interest in a legal person; and
(b) to the extent that there is doubt under (a) as to whether the person(s) with the controlling ownership interest is the beneficial owner(s) or where no natural person exerts control through ownership interests, the identity of the natural person(s) (if any) exercising control of the legal person or arrangement through other means; and
(c) where no natural person is identified under (a) or (b) above, the identity of the relevant natural person who holds the position of senior managing official.[277]

---

272. Stolen Asset Recovery Initiative (StAR), The Puppet Masters: How the Corrupt Use Legal Structures to Hide Stolen Assets and What to Do About It, E. van der Does de Willebois et al., World Bank, Washington, D.C., p.19, available at https://openknowledge.worldbank.org/entities/publication/ec364fd2-92f8-58a0-bd4e-155ac0f644d6 accessed 21 August 2024.
273. FATF, *FATF Recommendations: International Standards on Combating Money Laundering and the Financing of Terrorism & Proliferation* (FATF 2023), Paris, France, p. 132, available at www.fatf-gafi.org/en/publications/Fatfrecommendations/Fatf-recommendations.html accessed 21 August 2024.
274. *Ibid.*
275. FATF, *FATF Recommendations: International Standards on Combating Money Laundering and the Financing of Terrorism & Proliferation* (FATF 2023), Paris, France, p. 44, available at www.fatf-gafi.org/en/publications/Fatfrecommendations/Fatf-recommendations.html accessed 21 August 2024.
276. FATF, *FATF Recommendations: International Standards on Combating Money Laundering and the Financing of Terrorism & Proliferation* (FATF 2023), Paris, France, p. 67, available at www.fatf-gafi.org/en/publications/Fatfrecommendations/Fatf-recommendations.html accessed 21 August 2024.
277. FATF, *FATF Recommendations: International Standards on Combating Money Laundering and the Financing of Terrorism & Proliferation* (FATF 2023), Paris, France, p. 44, available at www.fatf-gafi.org/en/publications/Fatfrecommendations/Fatf-recommendations.html accessed 21 August 2024.

Further, controlling ownership interest has been clarified as 'dependent on the ownership structure of the company and may be based on a threshold, e.g. any person owning more than a certain percentage of the company (e.g. 25%)'.[278]

This criteria in the interpretative notes make it clear that the term 'ultimately owns or controls/ultimate effective control' means, in a cascading manner, (a) controlling ownership interest, which may be dependent on the threshold, (b) if not, then control through other means (c) if not, senior managing officials. However, there is no guidance by FATF on the meaning of 'exercising control … through other means'.

In the case of legal arrangements, the term BO has been defined inclusively. It states that:

> 'In the context of legal arrangements, beneficial owner includes (i) the settlor(s); (ii) the trustee(s); (iii) the protector(s) (if any); (iv) each beneficiary, or where applicable, the class of beneficiaries and objects of power; and (v) any other natural person(s) exercising effective control over the arrangement.'[279]

> 'In the case of a legal arrangement similar to an express trust, beneficial owner refers to the natural person(s) holding an equivalent position to those referred to above. When the trustee and any other party to the legal arrangement is a legal person, the beneficial owner of that legal person should be identified.'[280]

The interpretative notes also suggest the same definition. It states:

(a) for trusts, the identity of the settlor, the trustee(s), the protector (if any), the beneficiaries or class of beneficiaries, and any other natural person exercising ultimate effective control over the trust (including through a chain of control/ownership);
(b) for other legal arrangements, the identity of persons in equivalent or similar positions.[281]

The term 'ultimate effective control' has been clarified inclusively as 'including situations in which ownership/control is exercised through a chain of ownership/control'.[282] It has the same characteristics as the definition of the BO of a legal person. Settlors, trustees, beneficiaries, or natural persons 'exercising ultimate

278. FATF, *FATF Recommendations: International Standards on Combating Money Laundering and the Financing of Terrorism & Proliferation* (FATF 2023), Paris, France, p. 67, available at www.fatf-gafi.org/en/publications/Fatfrecommendations/Fatf-recommendations.html accessed 21 August 2024.
279. FATF, *FATF Recommendations: International Standards on Combating Money Laundering and the Financing of Terrorism & Proliferation* (FATF 2023), Paris, France, p. 123, available at www.fatf-gafi.org/en/publications/Fatfrecommendations/Fatf-recommendations.html accessed 21 August 2024.
280. *Ibid.*
281. FATF, *FATF Recommendations: International Standards on Combating Money Laundering and the Financing of Terrorism & Proliferation* (FATF 2023), Paris, France, p. 67, available at www.fatf-gafi.org/en/publications/Fatfrecommendations/Fatf-recommendations.html accessed 21 August 2024.
282. FATF, *FATF Recommendations: International Standards on Combating Money Laundering and the Financing of Terrorism & Proliferation* (FATF 2023), Paris, France, p. 123, available at www.fatf-gafi.org/en/publications/Fatfrecommendations/Fatf-recommendations.html accessed 21 August 2024.

effective control' have been considered beneficial owners. Furthermore, it provides that the beneficiary needs to be identified during the payout or when exercising vested rights.[283]

4.2.2.3 On Whose Behalf a Transaction Is Being Conducted

The term 'on whose behalf a transaction is being conducted' is included 'to ensure that the financial institution or DNFPBs while identifying the beneficial owners know if the natural person undertaking the transaction is acting on its own accord or on the directions of someone else'.[284]

4.2.3 Critical Assessment of the FATF Definition

The definition of beneficial ownership provided by FATF is straightforward.[285] However, a fundamental problem with the FATF definition is the use of the terms 'ultimately owns or controls' and 'ultimate effective control'. Both the terms have been clarified as 'a chain of ownership or by means of control other than direct control', i.e., indirect ownership and indirect control.[286] However, it is essential to distinguish between the terms 'ultimately owns or controls' and 'ultimate effective control'.

While the word 'ultimately' indicates the natural person at the end of the chain of ownership or control, no definition of the term 'control' or 'effective control' has been provided. In cases where ownership and control are with different persons, interpreting the term 'control' or 'effective control' becomes challenging. Global Forum uses the FATF definition in its country assessments and interchangeably uses the terms 'ultimate' and 'effective', suggesting the same meaning.[287] However, the influence of the Global Forum's country assessment on interpreting the meaning of the terms

283. FATF, *FATF Recommendations: International Standards on Combating Money Laundering and the Financing of Terrorism & Proliferation* (FATF 2023), Paris, France, p. 68, available at www.fatf-gafi.org/en/publications/Fatfrecommendations/Fatf-recommendations.html accessed 21 August 2024.
284. Stolen Asset Recovery Initiative (StAR), The Puppet Masters: How the Corrupt Use Legal Structures to Hide Stolen Assets and What to Do about It, by E. van der Does de Willebois et al., World Bank, Washington, D.C., p. 22, available at https://openknowledge.worldbank.org/entities/publication/ec364fd2-92f8-58a0-bd4e-155ac0f644d6 accessed 21 August 2024.
285. FATF, *Transparency and Beneficial Ownership*, FATF Guidance (2014) (as amended in November 2023), available at http://www.fatf-gafi.org/media/fatf/documents/reports/Guidance-transparency-beneficial-ownership.pdf accessed on 29 September 2020.
286. FATF, *FATF Recommendations: International Standards on Combating Money Laundering and the Financing of Terrorism & Proliferation* (FATF 2023), Paris, France, p. 123, available at www.fatf-gafi.org/en/publications/Fatfrecommendations/Fatf-recommendations.html accessed 21 August 2024.
287. G.P. Hook, *Beneficial Ownership and Trusts: A Critical Analysis of a Central FATF Definition and Its Failure to Meet Policy Objective*, University of Sydney, Master Thesis, p. 108, available at https://ses.library.usyd.edu.au/handle/2123/29387 accessed 21 August 2024; Global Forum on Transparency and Exchange of Information for Tax Purposes (OECD) and Inter-American Development Bank, *A Beneficial Ownership Implementation Toolkit* (OECD Publishing March 2019), Paris, France, available at https://publications.iadb.org/en/beneficial-ownership-implementation-toolkit accessed 21 August 2024.

'ultimate' and 'effective' is unclear. Therefore, a common term should be used to indicate 'ultimately owns or controls' and 'ultimate effective control', which mean the same.

The meaning of the term 'control' has been interpreted in various ways, and various jurisdictions worldwide have varying perspectives on its meaning.[288] Its meaning also varies depending on the legal entity or arrangement type and the ultimate person with a 'controlling ownership interest'[289] of the legal entity or 'chain of ownership/control'[290] of the legal arrangements. The FATF also acknowledges that control can be exercised through various ways and suggests that 'countries should consider various types of ownership interests and ways to exercise control over a legal person that exists within their jurisdiction, under commercial and administrative law, including voting rights, economic rights, convertible stock or outstanding debt that is convertible into voting equity. They should also consider ownership interests and ways to exercise control as the two aspects may have evolved in practice'.[291] For instance, in a company, controlling ownership interests could rest with shareholders, directors, or the board of directors. Shareholders often control the company because they have the power to elect the composition of the board of directors and vote on the critical decisions of the company. However, it may be more complex in other legal arrangements where ownership is separated from control, such as in the case of trust, where multiple parties are involved, including trustees, beneficiaries, and settlors. In such cases, multiple individuals could be considered to have controls when identifying BO.

The FATF uses the term 'controlling ownership interest' to clarify control and suggests the use of threshold, i.e., 'person owning more than a certain percentage of the company (e.g. 25%)'.[292] Andres Knobel notes that several countries use 'ownership thresholds or voting rights' to identify the controlling ownership interest.[293] For instance, the EU Anti-Money Laundering Directive employs a threshold of 25% or more

288. Financial Action Task Force (FATF), *Guidance to Beneficial Ownership of Legal Persons (Recommendation 24)* (FATF March 2023), Paris, France; Financial Action Task Force (FATF), available at https://www.fatf-gafi.org/en/publications/Fatfrecommendations/Guidance-Beneficial-Ownership-Legal-Persons.html accessed 21 August 2024.
289. FATF, *FATF Recommendations: International Standards on Combating Money Laundering and the Financing of Terrorism & Proliferation* (FATF 2023), Paris, France, p. 123, available at www.fatf-gafi.org/en/publications/Fatfrecommendations/Fatf-recommendations.html accessed 21 August 2024.
290. *Ibid.*
291. FATF, *FATF Recommendations: International Standards on Combating Money Laundering and the Financing of Terrorism & Proliferation* (FATF 2023), Paris, France, p. 16, available at www.fatf-gafi.org/en/publications/Fatfrecommendations/Fatf-recommendations.html accessed 21 August 2024.
292. FATF 2023, *FATF Recommendations: International Standards on Combating Money Laundering and the Financing of Terrorism & Proliferation* (FATF 2023), Paris, France, p. 67, available at www.fatf-gafi.org/en/publications/Fatfrecommendations/Fatf-recommendations.html accessed 21 August 2024.
293. A. Knobel, *Beneficial Ownership Definitions: Determining 'Control' Unrelated to Ownership*, Tax Justice Network (23 July 2020), available at https://www.taxjustice.net/2020/07/23/beneficial-ownership-definitions-determining-control-unrelated-to-ownership/ accessed 21 August 2024.

of the company's share capital to determine control.[294] The US Financial Crime Enforcement Network Rule mandates that financial institutions subject to its rule report any individuals owning 25% or more of the legal entity.[295] The CRS for the AEOI also employs a 25% threshold for reporting.[296] Asian Development Bank notes the same trend in Asian Countries.[297] This indicates that the term control has been defined in relation to ownership (holding a certain percentage) in countries' domestic legislation.

Although the threshold approach is a straightforward method for determining control, it has drawbacks. One of the significant drawbacks is the potential for the manipulation of thresholds, which could be used to circumvent the reporting of BO. For instance, an individual may divide the 25% threshold into minor shareholdings held by the other individuals on whom the primary shareholder has influence. Such tactics allow an individual to circumvent reporting as a beneficial owner under the definition of control. Knobel from the Tax Justice Network has shown evidence of the potential to manipulate thresholds.[298]

There can also be situations in which control may exist without ownership (holding a certain percentage). For instance, an individual may exert control via influence through close persons, such as relatives, nominees, internal agreements, or other arrangements that enable the individual to have control without directly holding legal ownership.[299] A global witness investigation revealed that over 410,000 individuals in the United Kingdom hold indirect ownership of UK companies. Indirect ownership 'can be exploited for money laundering and tax evasion'.[300] Professional

294. Directive (EU) 2015/849 of the European Parliament and of the Council of 20 May 2015 on the prevention of the use of the financial system for the purposes of money laundering or terrorist financing, amending Regulation (EU) No 648/2012 of the European Parliament and of the Council, and repealing Directive 2005/60/EC of the European Parliament and of the Council and Commission Directive 2006/70/EC, available at https://eur-lex.europa.eu/legal-content/EN/TXT/?uri=CELEX%3A32015L0849 accessed 21 August 2024.
295. Financial Crimes Enforcement Network, *FinCEN Reminds Financial Institutions CDD Rule Becomes Effective Today*, available at https://www.fincen.gov/news/news-releases/fincen-reminds-financial-institutions-cdd-rule-becomes-effective-today accessed 21 August 2024.
296. Government of Jersey, *Annotated Versions Jersey CRS Guidance Notes*, available at https://www.gov.je/sitecollectiondocuments/tax%20and%20your%20money/id%20annotated%20versions%20jersey%20crs%20guidance%20notes%2010272017%20vp.pdf accessed on 23 August 2024.
297. R. Chhina, *Beneficial Ownership Transparency in Asia and the Pacific*, Asian Development Bank (December 2022), available at https://www.adb.org/publications/beneficial-ownership-transparency-asia-pacific accessed 21 August 2024.
298. A. Knobel, *Beneficial Ownership Definitions: Determining Control Unrelated to Ownership*, Tax Justice Network (23 July 2020), at https://www.taxjustice.net/2020/07/23/beneficial-ownership-definitions-determining-control-unrelated-to-ownership/ accessed on 17 September 2020.
299. Global Witness, *The Great Rip-off: Anonymous Companies and Their Victims*, available at http://greatripoffmap.globalwitness.org/#!/ accessed 9 August 2023.
300. Global Policy Forum, *No Transparency Among UK's Leading Companies* (2014), available at https://archive.globalpolicy.org/component/content/article/221-transnational-corporations/52625-shocking-evidence-shows-scope-of-company-secrecy-in-the-uk.html accessed 21 August 2024.

beneficiaries may also lend their names to circumvent reporting requirements.[301] This means that individuals can influence decisions without direct control through legal ownership. The implication of such control without legal ownership is that the concept will depend on the facts of each case. Pablo Hernández also notes that in identifying control, 'it is probable that both legal and economic analyses are needed to reach a conclusion. However, as the concept will greatly depend on the case at stake, the results could be inconsistent'.[302] The Tax Justice Network advocates for a broad scope of effective control which includes in its scope identification of BO in such cases.[303] Therefore, the scope of the term 'ultimately owns or controls' and 'ultimate effective control' should be broadened to include cases of control without legal ownership.

4.2.4 Summary and Conclusions

Three key elements emerge from the FATF's definition of BO. It is a natural person, distinct from a legal person, who controls the legal person or legal arrangement. Control can be either direct or indirect. The inclusion of the term 'ultimate effective control' signifies control at the end of the chain of ownership. The critical assessment of the definition of BO highlights the need for clarity between the terms 'ultimately owns or controls' and 'ultimate effective control'. The use of a threshold to determine control carries the risk of manipulation. Control can also exist without ownership; therefore, a broad definition is required to cover such situations in its scope.

4.3 THE BENEFICIAL OWNERSHIP DEFINITION IN COMBATING CORRUPTION AND STOLEN ASSET RECOVERY: THE UNCAC AND THE WORLD BANK

4.3.1 Background

The discussion of the United Nations Convention against Corruption (UNCAC) is essential, as it is the only 'legally binding international anti-corruption instrument'.[304] It was established in 2005, and 190 parties are presently members of the UNCAC.[305]

301. FATF, *Professional Money Laundering* (FATF 2018), Paris, France, available at https://www.fatf-gafi.org/en/publications/Methodsandtrends/Professional-money-laundering.html accessed 21 August 2024.
302. P.H. González-Barreda, *Beneficial Ownership in Tax Law and Tax Treaties*, New York: Hart Publishing, 2020, p. 287.
303. A. Knobel, *Beneficial Ownership Definitions: Determining 'Control' Unrelated to Ownership*, Tax Justice Network (23 July 2020), available at https://www.taxjustice.net/2020/07/23/beneficial-ownership-definitions-determining-control-unrelated-to-ownership/ accessed 21 August 2024.
304. United Nations Office on Drugs and Crime (UNODC), *Implementation of Beneficial Ownership Transparency in ASEAN Member States and Timor-Leste* (May 2024), p. 3, available at https://www.unodc.org/roseap/uploads/documents/Publications/2024/Implementation_of_Beneficial_Ownership_Transparency_in_ASEAN_Member_States_and_Timor-Leste.pdf accessed 21 August 2024.
305. United Nations Office on Drugs and Crime (UNODC), *United Nations Convention Against Corruption (UNCAC)*, Vienna, Austria, available at https://www.unodc.org/corruption/en/uncac/learn-about-uncac.html accessed 21 August 2024.

Its three main objectives are (Article 1): '(a) to prevent and combat corruption; (b) to promote, facilitate and support international cooperation and technical assistance including in asset recovery; (c) to promote integrity, accountability and proper management of public affairs and public property'.[306] Its scope is restricted to (Article 2) *'prevention, investigation, and prosecution of corruption, the freezing, seizure, confiscation, and return of the proceeds of offences established in accordance with the Convention'.*[307] *(Emphasis added)*

To achieve its objectives, it provides obligations to the contracting parties such as 'preventive measures, criminalisation and law enforcement, international cooperation, asset recovery, technical assistance and information exchange'.[308]

The process of review of implementation of UNCAC provisions is conducted through a peer review process referred to as the 'implementation review mechanism'.[309] This mechanism assesses the measures taken by countries to implement articles of the UNCAC and provides specific examples to assess such measures.

Chapter 2 of the convention, which addresses the obligation of the contracting parties to undertake preventive measures, includes the provisions governing BO transparency.

Paragraph 2(c) of Article 12 promotes BO transparency to prevent corruption among its parties.[310] Its implementation is reviewed by assessing the measures 'aimed at promoting transparency among private entities, such as through public corporate registration requirements, disclosure of beneficial ownership information and ensuring that such information is available to competent authorities'.[311] It is evaluated through examples such as 'the availability and accessibility of BO information of legal persons and legal arrangements'.[312]

306. Article 1. Statement of purpose, UNCAC, available at https://uncaccoalition.org/the-uncac/united-nations-convention-against-corruption/ accessed 21 August 2024.
307. Article 3. Scope of application, UNCAC, available at https://uncaccoalition.org/the-uncac/united-nations-convention-against-corruption/ accessed 21 August 2024.
308. Chapter II to VI of UNCAC, available at https://uncaccoalition.org/the-uncac/united-nations-convention-against-corruption/ accessed 21 August 2024.
309. United Nations Office on Drugs and Crime (UNODC), *Implementation Review Mechanism*, available at https://www.unodc.org/corruption/en/uncac/implementation-review-mechani sm.html accessed 21 August 2024.
310. (c)Promoting transparency among private entities, including, where appropriate, measures regarding the identity of legal and natural persons involved in the establishment and management of corporate entities.
311. United Nations Office on Drugs and Crime (UNODC), *Guidance to Filling in the Revised Draft Self-Assessment Checklist on the Implementation of Chapters II (Preventive Measures) and V (Asset Recovery) of the United Nations Convention Against Corruption*, CAC/COSP/IRG/2016/CRP.1, 16 June 2016, pp. 51-52, 63, 70, available at https://www.unodc.org/documents/treaties/UNCAC/WorkingGroups/ImplementationReviewGroup/20-24June2016/V1603598e.pdf accessed 21 August 2024.
312. United Nations Office on Drugs and Crime (UNODC), *Guidance to Filling in the Revised Draft Self-Assessment Checklist on the Implementation of Chapters II (Preventive Measures) and V (Asset Recovery) of the United Nations Convention Against Corruption*, CAC/COSP/IRG/2016/CRP.1, 16 June 2016, p. 52, available at https://www.unodc.org/documents/treaties/UNCAC/WorkingGroups/ImplementationReviewGroup/20-24June2016/V1603598e.pdf accessed 21 August 2024.

Paragraph 1(a) of Article 14 provides for measures to prevent money laundering and advocates that countries mandatorily oblige financial institutions to collect and store information on the BO of their customers as part of customer due diligence.[313] Its implementation is reviewed by assessing the measures such as 'the legal provisions, regulations, policies or other forms of guidance issued by regulatory or supervisory bodies'.[314] It is evaluated through examples such as 'compliance reviews by financial sector regulators; sanctions issued for non-compliance, the number of suspicious transaction reports received by the financial intelligence Unit (FIU) or similar body, as well as information on whether those reports led to investigations and/or prosecutions'.[315]

Asset recovery is also considered one of the fundamental implementation principles of the convention under Article 51.[316] Paragraph 1 of Article 52 obliges parties to the convention explicitly '*to require financial institutions within its jurisdiction to verify the identity of customers, to take reasonable steps to determine the identity of beneficial owners of funds deposited into high-value accounts and to conduct enhanced scrutiny of accounts sought or maintained by or on behalf of individuals who are, or have been, entrusted with prominent public functions and their family members and close associates*'.[317] (*emphasis added*) In implementing this article, the UNCAC in its technical guide recommends that parties may '*prohibit financial institutions from accepting a corporate vehicle or a legal entity the identity of which cannot be established as a beneficial owner*' in defining 'beneficial owner'.[318] (*emphasis added*)

Its implementation is reviewed by assessing the measures such as 'types of financial institutions and, where applicable, any other entities subject to customer due diligence requirements, record keeping and other preventive measures and the systems

313. United Nations Office on Drugs and Crime (UNODC), Art. 14(1)(a), *United Nations Convention Against Corruption (UNCAC)*, Vienna, Austria. *(a) Institute a comprehensive domestic regulatory and supervisory regime for banks and non-bank financial institutions, including natural or legal persons that provide formal or informal services for the transmission of money or value and, where appropriate, other bodies particularly susceptible to money laundering, within its competence, in order to deter and detect all forms of money-laundering, which regime shall emphasize requirements for customer and, where appropriate, beneficial owner identification, record-keeping and the reporting of suspicious transactions.*
314. United Nations Office on Drugs and Crime (UNODC), *Guidance to Filling in the Revised Draft Self-Assessment Checklist on the Implementation of Chapters II (Preventive Measures) and V (Asset Recovery) of the United Nations Convention Against Corruption*, CAC/COSP/IRG/2016/CRP.1, 16 June 2016, p. 63, available at https://www.unodc.org/documents/treaties/UNCAC/WorkingGroups/ImplementationReviewGroup/20-24June2016/V1603598e.pdf accessed 21 August 2024.
315. *Ibid.*
316. Stolen Asset Recovery Initiative (StAR), *Mandate*, available at https://star.worldbank.org/focus-area/uncac accessed 21 August 2024.
317. UN Secretariat, *Thematic Report: Implementation of Provisions of a Cross-Cutting Nature in Chapters II and V of the United Nations Convention Against Corruption*, CAC/COSP/IRG/2022/8, p. 2, available at https://www.unodc.org/documents/treaties/UNCAC/WorkingGroups/ImplementationReviewGroup/7-11Nov2022/CAC-COSP-IRG-2022-8/2211181E.pdf accessed 21 August 2024.
318. UNODC, *Technical Guide to the United Nations Convention Against Corruption* (2009), p. 195, available at https://www.unodc.org/documents/treaties/UNCAC/Publications/TechnicalGuide/09-84395_Ebook.pdf accessed 21 August 2024.

in place to identify PEPs'.[319] Examples of the implementation of those measures 'include relevant jurisprudence, regulations, policies and/ or guidance notes reports, studies, statistics or any other relevant information that illustrates the measures your country has taken to implement this provision in practice'.[320]

Article 57 provides the legal basis for recovering stolen assets from 'public funds'. The Stolen Asset Recovery (StAR) Initiative was established by the World Bank to assist countries in implementing Chapter V of the UNCAC on asset recovery.[321]

The StAR Initiative in its 2011 report, 'the puppet masters' revealed the misuse of legal persons and legal arrangements.[322] The report showed the ease with which legal persons and arrangements could be created and misused for money laundering and concealing the true identities of their owners. Moreover, it emphasized its implications for law enforcement agencies to prosecute and investigate such cases. While providing evidence of such misuse, the report, through its recommendations, also proposed best practices, drafted definitions to address such misuse, and defined BO.[323]

4.3.2 Definition of Beneficial Ownership under UNCAC and World Bank Standards

4.3.2.1 The UNCAC

Although the term 'Beneficial Ownership' is not explicitly defined in the UNCAC, the technical guide prepared by the UNODC and the UNICRI for the UNCAC states that it must be interpreted as:

> Any person with a direct or indirect interest in or control over assets or transactions.[324]

319. UNODC, *Guidance to Filling in the Revised Draft Self-Assessment Checklist on the Implementation of Chapters II (Preventive Measures) and V (Asset Recovery) of the United Nations Convention Against Corruption*, CAC/COSP/IRG/2016/CRP.1, 16 June 2016, pp. 51-52, 63, 70, available at https://www.unodc.org/documents/treaties/UNCAC/WorkingGroups/ImplementationReviewGroup/20-24June2016/V1603598e.pdf accessed 21 August 2024.
320. UNODC, *Guidance to Filling in the Revised Draft Self-Assessment Checklist on the Implementation of Chapters II (Preventive Measures) and V (Asset Recovery) of the United Nations Convention Against Corruption*, CAC/COSP/IRG/2016/CRP.1, 16 June 2016, p. 70, available at https://www.unodc.org/documents/treaties/UNCAC/WorkingGroups/ImplementationReviewGroup/20-24June2016/V1603598e.pdf accessed 21 August 2024.
321. Stolen Asset Recovery Initiative (StAR), *Mandate*, available at https://star.worldbank.org/focus-area/uncac accessed 21 August 2024.
322. Stolen Asset Recovery Initiative (StAR), The Puppet Masters: How the Corrupt Use Legal Structures to Hide Stolen Assets and What to Do about It, E. van der Does de Willebois et al., World Bank, Washington, D.C., p. 21, available at https://openknowledge.worldbank.org/entities/publication/ec364fd2-92f8-58a0-bd4e-155ac0f644d6 accessed 21 August 2024.
323. UNODC, *Guidance to Filling in the Revised Draft Self-Assessment Checklist on the Implementation of Chapters II (Preventive Measures) and V (Asset Recovery) of the United Nations Convention Against Corruption*, CAC/COSP/IRG/2016/CRP.1, 16 June 2016, p. 70, available at https://www.unodc.org/documents/treaties/UNCAC/WorkingGroups/ImplementationReviewGroup/20-24June2016/V1603598e.pdf accessed 21 August 2024.
324. UNODC and UNICRI, *Technical Guide to the United Nations Convention Against Corruption* (2009), p. 69, available at https://www.unodc.org/documents/treaties/UNCAC/Publications

Several distinct elements emerge from this definition. First, the use of the term 'any person' in the definition suggests that legal persons can be identified as beneficial owners. Article 12(2)(c) of the UNCAC, which mandates the identification of BO, confirms this as it requires the identification of natural and legal persons. It states, 'promoting transparency among private entities, including, where appropriate, measures regarding the identity of legal and natural persons involved in the establishment and management of corporate entities'.[325]

Second, the term 'direct interest ... in' implies direct legal ownership or rights and entitlements over assets or transactions. Instances of such direct interest include ownership of land or holding shares in a company.

Third, the term 'indirect interest ... in' expands the scope of BO to include persons who may not hold assets or transactions in their name but still benefit from or exert influence on such assets or transactions.

Finally, the use of the term 'control over assets or transactions' indicates that not only direct and indirect interests are included, but also control, which allows the person to influence the decision or use of the asset or the transaction.

On the legal interpretation of the term beneficial owner, the UNCAC urges parties to adopt a 'common understanding of the essential elements of BO'.[326] It also suggests that law enforcement agencies consistently understand the methods available for collecting BO information and the limitations on sharing such information under the domestic legal framework.[327]

4.3.2.2 The World Bank StAR

The Puppet Master's report issued by the World Bank's Stolen Asset Recovery Initiative presents its definition of BO used by the World Bank in funding countries.

It defines BO as:

> The natural person who ultimately owns or controls the corporate vehicle or benefits from its assets, the person on whose behalf a transaction is being conducted, or both. Beneficial owners also include those who exercise ultimate effective control over a legal person or arrangement.[328]

/TechnicalGuide/09-84395_Ebook.pdf accessed 21 August 2024; United Nations Office on Drugs and Crime (UNODC), *Implementation of Beneficial Ownership Transparency in ASEAN Member States and Timor-Leste* (May 2024), p. 3, available at https://www.unodc.org/roseap/uploads/documents/Publications/2024/Implementation_of_Beneficial_Ownership_Transparency_in_ASEAN_Member_States_and_Timor-Leste.pdf accessed 21 August 2024.

325. UNODC, *United Nations Convention Against Corruption (UNCAC), Article 12(2)(c)*, Vienna, Austria.
326. UNODC, Point 9, Resolution 9/7: Promoting Beneficial Ownership Transparency, 9th Session, UN Convention Against Corruption, Vienna, Austria, available at https://www.unodc.org/unodc/en/corruption/COSP/session9-resolutions.html#Res.9-7 accessed on 16 August 2023.
327. *Ibid.*
328. Stolen Asset Recovery Initiative (StAR), The Puppet Masters: How the Corrupt Use Legal Structures to Hide Stolen Assets and What to Do about It, E. van der Does de Willebois et al., World Bank, Washington, D.C., p. 265, available at https://openknowledge.worldbank.org/entities/publication/ec364fd2-92f8-58a0-bd4e-155ac0f644d6 accessed 21 August 2024.

The definition proposed by the World Bank's Stolen Asset Recovery Initiative has the same elements as the FATF Definition. The primary distinction between them is the use of the terms 'corporate vehicles' and 'the beneficiary of the assets on whose behalf the transaction is being undertaken'.[329]

It defines corporate vehicles as a 'broad concept that refers to all forms of legal entities and legal arrangements through which a wide variety of commercial activities are conducted, and assets are held (for example, corporations, trusts, partnerships, foundations, and others)'.[330]

In addition, it suggests two distinct approaches for identifying BO.[331] The first approach utilizes a formal definition, such as the one suggested above, that establishes a stringent set of conditions to identify BO.[332] This is based on the rationale that legal ownership is necessary for an individual to exercise ownership, control, or benefit from the asset.[333] Without legal ownership, an individual may be unable to control a legal entity or arrangement effectively. Its key focus is not on identifying the person who effectively controls but who fulfils the conditions set out to identify legal ownership. The first approach combines a formal definition with a threshold to identify ownership.[334] For example, holding a certain percentage of shareholding or voting rights in a company may be sufficient to fulfil the formal definition for the identification of BO.

The second approach focuses on substance over form.[335] The key focus of the substance over form approach is to identify the natural person who owns, controls, or

329. Stolen Asset Recovery Initiative (StAR), The Puppet Masters: How the Corrupt Use Legal Structures to Hide Stolen Assets and What to Do about It, Emile van der Does de Willebois et al., World Bank, Washington, D.C., p. 21, available at https://openknowledge.worldbank.org/entities/publication/ec364fd2-92f8-58a0-bd4e-155ac0f644d6 accessed 21 August 2024.
330. Stolen Asset Recovery Initiative (StAR), The Puppet Masters: How the Corrupt Use Legal Structures to Hide Stolen Assets and What to Do about It, by E. van der Does de Willebois et al., World Bank, Washington, D.C., p. 265, available at https://openknowledge.worldbank.org/entities/publication/ec364fd2-92f8-58a0-bd4e-155ac0f644d6 accessed 21 August 2024.
331. Stolen Asset Recovery Initiative (StAR), *Glossary of Asset Recovery Terms*, available at https://star.worldbank.org/glossary-asset-recovery-terms accessed 21 August 2024.
332. Financial Action Task Force (FATF), *Guidance to Beneficial Ownership of Legal Persons (Recommendation 24)* (FATF March 2023), Paris, France; Financial Action Task Force (FATF), available at https://www.fatf-gafi.org/en/publications/Fatfrecommendations/Guidance-Beneficial-Ownership-Legal-Persons.html accessed 21 August 2024; Stolen Asset Recovery Initiative (StAR), The Puppet Masters: How the Corrupt Use Legal Structures to Hide Stolen Assets and What to Do about It, E. van der Does de Willebois et al., World Bank, Washington, D.C., p. 24, available at https://openknowledge.worldbank.org/entities/publication/ec364fd2-92f8-58a0-bd4e-155ac0f644d6 accessed 21 August 2024.
333. World Bank, Chapter 9: Beneficial Ownership Transparency, *in* Enhancing Government Effectiveness and Transparency: The Fight Against Corruption, World Bank (2020), Washington, D.C., available at https://www.worldbank.org/en/topic/governance/publication/enhancing-government-effectiveness-and-transparency-the-fight-against-corruption accessed on 23 August 2024.
334. Extractive Industries Transparency Initiative (EITI) and Open Ownership, *Technical Guidance: Defining and Capturing Data on the Ownership and Control of State-Owned Enterprises* (February 2023), available at https://eiti.org/guidance-notes/defining-and-capturing-data-ownership-and-control-state-owned-enterprises accessed 21 August 2024.
335. Stolen Asset Recovery Initiative (StAR), The Puppet Masters: How the Corrupt Use Legal Structures to Hide Stolen Assets and What to Do about It, E. van der Does de Willebois et al., World Bank, Washington, D.C., p. 25, available at https://openknowledge.worldbank.org/entities/publication/ec364fd2-92f8-58a0-bd4e-155ac0f644d6 accessed 21 August 2024.

benefits, rather than merely relying on a threshold approach that may reveal legal ownership but not BO. For example, nominees, trustees, or relatives of the owner may be legal owners and fulfil the criteria prescribed by the threshold approach. However, they may not be considered the beneficial owners.

4.3.3 Critical Assessment of the UNCAC and World Bank Definition on BO

While the UNCAC definition includes crucial elements such as direct and indirect interest and control, its fundamental problem is not using the term 'natural person' to identify the beneficial owner. It uses the term 'any person'. Evidence has shown that most countries use the term 'natural person' to identify the BO that hides behind legal persons and legal arrangements.[336] For instance, 'Afghanistan, Cameroon, Colombia, the Republic of Congo, Kazakhstan, Liberia, and Malawi' do not use the term 'natural person' in their definition of BO.[337]

The StAR definition departs from the wording of the FATF definition and uses the terms 'corporate vehicle' and 'benefits from the assets'. Using the term 'corporate vehicle' does not make any difference, as it achieves the same objective as the FATF definition of identifying beneficial owners of legal persons and legal arrangements. However, using the term 'benefits from the assets' widens its scope and includes identifying beneficial owners of assets.

4.3.4 Summary and Conclusions

The definitions from the UNCAC and StAR emphasize the importance of BO legislation. The UNCAC definition lacks clarity as it does not use 'natural persons'. This shortcoming of the UNCAC emphasizes the importance of including the term 'natural person' in the definition. In contrast, the StAR definition aligns with the FATF Definition. It broadens the scope of the BO by including the term 'benefits from the assets' to include the identification of the BO of assets.

---

336. Extractive Industries Transparency Initiative (EITI), *Legal Approaches to Beneficial Ownership Transparency in EITI Countries* (June 2019), p. 6, available at https://eiti.org/sites/default/files/attachments/legal_approaches_to_beneficial_ownership_transparency_in_eiti_countries.pdf accessed 29 September 2020.
337. Open Ownership, *Beneficial Ownership in Law: Definitions and Thresholds*, Policy Briefing (October 2020), p. 6, available at https://www.openownership.org/en/publications/beneficial-ownership-in-law-definitions-and-thresholds/ accessed on 21 August 2024; Extractive Industries Transparency Initiative (EITI), *Legal Approaches to Beneficial Ownership Transparency in EITI Countries* (June 2019), p. 6, available at https://eiti.org/files/documents/legal_approaches_to_beneficial_ownership_transparency_in_eiti_countries.pdf accessed 29 September 2020.

4.4 THE BENEFICIAL OWNERSHIP DEFINITION IN COMBATING TAX EVASION AND AVOIDANCE: TAX TREATIES AND THE GLOBAL FORUM ON TRANSPARENCY AND EXCHANGE OF INFORMATION FOR TAX PURPOSES

4.4.1 Introduction

4.4.1.1 Tax Treaties

The concept of BO was first introduced in 1966 in a protocol to the US-UK tax treaty, which provided 15% withholding tax in the case of dividends and exemption from tax in the United States when the recipient of such income is the beneficial owner.[338] Following the lead of the US-UK treaty, the OECD introduced this concept in its Model Tax Convention in 1977.[339] This concept was also included in the UN Model Tax Convention.[340]

It is essential to first understand the context in which they are introduced. The term was introduced to determine the person entitled to receive treaty benefits characterized by reduced withholding tax rates on interest, dividends, and royalties. The concept of the beneficial owner was included in paragraph 2 of Articles 10 and 11 and paragraph 1 of Article 12 to ensure that the term 'paid to a resident' does not allow the use of the treaty by a conduit person on behalf of another person to receive dividends, interest, and royalties.[341]

The term BO serves distinct purposes in different contexts. In tax treaties, it is used to determine eligibility to determine the reduced withholding rates on interest, dividend and royalty income. However, the Global Forum has integrated the concept of BO into its standards for the exchange of information. It is essential to recognize that these two are separate legal frameworks with distinct objectives. In the case of tax treaties, the objective is to determine the eligibility of the reduced withholding rates in interest, dividends and royalties. In contrast, the focus of global forums is on access and exchange of BO information to tax authorities to prevent tax evasion and avoidance. While both frameworks use the term BO, they operate in different contexts and should not be confused.

338. C.P. du Toit, The Evolution of the Term 'Beneficial Ownership' in Relation to International Taxation over the Past 45 Years, *Bulletin for International Taxation* 64, no. 10 (2010), IBFD https://doi.org/10.59403/8x6ad6 accessed 3 September 2025; 1966 Protocol to the 1945 United Kingdom–United States Tax Treaty.
339. OECD, *Model Tax Convention on Income and on Capital* (1977).
340. United Nations, *Model Double Taxation Convention Between Developed and Developing Countries* (2017 Update), New York, United Nations, available at https://www.un.org/esa/ffd/wp-content/uploads/2018/05/MDT_2017.pdf accessed on 21 August 2024.
341. Paragraph 12.3, OECD, *OECD Model Commentary on Article 10* (2017).

4.4.1.2 *The Global Forum*

The Global Forum on Transparency and Exchange of Information for Tax Purposes (Global Forum) aims to promote tax transparency and the exchange of information standards among its members and other countries.[342] It achieves this aim through its two standards: '(1) the standard on the exchange of information on request (EOIR) and (2) the standard on the automatic exchange of information (AEOI).'[343]

EOIR standards require the contracting states to exchange 'foreseeably relevant information' on request, which also includes BO information.[344] 'The concept of beneficial owner has been incorporated into Global Forum's Terms of Reference for Peer Reviews for EOIR.'[345] It states that:

> 'A. Availability of information: Essential elements'
>
> 'A.1 Jurisdiction should ensure that ownership and identity information, including information on legal and beneficial owners, for all relevant entities and arrangements, is available to their competent authorities.'
>
>> 'A.1.1. Jurisdictions should ensure that information is available to their competent authorities that identifies the owners of companies and any bodies corporate. Owners include legal owners and beneficial owners (including, in any case where a legal owner acts on behalf of any other person as a nominee or under a similar arrangement, that other person), as well as persons in an ownership chain.'
>>
>> 'A.1.2. Where jurisdictions permit the issuance of bearer shares, they should have appropriate mechanisms in place that allow the owners of such shares to be identified. One possibility among others is a custodial arrangement with a recognised custodian or other similar arrangement to immobilise such shares.'
>>
>> 'A.1.3. Jurisdictions should ensure that information is available to their competent authorities that identifies the partners in, and the beneficial owners of, any partnership that has income, deductions or credits for tax purposes in the jurisdiction, (ii) carries on business in the jurisdiction or (iii) is a limited partnership formed under the laws of that jurisdiction.'
>>
>> 'A.1.4. Jurisdictions should take all reasonable measures to ensure that BO information is available to their competent authorities in respect of express

---

342. OECD, *Beneficial Ownership and Tax Transparency: Implementation and Remaining Challenges: OECD and Global Forum Report to G20 Finance Ministers and Central Bank Governors* (OECD Publishing 2024), Paris, available at https://doi.org/10.1787/f95790b1-en accessed 21 August 2024.
343. OECD, *Beneficial Ownership and Tax Transparency: Implementation and Remaining Challenges: OECD and Global Forum Report to G20 Finance Ministers and Central Bank Governors* (OECD Publishing 2024), Paris, p. 11, available at https://doi.org/10.1787/f95790b1-en accessed 21 August 2024.
344. OECD and Inter-American Development Bank (IDB), *Building Effective Beneficial Ownership Frameworks: A Joint Global Forum and IDB Toolkit – Second Edition* (OECD Publishing 2024), Paris, p. 32, available at www.oecd.org/tax/transparency/documents/effective-beneficial-ownership-frameworks-toolkit-second-edition-2024.pdf.
345. OECD, *Handbook for Peer Reviews on Transparency and Exchange of Information on Request: Second Round*, Global Forum on Transparency and Exchange of Information for Tax Purposes (OECD Publishing 2023), Paris, p. 12, available at https://www.oecd.org/tax/transparency/documents/handbook-for-peer-reviews-on-transparency-and-exchange-of-information-on-request.pdf accessed 21 August 2024.

> trusts (i) governed by the laws of that jurisdiction, (ii) administered in that jurisdiction, or (iii) in respect of which a trustee is resident in that jurisdiction.'
> 'A.1.5. Jurisdictions that allow for the establishment of foundations should ensure that information is available to their competent authorities for foundations formed under those laws to identify the founders, members of the foundation council, and beneficiaries (where applicable), as well as any beneficial owners of the foundation or persons with the authority to represent the foundation.'

'A.3 Banking information should be available for all account holders.'

> 'A.3.1. Banking information should include all records pertaining to the accounts as well as to related financial and transactional information, including information regarding the legal and beneficial owners of the accounts.'[346]

The Global Forum adopts FATF recommendations 10, 11, 17, 22, 24, and 25 to interpret BO in principles A.1 and A.2.[347]

AEOI standards also include BO, which requires financial institutions to collect and report BO information of 'controlling persons'.[348]

4.4.2 Definition of Beneficial Ownership under the OECD Model and the Global Forum

It is essential to differentiate between the concept of BO in the context of tax treaties and in the context of IFFs. While these concepts seem similar, they are fundamentally different. They serve distinct purposes and applications.

4.4.2.1 The OECD Model

Before we discuss the meaning of the term 'BO' as a starting point, it would be beneficial to underline that the scope of the term is specific to the tax area. First, the concept is used and understood in the context of Articles 10 (dividends),[349] 11

346. *Ibid.*
347. OECD, *Handbook for Peer Reviews on Transparency and Exchange of Information on Request: Second Round*, Global Forum on Transparency and Exchange of Information for Tax Purposes (OECD Publishing 2023), Paris, para. 21, p. 23, available at https://www.oecd.org/tax/transparency/documents/handbook-for-peer-reviews-on-transparency-and-exchange-of-information-on-request.pdf accessed 21 August 2024; OECD and Inter-American Development Bank (IDB), *Building Effective Beneficial Ownership Frameworks: A Joint Global Forum and IDB Toolkit – Second Edition* (OECD Publishing 2024), Paris, p. 32, available at www.oecd.org/tax/transparency/documents/effective-beneficial-ownership-frameworks-toolkit-second-edition-2024.pdf accessed 21 August 2024.
348. Global Forum on Transparency and Exchange of Information for Tax Purposes (OECD) and Inter-American Development Bank, *A Beneficial Ownership Implementation Toolkit* (OECD Publishing March 2019), Paris, France, p. 10, available at https://publications.iadb.org/en/beneficial-ownership-implementation-toolkit accessed 21 August 2024.
349. Paragraph 2 of Art. 10 on Dividends: However, dividends paid by a company which is a resident of a Contracting State may also be taxed in that State according to the laws of that State, but if the beneficial owner of the dividends is a resident of the other Contracting State, the tax so charged shall not exceed ... .

(interest),[350] and 12 (royalties)[351] of the OECD Model Convention, which seeks to ensure that treaty benefits (including reduced withholding tax rates) are available only to the beneficial owner of the income who is a resident of the other contracting state.

Second, the OECD Commentary (paragraph 12.1) clarifies that the term must be interpreted in 'context' to 'paid to a resident' and considering the 'object and purpose of the convention', rather than in 'narrow technical sense (such as the meaning that it has under the trust law of many common law countries)'.[352] The concept clarifies 'that the state of source is not obliged to give up taxing rights over dividend income merely because that income was paid directly to a resident of a State with which the State of the source had concluded a convention, but only if the recipient is the beneficial owner'.[353] Relief would thus 'not be available if the income is paid to a resident of the other Contracting State who is acting in the capacity of agent or nominee' or who acts as a mere conduit.

Third, the term should not be considered a general anti-abuse provision to prevent treaty shopping, as such abuse is dealt with by 'Article 29 and the principles on improper use of the Convention in the Commentary on Article 1'.[354] This means that even if the recipient of the income is the beneficial owner, the reduced rates do not need to be automatically granted, particularly in other cases of abuse, such as certain forms of treaty shopping addressed by Articles 1 and 29 of the OECD Model.

In addition, it should be noted that the 2014 OECD update provided crucial clarification to the term BO, making older definitions pre-2014 model less relevant for a '*de lege ferenda*' discussion. The discussion in this section will be based on the clarifications provided in the 2014 OECD Update. With this restrictive scope in mind, let us now discuss the meaning of the term 'BO', which is defined in neither the OECD Model Tax Convention nor the UN Model Tax Convention.

The term was introduced as a clarification of the term 'paid to a resident'.[355] In its commentary on Article 10, the OECD provides negative clarification of its meaning. It states that in the case of an agent, a nominee, or a conduit company:

> The direct recipient of the dividend is not the beneficial owner because that recipient's right to use and enjoy the dividend is constrained by a contractual or legal obligation to pass on the payment received to another person.[356]

Based on the negative clarification provided by the OECD, several distinct elements emerge in relation to the meaning of the term BO.

350. Paragraph 2 of Art. 11 on Interest: However, interest arising in a Contracting State may also be taxed in that State according to the laws of that State, but if the beneficial owner of the interest is a resident of the other Contracting State, the tax so charged shall not exceed … .
351. Paragraph 3 of Art. 12 on Royalties: The provisions of para. 1 shall not apply if the beneficial owner of the royalties, being a resident of a Contracting State, carries on business in the other Contracting State in which the royalties arise through a permanent establishment situated therein.
352. Paragraph 12.1, OECD, OECD Model commentary on Art. 10, 2017.
353. Paragraph 12, OECD, OECD Model commentary on Art. 10, 2017.
354. Paragraph 12.5, OECD, OECD Model commentary on Art. 10, 2017.
355. Paragraph 12, OECD, OECD Model commentary on Art. 10, 2017.
356. Paragraph 12.4, OECD, OECD Model commentary on Art. 10, 2017.

First, the definition refers to a 'direct recipient' of the dividends, as opposed to a person who receives the dividends at a later stage.

Second, the direct recipient's 'right to use and enjoy' the income received is constrained so that the recipient cannot freely decide on the use of the income. Thus, whereas the beneficial owner may either decide to use such income, spend it, or reinvest it, a direct recipient who acts as an intermediary, such as an agent, a nominee, or a conduit company, does not have that right and thus does not benefit from the income.[357]

Third, the direct recipient's right is constrained 'by a contractual or legal obligation to pass on' the income to another person. The OECD Commentary emphasizes the legal obligation to pass on funds rather than economic control in interpreting the term. A similar wording has been used in defining BO in the commentary to Article 11 and Article 12.[358]

Fourth, the requirement that the recipient must pass on the income under an agreement or legal requirement may be clear from legal documents or 'on the basis of facts and circumstances showing that, in substance, the recipient clearly does not have the right to use and enjoy the dividend'. It states that 'such an obligation will normally derive from relevant legal documents but may also be found to exist based on facts and circumstances showing that, in substance, the recipient clearly does not have the right to use and enjoy the dividend unconstrained by a contractual or legal obligation to pass on the payment received to another person'.[359] A similar wording has been used in the commentary to Article 11 and Article 12.[360]

4.4.2.2 The Global Forum

The Global Forum uses the concept of BO to exchange information between tax authorities. It does not use the OECD model's convention concept. Instead, it adopts the definition provided by the FATF, which refers to 'the natural person(s) who ultimately owns or controls a customer and/or the natural person on whose behalf a transaction is being conducted. It also includes those natural persons who exercise ultimate effective control over a legal person or arrangement. Only a natural person can be an ultimate beneficial owner, and more than one natural person can be the ultimate

357. *Ibid.*
358. Paragraph 10.2, OECD, OECD Model commentary on Art. 11, 2017; para. 4.3, OECD, OECD Model commentary on Art. 12, 2017, Preface to Arts 10-12, E. Kemmerson and A. Streicher, Introduction, in K. Vogel (ed.), *Klaus Vogel on Double Taxation Conventions* (2022), 5th ed., M. no. 33, p. 837.
359. Paragraph 12.4, OECD, OECD Model commentary on Art. 10, 2017.
360. Paragraph 10.2, OECD, OECD Model commentary on Art. 11, 2017; para. 4.3, OECD, OECD Model commentary on Art. 12, 2017, Preface to Arts 10-12, E. Kemmerson and A. Streicher, Introduction, in K. Vogel (ed.), *Klaus Vogel on Double Taxation Conventions* (2022), 5th ed., M. no. 33, p. 837.

beneficial owner of a given legal person'[361] in defining the term under the EOIR standard prescribed in principles A.1 and A.2.[362]

The term effective control in the definition is similar to the FATF definition and means 'situations in which ownership/control is exercised through a chain of ownership or by means of control other than direct control'.[363] This clarification states that the term refers to indirect ownership or control for EOIR Standards.

For the adoption of such a definition, the global forum advocates a legal framework where 'domestic definitions on BO are aligned as closely as possible'.[364] Further, if in substance, the goals of the definition are met, the wording of the definition is of less consequence, and it would be deemed as compliant with EOIR standards.[365] Therefore, the EOIR definition of BO has the same elements as the FATF definition, as discussed in section 1.2.2 earlier.

Element A of the EOIR on 'availability of information on legal and beneficial owners' requires compliance with the following aspects.

Table 4.1 Adapted from OECD Building Effective BO framework, A Joint IADB OECD Toolkit 2024, Page 25

Aspect	*Description*
A.1.1 – Companies	*Identification of legal and beneficial owners of companies, including nominees.*
A.1.2 – Bearer Shares	*If bearer shares are permitted in the jurisdiction, mechanisms must exist to identify their beneficial owners.*

361. FATF, *FATF Recommendations: International Standards on Combating Money Laundering and the Financing of Terrorism & Proliferation* (FATF 2023), Paris, France, p. 123, available at www.fatf-gafi.org/en/publications/Fatfrecommendations/Fatf-recommendations.html accessed 21 August 2024.
362. OECD, *Beneficial Ownership and Tax Transparency – Implementation and Remaining Challenges: OECD and Global Forum Report to G20 Finance Ministers and Central Bank Governors* (OECD Publishing 2024), Paris, p. 11, available at https://doi.org/10.1787/f95790b1-en accessed 21 August 2024.
363. Global Forum on Transparency and Exchange of Information for Tax Purposes (OECD) and Inter-American Development Bank, *A Beneficial Ownership Implementation Toolkit* (OECD Publishing March 2019), Paris, France, p. 10, available at https://publications.iadb.org/en/beneficial-ownership-implementation-toolkit accessed 21 August 2024, FATF, *FATF Recommendations: International Standards on Combating Money Laundering and the Financing of Terrorism & Proliferation* (FATF 2023), Paris, France, p. 123, available at www.fatf-gafi.org/en/publications/Fatfrecommendations/Fatf-recommendations.html accessed 21 August 2024.
364. Global Forum on Transparency and Exchange of Information for Tax Purposes (OECD) and Inter-American Development Bank, *A Beneficial Ownership Implementation Toolkit* (OECD Publishing March 2019), Paris, France, available at https://publications.iadb.org/en/beneficial-ownership-implementation-toolkit accessed 21 August 2024.
365. Global Forum on Transparency and Exchange of Information for Tax Purposes (OECD) and Inter-American Development Bank, *A Beneficial Ownership Implementation Toolkit* (OECD Publishing March 2019), Paris, France, p. 30, available at https://publications.iadb.org/en/beneficial-ownership-implementation-toolkit accessed 21 August 2024.

Aspect	*Description*
A.1.3 – Partnerships	*Identification of partners and beneficial owners of partnerships that: Have tax-related activities in the jurisdiction – Operate in the jurisdiction – Are limited partnerships formed under domestic legislation*
A.1.4 – Trusts	*Identify beneficial owners of express trusts that are: – Governed, administered by domestic legislation – Have a resident trustee*
A.1.5 – Foundations	*Identification of founders, members, council, beneficiaries, beneficial owners, or foundations' representatives.*
A.3.1-Banking Information	*Banking information must include all records related to the details of legal and beneficial owners of the accounts.*

For AEOI standards, the Global Forum requires the exchange of Information on 'Controlling Persons'. The term is defined as:

> The term 'Controlling Persons' means 'the natural persons who exercise control over an Entity. In the case of a trust, such term means the settlor(s), the trustee(s), the protector(s) (if any), the beneficiary(ies) or class(es) of beneficiaries, and any other natural person(s) exercising ultimate effective control over the trust. In the case of a legal arrangement other than a trust, such term means persons in equivalent or similar positions'.[366]

The Global Forum states that 'the term "Controlling Persons" must be interpreted in a manner consistent with the FATF Recommendations'.[367] Therefore, the AEOI definition of BO has the same meaning and elements as those of the FATF definition, as discussed in section 1.2.2.

4.4.3 Critical Assessment of the Concept of BO under Tax Treaties and the Global Forum

4.4.3.1 Tax Treaties

The OECD advocates that the term 'BO' should be interpreted autonomously, i.e., based on its context and purpose.[368] In the literature, Vogel's commentary, while

366. OECD, *Standard for Automatic Exchange of Financial Account Information in Tax Matters*, 2nd ed. (OECD Publishing 2017), Paris, p. 57, available at http://dx.doi.org/10.1787/9789264267992-en accessed 21 August 2024.
367. *Ibid.*
368. From the 2017 OECD Model Tax Convention Commentary: Article 10 (Dividends), para. 12.1:

> Since the term 'beneficial owner' was added to address potential difficulties arising from the use of the words 'paid to … a resident' in paragraph 1, it was intended to be interpreted in this context and not to refer to any technical meaning that it could have had under the domestic law of a specific country (in fact, when it was added to the paragraph, the term did not have a precise meaning in the law of many countries). The term 'beneficial owner' is therefore not used in a narrow technical sense (such as the meaning that it has under the trust law of many common law countries 1), rather, it should be understood in its context, in particular in relation to the words 'paid … to a

discussing various views, also advocates for such an approach for limiting the taxing rights of the source state as well as for the prevention of tax avoidance.[369] However, state practices differ.[370] Some countries refer to the meaning of the term in their domestic legislation when interpreting the term BO. For example, the US in its technical explanations to the US Model Convention (2006) states that 'the term beneficial owner is not defined in the Convention, and is, therefore, defined as under the internal law of the country imposing tax (i.e., the source country)'.[371] The Swiss Federal Tax Appeals Commission, in one of its cases from 2003, held that domestic law in the source state is crucial in interpreting the term BO.[372]

While different approaches to the interpretation of the term exist, there is a critical distinction between the concept of BO under a tax treaty and the concept of BO under AML legislation which is the central theme of this research. The concept of BO under Articles 10, 11, and 12 of the tax treaty is narrower than the concept of BO used in other contexts, which depends on ownership and control as the influencing factors. The former is restricted to the beneficial owner of the recipient of the dividend, interest, and royalty.

Articles 10, 11 and 12 emphasize 'legal and contractual obligations'[373] of the recipient to pass on the payment as a prerequisite for determining BO, whereas the concept of BO under AML legislation also includes indirect ownership and control, which may not involve 'legal and contractual obligations'. Under the tax treaties, according to OECD commentary, 'legal and contractual obligations' are primarily inferred from 'legal documents'.[374] The use of the word 'normally'[375] in the commentary indicates that legal documents are crucial in determining such an obligation.

---

resident', and in light of the object and purposes of the Convention, including avoiding double taxation and the prevention of fiscal evasion and avoidance.

For Art. 11 (Interest), the equivalent paragraph is 9.1, which uses identical language.
For Art. 12 (Royalties), the equivalent paragraph is 4.3, which also uses identical language.

369. Preface to Arts 10-12, E. Kemmerson and A. Streicher, in K. Vogel (ed.), *Klaus Vogel on Double Taxation Conventions* (2022), 5th ed., M. no. 29, p. 834.
370. For divergent state practices *see*: Preface to Arts 10-12, E. Kemmerson and A. Streicher in K. Vogel (ed.), *Klaus Vogel on Double Taxation Conventions* (2022), 5th ed., M. nos 65-163, p. 1245.
371. Preface to Arts 10-12, Eric Kemmerson and Anika Streicher in K. Vogel, in *Klaus Vogel on Double Taxation Conventions* (2022), 5th ed., M. no. 25, p. 832; United States Model Technical Explanation Accompanying the United States Model Income Tax Convention of 15 November 2006, p. 32.
372. Preface to Arts 10-12, E. Kemmerson and A. Streicher, in K. Vogel (ed.), *Klaus Vogel on Double Taxation Conventions* (2022), 5th ed., M. no. 25, p. 832; SRK 2003-159, X Holdings Aps: DTC Switzerland/Denmark; R. Matteotti and F.M. Sutter, Switzerland: Beneficial Ownership and EU Law, in Lang et al. (eds), *Beneficial Ownership: Recent Trends*, 2013, pp. 52-54.
373. 'In these various examples (agent, nominee, conduit company acting as a fiduciary or administrator), the direct recipient of the dividend is not the "beneficial owner" because that recipient's right to use and enjoy the dividend is constrained by a *contractual or legal obligation* to pass on the payment received to another person': Paragraph 12.4, OECD, OECD Model commentary on Art. 10, 2017; para. 10.2, OECD, OECD Model commentary on Art. 11, 2017; para. 4.3, OECD, OECD Model commentary on Art. 12, 2017.
374. 'Such an obligation will normally derive from relevant *legal documents* but may also be found to exist on the basis of facts and circumstances showing that, in substance ...' Paragraph 12.4,

However, legal documents 'may not always reflect reality'.[376] To address such cases, OECD commentary suggests reliance on 'facts and circumstances'.[377] However, such inference on 'facts and circumstances' raises a question whether the 'facts and circumstances' imply a legal obligation in substance or if a purely legal/contractual obligation is required. An example is when the legal/contractual obligation does not oblige the person to pass on the income. However, circumstances such as the relationship or actions of the person indicate that the person does not have the right to enjoy the income. In such a situation, facts and circumstances serve as evidence of obligation to pass on the income. While 'legal documents' and 'facts and circumstances' assist in the identification of obligations, they are only secondary to 'legal and contractual obligations', which are essential to be identified as BO. The facts and circumstance test fails without 'legal and contractual obligations'.[378] Therefore, the BO concept under the treaty focuses on legal and contractual obligations for determining BO.

4.4.3.2 Distinguishing BO in the Context of Tax Treaties and IFFs

In its commentary on the model tax convention, the OECD also takes the view that the concepts of BO are distinct and cannot be reconciled.[379] It states that (paragraph 12.6):

> 'The above explanations concerning the meaning of beneficial owner make it clear that the meaning given to this term in the context of the Article must be distinguished from the different meaning that has been given to that term in the context of other instruments that concern the determination of the persons (typically the individuals) that exercise ultimate control over entities or assets, that different meaning of beneficial owner cannot be applied in the context of the Article.'[380]
>
> 'Indeed, that meaning, which refers to natural persons (i.e. individuals), cannot be reconciled with the express wording of subparagraph 2 a), which refers to the situation where a company is the beneficial owner of a dividend. In the context of Article 10, the term beneficial owner is intended to address difficulties arising from the use of the words paid to in relation to dividends rather than difficulties related to the ownership of the shares of the company paying these dividends. For that

OECD, OECD Model commentary on Art. 10, 2017; para. 10.2, OECD, OECD Model commentary on Art. 11, 2017; para. 4.3, OECD, OECD Model commentary on Art. 12, 2017.

375. 'Such an obligation will *normally* derive from relevant legal documents but may also be found to exist on the basis of facts and circumstances showing that, in substance ...' Paragraph 12.4, OECD, OECD Model commentary on Art. 10, 2017; para. 10.2, OECD, OECD Model commentary on Art. 11, 2017; para. 4.3, OECD, OECD Model commentary on Art. 12, 2017.
376. Preface to Arts 10-12, E. Kemmerson and A. Streicher, in K. Vogel (ed.), *Klaus Vogel on Double Taxation Conventions* (2022), 5th ed., M. no. 35, p. 837.
377. 'Such an obligation will normally derive from relevant legal documents but may also be found to exist on the basis of *facts and circumstances*.' Paragraph 12.4, OECD, OECD Model commentary on Art. 10, 2017; para. 10.2, OECD, OECD Model commentary on Art. 11, 2017; para. 4.3, OECD, OECD Model commentary on Art. 12, 2017.
378. Preface to Arts 10-12, E. Kemmerson and A. Streicher, in K. Vogel (ed.), *Klaus Vogel on Double Taxation Conventions* (2022), 5th ed., M. no. 35, p. 837.
379. Paragraph 12.6, OECD, OECD Model commentary on Art. 10, 2017.
380. *Ibid.*

> reason, in the context of that Article, it would be inappropriate to consider a meaning developed to refer to the individuals who exercise ultimate effective control over a legal person or arrangement.'[381]

Therefore, it is essential to avoid confusion between the two concepts. The critical difference between the terms is that in the context of Tax Treaties, it only refers to legal persons and not natural persons, which is the focus of the definition of BO.

The teleological difference between the concepts is significant. In the context of tax treaties, its purpose is to ensure that the benefits of reduced withholding rates are only granted to the intended recipient. In the context of IFFs, its goal is to identify individuals who ultimately control or benefit from the legal person or legal arrangement, to prevent IFFs by use of such entities for concealing identity.

4.4.3.3 The Global Forum

The definition adopted by the Global Forum was similar to the FATF Definition. However, there are a few key differences. The primary difference lies in the focus of that definition. While using the FATF definition, the Global Forum clearly states that the definition is yet to be fully adopted as both have different aims, that is: the FATF (AML) and the Global Forum (Exchange of Information for tax purposes).[382] It clarifies that 'in applying and interpreting the FATF standards regarding "beneficial owner," care must be taken that such application and interpretation do not go beyond what is appropriate for ensuring effective exchange of information for tax purposes'.[383]

The most significant difference between the two definitions lies in their scope. The FATF adopts a principle-based approach to defining BO in its recommendations and assesses outcomes by evaluating them.[384] However, the Global Forum focuses primarily on tax issues and is limited to legal persons or arrangements at risk of being used for tax evasion.[385]

The two standards also differ in their evaluations. For instance, in the case of the FATF, the assessment is done on compliance with the legal framework and its effectiveness. By contrast, the Global Forum only assesses compliance with the legal framework. As a result, separate assessment outcomes for the legal framework and its effectiveness are possible in the case of the FATF. In contrast, this may not be the case for the Global Forum, as it provides a single rating after assessing the legal framework.[386]

381. *Ibid.*
382. Global Forum on Transparency and Exchange of Information for Tax Purposes (OECD) and Inter-American Development Bank, *A Beneficial Ownership Implementation Toolkit* (OECD Publishing March 2019), Paris, France, p. 10, available at https://publications.iadb.org/en/beneficial-ownership-implementation-toolkit accessed 21 August 2024.
383. *Ibid.*
384. *Ibid.*
385. *Ibid.*
386. *Ibid.*

In addition, no methodology has been prescribed to evaluate the outcome achieved by the Global Forum, whereas the FATF methodology applies to every type of legal entity and arrangement.

Another distinction between the EOIR and the FATF Standard is the use of a risk-based approach to assess the information needed, based on the risk posed by the legal entity or legal arrangements. Such a risk-based assessment could be based on the residence of the legal entity or legal arrangement or depending on the jurisdiction involved in the cross-border nature of the transaction. While the issues covered by FATF evaluations are of interest to EOIR for tax purposes, only some of the criteria assessed by the FATF are of interest to the EOIR. For instance, the EOIR assessment states that EOIR peer review may overlook recommendations 24 and 25 of the FATF if it finds that such irregularities do not impact the assessment under the EOIR for tax purposes. Such differences in assessment and evaluation may lead to different outcomes in review processes.[387]

4.4.4 Summary and Conclusions

The notion of BO used in tax treaties is limited in scope and is solely aimed at determining the eligibility for applying lower withholding tax rates under Articles 10, 11 and 12. By contrast, the Global Forum adopts a broader definition provided by the FATF for its exchange of information standards. BO under a tax treaty focuses on the legal and contractual obligations, whereas the FATF and the Global Forum use an economic test to determine BO. However, the definition of the Global Forum is restrictive as it focuses on legal compliance for tax purposes. At the same time, the FATF adopts a comprehensive approach in its evaluations that addresses aspects of money laundering. The OECD also notes that the concepts of BO under the FATF and the OECD are entirely different. Furthermore, a critical difference between the definitions of the FATF and the OECD is that while the former focuses on natural persons, the latter focuses on legal persons.

4.5 OTHER DEFINITIONS

4.5.1 Definition of Beneficial Ownership under the Extractive Industry Transparency Initiative

The Extractive Industry Transparency Initiative (EITI) is an international standard aimed at promoting transparency in extractive industries, including oil, gas, and minerals.[388] By becoming members of this initiative, countries 'commit to disclose information along the extractive industry value chain – from how extraction rights are awarded, to how revenues make their way through government and how they benefit

387. *Ibid.*
388. EITI, *Our Mission*, available at https://eiti.org/our-mission accessed on 12 August 2023.

the public'.[389] The countries that join the EITI are supported by 'government, companies as well as civil society' in implementing the standards.[390] Currently, forty-one countries are members.[391] Participating countries are evaluated on their progress in validation, which consists of 'stakeholder engagement, transparency, outcomes, and impact'.[392]

Notable progress has been achieved since the introduction of EITI standards for the extractive sector in 2013.[393] This includes expanding the disclosure requirements under the EITI standards, extending beyond financial indicators.[394] The success of the EITI can be measured by the fact that by 2006, more than twenty countries, including Nigeria and Ghana from Africa, had committed to complying with EITI extractive standards.[395] As a significant milestone for EITI standards, Nigeria enacted the EITI standards into national legislation as the NEITI Act, becoming the first country in the world to do so.[396] As of 2009, thirty countries were reporting under the EITI standards, and since then, over USD 200 billion in revenue has been reported under the EITI standard, indicating the EITI initiative's success.[397]

The EITI also includes BO transparency as a primary requirement for its implementation under 'requirement 2.5'.[398] It is to ensure oversight by the public to deter corrupt practices and 'monitoring the ownership of PEPs (Politically Exposed

389. *Ibid.*
390. *Ibid.*
391. EITI, *Countries*, available at https://eiti.org/countries accessed on 12 August 2023:

Validation Outcome	*Countries*
Fairly low	Chad, Guyana, Kyrgyz Republic, Madagascar, Mali, Netherlands, Timor-Leste
Moderate	Argentina, Burkina Faso, Colombia, Cote d'Ivoire, Ghana, Liberia, Malawi, Mongolia, Mozambique, Nigeria, Papua New Guinea, Philippines, Republic of the Congo, Tanzania, Uganda
Meaningful progress	Indonesia, Iraq, Kazakhstan, Mauritania, Peru, Seychelles, Tajikistan, Togo, Ukraine
High	Armenia, Democratic Republic of Congo, Germany, Guinea, Norway, Sierra Leone, Trinidad and Tobago, United Kingdom, Zambia
Very high	Senegal

392. EITI, *Validation*, available at https://eiti.org/validation accessed on 12 August 2023.
393. World Bank, *Building on Progress to Implement the EITI Standard Extractive Industries Transparency Initiative: Multi-Donor Trust Fund (EITI MDTF), Annual Report 2013*, available at https://www.worldbank.org/content/dam/Worldbank/document/Extractives/EITI-MDTF%20Annual%20Report%202013.pdf accessed on 12 August 2023.
394. EITI, *Our History*, available at https://eiti.org/our-history accessed on 12 August 2023.
395. *Ibid.*
396. *Ibid.*
397. *Ibid.*
398. Requirement 2.5 of 2023 EITI standards, available at https://eiti.org/eiti-requirements accessed on 12 August 2023.

Persons)'.[399] Companies and PEPs are required to disclose BO information, the accuracy and reliability of which is assessed by the multi-stakeholder group.

EITI defines BO in its Requirement 2.5(f)(i) of the EITI standards (2023).[400] It defines BO as:

> Beneficial owner in a company means the natural person(s) who directly or indirectly ultimately owns or controls the corporate entity.

This definition is similar to the FATF definition, although it is not identical. Its scope is restrictive, as the focus of the EITI standards is limited to companies operating in the oil, natural gas, and extractive industries. In addition, the EITI mandates that countries require PEPs to report BO in listed companies, including wholly owned subsidiaries and joint venture partners.[401] The EITI advocates a threshold of 10% for the identification of BO.[402]

The critical elements of BO requirements under EITI standards are identifying beneficial owners, transparency through the public register, verification through the multi-stakeholder group, a threshold of 10%, and PEP disclosure.[403] Enhanced transparency by identifying BO to prevent the risk of corruption, accountability of companies in extractive industries, and public disclosure to build public trust are critical strengths of the EITI standards.[404] Divergent national legislation creates challenges for implementation and undermines the accuracy and authenticity of data, particularly in jurisdictions with weak legal frameworks, where privacy concerns associated with public disclosure further exacerbate this weakness.

4.5.2 Definition of Beneficial Ownership under the 2015 G20 Principles

The G20 principles on BO were established in 2015 as guidelines designed to enhance the transparency of BO of legal persons and legal arrangements. Acknowledging the need to prevent the misuse of legal persons and legal arrangements,[405] the first core principles on BO were developed by the G20 in 2015, which aimed to identify the

399. 2023 EITI Standard Part 1: Principles and Requirements, section 2.5, p. 21, available at https://eiti.org/sites/default/files/2023-06/2023%20EITI%20Standard.pdf accessed on 12 August 2023.
400. Requirement 2.5(f)(i) of 2023 EITI standards, available at https://eiti.org/eiti-requirements accessed on 12 August 2023.
401. Requirement 2.5(f)(iii) and Requirement 2.5(f)(v) of 2023 EITI standards, available at https://eiti.org/eiti-requirements accessed on 12 August 2023.
402. Requirement 2.5(f)(iii) and Requirement 2.5(f)(v) of 2023 EITI standards, p. 257, available at https://eiti.org/eiti-requirements accessed on 12 August 2023.
403. Extractive Industries Transparency Initiative (EITI), *Doubling Down: Beneficial Ownership Transparency in the New EITI Standard*, available at https://eiti.org/blog-post/doubling-down-beneficial-ownership-transparency-new-eiti-standard accessed on 22 August 2024.
404. Open Ownership, *2023 EITI Standard Strengthened Requirements on Beneficial Ownership Transparency*, available at https://www.openownership.org/en/news/2023-eiti-standard-strengthened-requirements-on-beneficial-ownership-transparency/ accessed on 22 August 2024.
405. Transparency International, *Implementation of the G20 Beneficial Ownership Principles*, available at https://knowledgehub.transparency.org/assets/uploads/kproducts/2015_ImplementationG20BOPrinciples_EN.pdf accessed on 22 August 2024.

natural owners of legal vehicles and legal arrangements.[406] It is built on existing international standards and allows flexibility to be adapted to different jurisdictions and legal frameworks.[407]

These principles are anchored in FATF recommendations on BO.[408] However, these principles offer flexibility in the domestic legal framework for countries that implement them.[409] The G20 comprises nineteen countries and the EU.[410] Each member country, the FATF, and the OECD participated in the discussion and formulation of these principles. The principle was designed to be implemented in the G20 countries, emphasizing its future adoption as a global standard.

Principle 1 states that *'countries should have a definition of "beneficial owner" that captures the natural person(s) who ultimately owns or controls the legal person or legal arrangement'*.[411] *(Emphasis added)*

This principal advocates a BO definition focused on identifying 'natural persons' rather than legal persons. The FATF Definition satisfies this principle as its focus is on identifying natural persons. Furthermore, this principle suggests the importance of including ownership or control in identifying beneficial owners.

Principle 3 mandates that *'countries should ensure that legal persons maintain BO information onshore and that information is adequate, accurate, and current'*.[412]

Principle 4 emphasizes the need for *'ensuring that competent authorities (including law enforcement and prosecutorial authorities, supervisory authorities, tax authorities, and financial intelligence units) have timely access to adequate, accurate, and current information regarding the BO of legal persons. Countries could implement this, for example, through central registries of BO of legal persons or other appropriate mechanisms'*.[413] Countries such as the US[414] and Italy[415] have already taken steps to implement the G20 principle of BO in their domestic legislation.

406. G20, *High-Level Principles on Beneficial Ownership Transparency*, Australia (2014), available at https://star.worldbank.org/publications/g20-high-level-principles-beneficial-ownership-transparency accessed on 22 August 2024.
407. *Ibid.*
408. M. Martini, *Technical Guide: Implementing the G20 Beneficial Ownership Principles*, Transparency International, p. 2, available at https://knowledgehub.transparency.org/product/implementing-the-g20-beneficial-ownership-principles-a-technical-guide accessed on 22 August 2024.
409. *Ibid.*
410. Overview of G20 (in German), available at https://www.bmz.de/de/service/lexikon/gruppe-der-20-g20-14454 accessed on 22 August 2024.
411. G20, *Principle 1, High-Level Principles on Beneficial Ownership Transparency*, Australia (2014), available at https://star.worldbank.org/publications/g20-high-level-principles-beneficial-ownership-transparency accessed on 22 August 2024.
412. *Ibid.*
413. G20, *Principle 4, High-Level Principles on Beneficial Ownership Transparency*, Australia (2014), available at https://star.worldbank.org/publications/g20-high-level-principles-beneficial-ownership-transparency accessed on 22 August 2024.
414. U.S. Government, *U.S. Action Plan to Implement G-20 High-Level Principles on Beneficial Ownership*, available at https://obamawhitehouse.archives.gov/blog/2015/10/16/us-action-plan-implement-g-20-high-level-principles-beneficial-ownership accessed on 22 August 2024.
415. Italian Ministry of Economy and Finance, *Italy's Action Plan to Implement the G20 High-Level Principles on Beneficial Ownership Transparency*, available at https://www.dt.mef.gov.it/modules/documenti_it/prevenzione_reati_finanziari/g20_acwg_anti-corruption/ITALY_ACTI

The critical elements of BO under the G20 principles of BO include identifying beneficial owners, central registries of BO, and timely access to such information by law enforcement agencies.

The G20 principle of BO indicates a political push for global adoption of a standard definition of BO. The critical strengths of the BO principles of the G20 are enhanced transparency and international cooperation through the exchange of information to prevent IFFs.[416] Key weaknesses include implementation challenges due to weak legal and regulatory frameworks, privacy concerns due to the disclosure of BO information, and data reliability, especially concerning jurisdictions with weak legal and regulatory frameworks.

4.5.3 Definition of Beneficial Ownership under the 5th EU Anti-money Laundering Directive

The EU's 5th Anti Money Laundering Directive (5AMLD) took effect on 10 January 2020.[417] It builds on previous directives to enhance the measures undertaken in the EU to prevent money laundering and terrorist financing. It focuses on improving transparency and regulating BO to effectively prevent money laundering and other types of financial crimes.[418] It further identifies and documents BO, strengthens monitoring obligations and risk assessments, extends the oversight of politically exposed persons, and incorporates tax evasion as a predicate offence linked to money laundering.

The primary reasons for including BO transparency in the 5AMLD have been to combat IFFs, transparency, and accountability in using corporate structures to prevent their misuse, compliance with FATF standards, and providing the authorities with information to conduct due diligence.[419]

Article 3(6) of the 4AMLD updated by the 5th AMLD of the EU defines BO as follows:

> 'Any natural person(s) who ultimately owns or controls the customer and the natural person(s) on whose behalf a transaction or activity is being conducted and includes at least'
>
> '(a) in the case of corporate entities'
>
> '(i) the natural person(s) who ultimately owns or controls a legal entity through direct or indirect ownership of a sufficient percentage of the shares or voting rights or ownership interest in that entity, including through bearer shareholdings or control via other means, other than a

ON_PLAN_TO_IMPLEMENT_THE_G20_HIGH-LEVEL_PRINCIPLES_ON_BENEFICIAL_OWNERSHIP_TRANSPARENCY.pdf accessed on 22 August 2024.

416. Transparency International, *Six Things to Know about the New G20 Beneficial Ownership Principles*, available at https://www.transparency.org/en/news/six-things-to-know-new-g20-beneficial-ownership-principles accessed on 22 August 2024.
417. European Parliament and Council, Directive (EU) 2018/843 amending Directive (EU) 2015/849 on the prevention of the use of the financial system for money laundering or terrorist financing and amending Directives 2009/138/EC and 2013/36/EU, 30 May 2018, available at https://eur-lex.europa.eu/legal-content/EN/TXT/?uri=CELEX:32018L0843 accessed on 22 August 2024.
418. *Ibid.*
419. *Ibid.*

company listed on a regulated market that is subject to disclosure requirements consistent with union law or subject to equivalent international standards which ensure adequate transparency of ownership information. A shareholding of 25 % plus one share or an ownership interest of more than 25 % in the customer held by a natural person shall indicate direct ownership.'

'A shareholding of 25 % plus one share or an ownership interest of more than 25 % in the customer held by a corporate entity, which is under the control of a natural person(s), or by multiple corporate entities, which are under the control of the same natural person(s), shall be an indication of indirect ownership.'

'This applies without prejudice to the right of Member States to decide that a lower percentage may indicate ownership or control.'

'Control through other means may be determined, among other things in accordance with the criteria in Article 22(1) to (5) of Directive 2013/34/EU of the European Parliament and the Council (3)'

'(ii) if, after having exhausted all possible means and provided there are no grounds for suspicion, no person under point (i) is identified, or if there is any doubt that the person(s) identified are the beneficial Owner (s), the natural person(s) who hold the position of senior managing official(s), the obliged entities shall keep records of the actions taken in order to identify the BO under point (i) and this point;'

'(b) in the case of trusts'

'(i) the settlor; (ii) the trustee(s); (iii) the protector, if any;

(iv) the beneficiaries, or where the individuals benefiting from the legal arrangement or entity have yet to be determined, the class of persons in whose main interest the legal arrangement or entity is set up or operates;

(v) any other natural person exercising control over the trust using direct or indirect ownership or by other means;'

'(c) in the case of legal persons such as foundations, and legal arrangements similar to trusts, the natural person(s) holding equivalent or similar positions to those referred to in point (b).'[420]

This definition is similar to the FATF definition and focuses on the natural person as a beneficial owner rather than a legal entity. It also addresses direct and indirect ownership and control in the case of legal persons, trusts, and other similar legal arrangements. According to Article 3(6)(a)(i) of the AMLD, a natural person may be deemed to be the beneficial owner of the legal entity under certain conditions. The directive specifies the conditions under which direct or indirect ownership is considered. To be considered the beneficial owner through direct ownership, a natural person must hold 25% plus one or more of the company shares.[421] Similar to direct ownership, indirect ownership through ownership of 25% plus one or more shares of the company qualifies the natural person as the beneficial owner. However, this must occur through a layer of multiple legal persons controlled by the same natural person.[422]

420. Article 3, para. 6 of the 4th AMLD of the EU.
421. Article 3(6), Directive (EU) 2018/843, 30 May 2018.
422. Article 3(6)(a), Directive (EU) 2018/843, 30 May 2018.

Article 3(6)(b) of the AMLD Directive provides that, in the case of trusts, the beneficial owner could be the settlor, trustee, beneficiary, or any other natural person who ultimately exercises control and ownership of the trust's assets. Similarly, Article 3(6)(c) of the AMLD Directive specifies that in case of foundations or any other legal arrangements that exhibit similar characteristics as trusts, the beneficial owner could be the natural person who occupies the position analogous to trustee, settler, or beneficiary and who ultimately exercises control and ownership over the assets of such foundations and other legal arrangements.

The key strength of the BO concept in the 5AMLD includes access to information for enhanced due diligence, alignment with the FATF standards, accountability and transparency in the use of structures and entities for deterring misuse of illicit activities, and enhanced cooperation among EU Member States through the exchange of information.[423] Privacy concerns, as highlighted in the decision of the ECJ in Luxembourg Business Registers (Case C-37/20, C-601/20), are its weakness.[424] In addition, compliance costs on businesses are also considered a weakness of 5AMLD.

4.5.4 Definition of Beneficial Ownership under Open Ownership

Open Ownership is an initiative that aims to promote BO transparency of companies.[425] It collaborates with countries to generate information on the BO of companies that comply with existing international standards on BO transparency and meet the needs of stakeholders such as academics, civil society, and non-governmental organizations. Since 2017, it has cooperated with forty countries to establish BO transparency regimes that comply with international standards and effectively address corruption and tax evasion issues.[426] Currently, forty-seven countries engage in open ownership for BO transparency reforms. The principles of BO transparency developed by Open Ownership are considered best practices and are intended to assist governments in implementing policy reforms in this area.[427]

Open Ownership defines 'a beneficial owner is a natural person who has the right to some share or enjoyment of a legal entity's income or assets (ownership or the right to direct or influence the entity's activities (control). Ownership and control can be exerted either directly or indirectly'.[428]

---

423. L. Partners, *5 Main Changes Made by 5th AMLD,* available at https://lavenpartners.com/thought-leadership/5-main-changes-made-5th-amld/ accessed on 22 August 2024.
424. Luxembourg Business Registers ('LBR'), WM and Luxembourg Business Registers ('LBR') (Case C-37/20), available at https://curia.europa.eu/juris/document/document.jsf?docid=268059&mode=req&p.Index=1&dir=&occ=first&part=1&text=&doclang=EN&cid=9481 accessed on 22 August 2024.
425. Open Ownership, *What We Do,* available at https://www.openownership.org/en/about/what-we-do/ accessed on 18 August 2023.
426. *Ibid.*
427. Extractive Industries Transparency Initiative (EITI), *Supporters: Open Ownership,* available at https://eiti.org/supporters/open-ownership accessed on 18 August 2023.
428. Open Ownership, *Beneficial Ownership in Law: Definitions and Thresholds,* Policy Briefing (October 2020), p. 3, available at https://www.openownership.org/en/about/what-we-do/ accessed on 18 August 2023.

This definition is similar to the FATF definition, except that the focus is restricted to the legal entity rather than to legal arrangements. The critical mission of Open Ownership is to provide for BO transparency of companies, as the definition emphasizes a 'Legal entity's Incomes', in addition to assets of legal persons, thereby making it helpful in tackling money laundering and identifying beneficial owners in case of tax evasion.

According to the definition of open ownership, a threshold test must be employed to determine control and ownership, and to identify BO. It states, *'BO must be disclosed when an individual's aggregate control of, or economic benefit from, a company reaches or exceeds 5% of the company's stock, votes, profits or assets; or the right to appoint board members or company officers.'*[429] *(Emphasis added)*

It suggests a lower threshold of 5% compared with the EU 5th AMLD and CRS, which prescribe a threshold of 25%. Furthermore, the threshold test is not applicable when an individual possesses the right to appoint a director to a company's board. Nonetheless, that individual can still be deemed the beneficial owner based on their power to appoint directors to the company's board. Policy frameworks defining BO primarily employ the threshold test as the primary means of identification. However, these definitions do not specify consequences when the threshold is not crossed and no beneficial owner is identified. In such cases, the definition of open ownership provides a solution that goes beyond the traditional definition. It stipulates that, 'Where no beneficial owners of a company reach the thresholds for disclosure, all board members and senior managing officials must be disclosed as the parties responsible for the declaration.'[430]

This approach places responsibility on the board of directors and senior management when no BO can be reported due to unmet thresholds. In such cases, senior management individuals must be considered the beneficial owners. However, the scope of the definition provided by Open Ownership is restrictive, as it only applies to legal persons and legal arrangements which do not fall within the scope of its definition.

Open Ownership provides a good case by highlighting the identification of senior managing officials as beneficial owners when no natural person is identified. In addition, its strengths include enhanced transparency through public disclosure of BO data, fostering trust among investors, regulators, and the public, providing valuable information to policymakers and regulators, and an initiative to contribute to creating a global standard for the definition of BO.[431] However, compliance costs to businesses to identify and verify BO, challenges in verifying BO data, implementation challenges,

429. *Ibid.*
430. *Ibid.*
431. Open Ownership, *The Open Ownership Principles*, available at https://www.openownership.org/en/principles/ accessed on 22 August 2024.

and privacy concerns[432] are critical weaknesses of the BO framework provided by Open Ownership.

4.6 COUNTRY EXPERIENCES UNDER TAX TRANSPARENCY AND CORRUPTION PROJECT

Tax Transparency and Corruption (an African perspective) was a project by the WU Global Tax Policy Center at the Institute for Austrian and International Tax Law of Vienna University of Economics and Business.[433] It was a four-year program (2019-2023) in cooperation with the United Nations Office on Drugs and Crime (UNODC), the World Bank and the African Tax Institute to prevent corruption, money laundering, tax evasion and avoidance and other related IFFs in Africa. The key aim of the project were 'identifying and mobilizing stakeholders in national tax and customs administrations, FIUs, other law enforcement agencies and private sector; drafting model national tax legislation and international tax agreements to strengthen country-specific anti-avoidance rules, improving the effectiveness of the tax administrations to get access to information on assets held offshore; building up institutional capacity in African countries and ensuring sustainability by establishing network of "ambassadors" of key institutions in Africa who will disseminate and promote the acquired knowledge on the role of tax authorities in detection of the corruption practices'.[434] The project identified the following issues with respect to BO definition in the target countries, which has been discussed in the next paragraph.

The Companies Act 2008 in South Africa, defines BO 'in respect of a company, means an individual who, directly or indirectly, ultimately owns that company or exercises effective control of that company, including through (a) the holding of beneficial interests in the securities of that company (b) the exercise of, or control of the exercise of the voting rights associated with securities of that company (c) the exercise of, or control of the exercise of the right to appoint or remove members of the board of directors of that company (d) the holding of beneficial interests in the securities, or the ability to exercise control including through a chain of ownership or control, of a holding company of that company (e) the ability to exercise control, including through a chain of ownership or control, of (i) a juristic person other than a holding company

432. Open Ownership, *The Open Ownership Principles: Setting the Standard for Beneficial Ownership Transparency*, available at https://www.openownership.org/en/news/the-open-ownership-principles-setting-the-standard-for-beneficial-ownership-transparency/ accessed on 18 August 2023.
433. WU Global Tax Policy Center at the Institute for Austrian and International Tax Law, *Tax Transparency and Corruption* (2019-2023), Vienna University of Economics and Business, available at www.wu.ac.at/en/taxlaw/institute/gtpc/current-projects/tax-transparency-and-corruption accessed on 13 August 2024; J. Owens and J. Ndubai, *Beneficial Ownership Focus Group, Focus Group Call Summary*, Tax Transparency and Corruption Project (2019-2023), WU Global Tax Policy Centre.
434. Project Flyer, *WU Global Tax Policy Center at the Institute for Austrian and International Tax Law*, Tax Transparency and Corruption (2019-2023), Vienna University of Economics and Business, available at https://www.wu.ac.at/fileadmin/wu/d/i/taxlaw/Institute/WU_Global_Tax_Policy_Center/TT_C/Flyer_final.pdf accessed on 13 August 2024.

of that company (ii) a body of persons, corporate or unincorporated (iii) a person acting on behalf of a partnership (iv) a person acting in pursuance of the provisions of a trust agreement or (f) the ability to otherwise materially influence the management of that company'.[435] It used the term 'beneficial interest' before the introduction of the definition of BO. Information gathered under the project indicated that before the introduction of the definition of BO in the Companies Act in 2022, South Africa faced challenges in aligning its definition of BO (which was beneficial interest) with effective control rather than legal ownership.[436] It was acknowledged through the information gathered under the project that the trust registers and register of shares that consider 'beneficial interest' did not capture effective control, leading to non-alignment with the BO Definition in the FATF Standards, where effective control is a crucial criterion.

In the case of Nigeria, the BO definition of Nigeria was influenced by open government partnerships, as well as by the FATF. Section 868 of the Companies and allied matters Act, 2020 uses the term 'person of significant control' to define beneficial ownership as: 'any person (a) directly or indirectly holding at least 5 % of the shares or interest in a company or limited liability partnership; (b) directly or indirectly holding at least 5 % of the voting rights in a company or limited liability partnership; (c) directly or indirectly holding the right to appoint or remove a majority of the directors or partners in a company or limited liability partnership; (d) otherwise having the right to exercise or exercising significant influence or control over a company or limited liability partnership or (e) having the right to exercise, or exercising significant influence or control over the activities of a trust or firm whether or not it is a legal entity but would satisfy any of the first four conditions if it were an individual'. Information gathered under the project showed that Nigeria faced challenges in the implementation of BO regulations. The key challenges identified in the implementation were the use of nominee ownership and fictitious names to register BO.

In case of Zambia, the Companies Act of 2017 before its amendment did not include critical elements such as 'indirect control' and 'indirect ownership' in the definition of BO. Zambia amended its definition of 'BO' as 'a natural person who (a) directly or indirectly, through any contract, arrangement, understanding, relationship or any other means ultimately owns, controls, exercises substantial interest in, or receives substantial economic benefit from a body corporate; or (b) exercises ultimate and effective control over a legal person or legal arrangement; and the terms "beneficially own" and "beneficial ownership" shall be construed accordingly' to include indirect ownership and indirect control within the scope of the definition. It had legislation to identify BO for specific sectors. A key challenge Zambia faced was such sector-specific legislation in the absence of overriding provisions by the FIC Act which is the anti-money laundering act in Zambia which did not align with the FIC Act and the FATF standards. It created inconsistencies in the collection of BO information.

435. Section 1 of the Companies Act 2008, South Africa as amended in 2022.

436. J.W. Ndubai, *Best Practices and Guidance for the Implementation of Standards on Beneficial Ownership: A Case Study Approach*, WU Global Tax Policy Centre, section 3.1.3 which identified the issue of effective control.

In case of Kenya, the information collected under the project indicated that only 45% of companies followed the BO compliance requirements, which shows a low level of compliance. Kenya also faced issues in obtaining BO information related to Trusts and verifying BO information.

A critical issue which was noted across countries was the difference between legal ownership and effective control per the FATF standards. It was found that most countries still focus on legal ownership, which fails to capture the complex ownership structures with indirect or informal control. Further, countries also found the use of nominee ownership and fictitious names as critical challenges in the implementation of the BO definition. Nigeria and Zambia showed concerns about defining their legal definition of BO to capture such ownerships.

4.7 TOWARDS A NORMATIVE FRAMEWORK: A GOOD PRACTICE DEFINITION OF BENEFICIAL OWNERSHIP

Based on the discussion on the definition of BO, some essential elements emerge that can be used to develop a 'good practice' definition of BO.

4.7.1 Element 1: Natural Person(s)

First, an essential element derived from all the definitions of BO provided by international policy organizations is that a beneficial owner is 'the natural person' who is behind the legal person or arrangement that receives income.[437] The definition must explicitly use the term 'natural person(s)' to identify the beneficial owner. This is imperative, as a natural person ultimately owns and controls the legal person or arrangement at the end of any ownership chain. Legal ownership differs from BO. While an individual may hold the legal ownership of a legal entity or arrangement, they may not necessarily benefit from legal ownership. Identifying a natural person is the primary objective of defining BO.[438] Therefore, the 'natural person' element for inclusion in the BO definition is assessed 'positively'.

4.7.2 Element 2: Ownership (Threshold) with 15% as Benchmark for Identification

The threshold approach is widely used for defining control and ownership. It establishes a clear and measurable criterion for defining control, such as the percentage of share capital, voting rights, or other indicators to identify the beneficial owner. This

437. FATF, *Transparency and Beneficial Ownership*, FATF Guidance (2014), available at http://www.fatf-gafi.org/media/fatf/documents/reports/Guidance-transparency-beneficial-ownership.pdf accessed on 29 September 2020 this guidance is from 2014 but the recommendation has been amended in November 2023, while the main principle remain identical.
438. Open Ownership, *Beneficial Ownership in Law: Definitions and Thresholds*, available at https://www.openownership.org/en/publications/beneficial-ownership-in-law-definitions-and-thresholds/defining-beneficial-ownership/ accessed 21 August 2024.

approach provides a legalistic and precise way to identify BO with legal certainty. Several countries also employ a threshold approach to define control in their BO definitions.[439] However, there are potential risks associated with such an approach, such as individuals circumventing the thresholds through manipulation or not being reported as BO if the threshold is too high. Therefore, to mitigate such risks, it is essential to consider both the direct and indirect means of control and ownership when determining the breach of the BO identification threshold. The threshold approach is vital for identifying BO but must be used responsibly to ensure accurate and timely reporting.

Threshold rates play a vital role in a country's decision to use such an approach when drafting definitions of BO to identify control and ownership. The threshold between countries varies between 5% and 25% to identify BO.[440] There is no specific evidence regarding the optimal threshold ceiling for identifying ownership and control. Recently, there has been a trend among countries to choose lower thresholds.[441]

A key aspect often overlooked is that the threshold serves as the trigger point for BO identification.[442] There may be situations in which legal persons or legal arrangements operating in sectors prone to tax evasion and corruption and with a history of

439. Extractive Industries Transparency Initiative, *Legal Approaches to Beneficial Ownership Transparency in EITI Countries* (June 2019), p. 5, available at https://eiti.org/sites/default/files/attachments/legal_approaches_to_beneficial_ownership_transparency_in_eiti_countries.pdf accessed on 29 September 2020.

440. Extractive Industries Transparency Initiative, *Legal Approaches to Beneficial Ownership Transparency in EITI Countries* (June 2019), p. 6, available at https://eiti.org/sites/default/files/attachments/legal_approaches_to_beneficial_ownership_transparency_in_eiti_countries.pdf accessed on 29 September 2020. The table below has been summarized from this publication by EITI:

Threshold Rate	*Country*
5% of shareholding	Cameroon, Malawi, Nigeria
10% of shareholding	Kyrgyz Republic, Peru, Paraguay, Kenya, Cayman Island
25% of shareholding 25% of Voting shares	UK, Ukraine, EU Countries (EU's AMLD4)
25% of shareholding 25% of Voting shares 25% of Profit	Indonesia, Kazakhstan
2% of shareholding	Senegal
Holding one share capital or more	Argentina

441. Examples: Argentina, where holding even one share is used to identify beneficial owner, Senegal uses 2% of share capital as the threshold for reporting.

442. Stolen Asset Recovery Initiative (StAR), The Puppet Masters: How the Corrupt Use Legal Structures to Hide Stolen Assets and What to Do about It, E. van der Does de Willebois et al., World Bank, Washington, D.C, available at https://openknowledge.worldbank.org/entities/publication/ec364fd2-92f8-58a0-bd4e-155ac0f644d6 accessed 21 August 2024.

misuse will be subject to further investigation, even when the threshold is unmet.[443] However, the existence of a threshold in the definition of BO for identification may also create obstacles to further investigation. A high threshold for reporting BO can facilitate exploitation. The 'Russian Laundromat' case is the most well-known case of such exploitation.[444] It demonstrated how the threshold for identifying ownership and control could be circumvented to evade the reporting of BO. In that case, an estimated USD 70 billion was transferred from nineteen Russian Banks into Moldova,[445] which was then transferred to other countries. For reporting purposes, Moldova had a BO threshold of 5% shareholding.[446] The individuals involved in this case avoided the BO reporting by using companies as well as legal arrangements for keeping the threshold below the reporting level of 5% for each company as well as each legal arrangement. When Moldova amended its BO threshold to 1%, the individuals reduced their share ownership by 0.9%.[447] This case highlights the potential of exploiting thresholds to evade BO reporting, which can lead to tax evasion, money laundering, and IFFs.

Another interesting case from the Cayman Islands highlights how thresholds can impede the collection of information in cases that require further investigation.[448] Under the Companies Law in the Cayman Islands, a beneficial owner is defined as: 'someone who holds more than 25% of shares or voting rights in a company, or any individual who can vote to remove a majority of the company's board of directors'.[449] In this case, the registrar requested an individual who owned 1% of the company's share capital on the Cayman Islands to provide information on the ownership of the shares. The individual appealed to the ombudsman, objecting to the registrar's request. The Ombudsman ruled that the registrar could not collect such information as it did not breach the threshold, and that any collection of information was without a legal basis.[450] This decision presents challenges for law enforcement agencies' investigation and prosecution efforts, as it hinders their ability to collect crucial information required to identify BO to build their case.

---

443. Open Ownership, *Beneficial Ownership in Law: Definitions and Thresholds*, p. 16, available at https://www.openownership.org/en/publications/beneficial-ownership-in-law-definitions-and-thresholds/defining-beneficial-ownership/ accessed 21 August 2024.
444. OCCRP, *The Russian Laundromat* (August 2014), available at https://www.reportingproject.net/therussianlaundromat/russian-laundromat.php accessed on 29 September 2020.
445. Open Ownership, *Beneficial Ownership in Law: Definitions and Thresholds*, p. 16, available at https://www.openownership.org/en/publications/beneficial-ownership-in-law-definitions-and-thresholds/defining-beneficial-ownership/ accessed 21 August 2024.
446. *Ibid.*
447. Committee of Inquiry into Money Laundering, *Tax Avoidance and Tax Evasion, Public Hearing Financial Intelligence Units (FIUs): 'Ins and Outs' and the Russian 'Laundromat' Case* (21 June 2017), available at https://www.europarl.europa.eu/cmsdata/128621/PANA%2021%20June%20pm_Verbatim%20Report_EN.pdf accessed on 29 September 2020; *Open Ownership, Beneficial Ownership in Law: Definitions and Thresholds*, p. 16, available at https://www.openownership.org/en/publications/beneficial-ownership-in-law-definitions-and-thresholds/defining-beneficial-ownership/ accessed 21 August 2024.
448. Case 202000507, *Enforcement Order Registrar of Companies, Ombudsman Cayman Islands* (12 August 2020), available at https://ombudsman.ky/images/pdf/decisions/dp_decisions/DP_Case_202000507.pdf accessed on 30 August 2023.
449. *Ibid.*
450. *Ibid.*

In contrast, a low threshold may present challenges, such as increased compliance costs, the need for detailed guidance from the government, and difficulties in collecting information on BO. To address this issue while devising a threshold, an analysis of the costs and benefits must be undertaken before implementing such a policy.[451] However, concerns regarding compliance could be mitigated, as seen from VAT compliance, where technology has assisted tremendously in reducing the compliance burden.[452]

A solution to mitigate the risk posed by the use of a threshold is using the 'Risk Based Approach to Threshold (RBA)' advocated by open ownership, which uses a threshold based on specific risks associated with a particular sector or reporting a legal person or arrangement.[453] RBA may result in varying thresholds across jurisdictions for different sectors of legal persons or legal arrangements. RBA can mitigate some disadvantages of using a threshold to determine ownership and control. This approach proposes setting thresholds that depend on the level of risk associated with tax evasion, corruption, money laundering, and bribery in a specific sector. A lower threshold may be established for sectors with higher risks. Examples include gambling, extractives, and real estate.

Countries with abundant mineral resources rely heavily on revenue generated from extractive activities to finance public budgets. However, sectors such as mining and extractives are particularly susceptible to bribery and corruption.[454] Africa is rich in natural resources, with several countries holding significant reserves of minerals, oils, and other extractives.[455] Therefore, it is necessary to pay special attention to the mining and extractive sectors when establishing a threshold based on risk.[456] However, such a risk-based threshold in the BO definition needs to be carefully drafted as lack of clarity could lead to manipulations, disputes, and potential loopholes. A clear and concise definition indicating the sector to which the threshold applies is essential for

451. Tax Justice Network, *Argentina Finally Has a Beneficial Ownership Register* (20 April 2020), available at https://www.taxjustice.net/2020/04/20/argentina-finally-has-a-beneficial-ownership-register-now-it-should-make-it-public/ accessed on 29 August 2020.
452. Feedback by Prof. Dr Robert Risse in his roundtables chaired at the Institute for Austrian and International Tax Law, WU, Vienna.
453. Open Ownership, *Beneficial Ownership in Law: Definitions and Thresholds*, p. 13, available at https://www.openownership.org/en/publications/beneficial-ownership-in-law-definitions-and-thresholds/defining-beneficial-ownership/ accessed 21 August 2024.
454. The Economist, *Bribery Pays if You Don't Get Caught* (August 2020), available at https://www.economist.com/business/2020/08/27/bribery-pays-if-you-dont-get-caught accessed on 29 September 2020; Transparency International, *Our Priorities: Extractive Industries*, available at https://www.transparency.org/en/our-priorities/extractive-industries accessed on 1 September 2024.
455. International Monetary Fund (IMF), *Harnessing Sub-Saharan Africa's Critical Mineral Wealth*, available at https://www.imf.org/en/News/Articles/2024/04/29/cf-harnessing-sub-saharan-africas-critical-mineral-wealth accessed on 24 August 2024; United Nations Environment Programme (UNEP), *Our Work in Africa*, available at https://www.unep.org/regions/africa/our-work-africa accessed on 24 August 2024.
456. UNODC, *Enhancing Beneficial Ownership Transparency: A Study of Beneficial Ownership Registration Systems* (December 2023), p. 25, available at https://www.unodc.org/documents/treaties/UNCAC/COSP/session10/CAC-COSP-2023-CRP.5.pdf accessed 2 September 2024.

the application of a risk-based threshold approach to the definition of BO.[457] Utilizing sectors specific to the threshold enables law enforcement agencies, such as tax authorities and anti-corruption agencies, to focus their limited financial and personnel resources on sectors that pose a risk to BO transparency.[458] This approach reduces the focus on sectors that are less likely to pose a risk to BO transparency. Along with the efficient use of limited resources, a threshold applicable to a specific sector allows law enforcement agencies to efficiently and effectively identify the BO of legal persons and arrangements, as these agencies are familiar with the legal persons and arrangements operating in a particular sector and can focus on scrutinizing and auditing the legal persons and arrangements within that sector.[459] However, implementing different thresholds based on sector-specific risks may lead to inconsistencies and complexities regarding compliance and reporting. This could create confusion for businesses operating in multiple sectors or across jurisdictions.

The responsibility of identifying BO and filing relevant reports falls on compliance officers in legal persons or legal arrangements. Non-compliance in reporting obligations carries financial and administrative risks, including potential penalties for money laundering and terrorism financing as well as temporary blocks on accepting new clients, difficulties in raising new finances, and challenges with conducting KYC (Know Your Customer) for which information on BO is required. In practice, compliance officers often rely on proprietary databases on BO maintained by private organizations that source their data from government agencies.[460] However, such databases may only provide sufficient information to accurately identify the actual BO of legal persons and legal arrangements. A higher threshold can prevent the reporting of legal persons and arrangements if the threshold is not crossed, and is prone to manipulation to avoid reporting.

There are also drawbacks to using a lower threshold to identify control and ownership to determine BO. One of the significant disadvantages of using a lower threshold is the increased reporting and compliance responsibilities of the parties responsible for the legal persons or legal arrangements.[461] Further, the cost of compliance would also increase for such parties, as they would need to collect, maintain, and report the required information.[462] Such an increased cost could lower the 'ease of

457. UNODC, *Enhancing Beneficial Ownership Transparency: A Study of Beneficial Ownership Registration Systems* (December 2023), p. 17, available at https://www.unodc.org/documents/treaties/UNCAC/COSP/session10/CAC-COSP-2023-CRP.5.pdf accessed 2 September 2024.
458. For detailed discussion on risk based approach to threshold: *see* Open Ownership, *Beneficial Ownership in Law: Definitions and Thresholds*, p. 11, available at https://www.openownership.org/en/publications/beneficial-ownership-in-law-definitions-and-thresholds/defining-beneficial-ownership/ accessed 2 September 2024.
459. UNODC, *Enhancing Beneficial Ownership Transparency: A Study of Beneficial Ownership Registration Systems* (December 2023), p. 17, available at https://www.unodc.org/documents/treaties/UNCAC/COSP/session10/CAC-COSP-2023-CRP.5.pdf accessed 2 September 2024.
460. Open Ownership, *Beneficial Ownership in Law: Definitions and Thresholds*, p. 16, available at https://www.openownership.org/en/publications/beneficial-ownership-in-law-definitions-and-thresholds/defining-beneficial-ownership/ accessed 2 September 2024.
461. *Ibid.*
462. *Ibid.*

doing business'[463] due to compliance costs and reporting. In addition to rising compliance costs, the individual responsible for reporting BO is burdened with obtaining and updating current information.[464]

For instance, in the case of complex ownership structures involving multiple legal persons and legal arrangements involving different countries, a reportable person may need help to obtain current information on BO. This may be due to changes in ownership and control at any time in the ownership and control chain, making it challenging for the reportable person to furnish accurate and current information on BO.[465]

There will also be an increased need for guidance from the government on reporting. Such guidance is necessary to address any uncertainties that may arise during the reporting process for reporting entities. This will necessitate the hiring and training of specialized personnel by the government. Furthermore, additional resources will be required to communicate new guidance and policies to reporting individuals and to analyse, investigate, and prosecute cases based on the information gathered on BO. Such additional costs may be challenging for law enforcement agencies in countries that have limited financial resources.

The above discussion shows that the use of a threshold for the identification of BO has both advantages and disadvantages. Open Ownership indicates a threshold between 5% and 15% as a good range to set the threshold.[466] A relatively low threshold, such as 5% would be prone to the risks discussed above, whereas a higher threshold of 25% which has been prescribed by FATF would be at risk of manipulation. Therefore, a relatively balanced threshold between 5% and 25% such as 15%, would help mitigate some of the drawbacks of having no threshold or a higher threshold and would make the scope of the definition broader. Based on the discussion above, the element of 'threshold' with 15% as a benchmark is assessed 'positively' for inclusion in the BO definition.

4.7.3 Element 3: Control Including Informal Control

Ownership and control can be held, either directly or indirectly. Direct ownership and control are straightforward, where an individual owns or controls the legal person or legal arrangement directly and can be easily identified without extensive investigation of ownership and control. In contrast, indirect ownership and control are held through various legal persons, legal arrangements, or individuals transposed between the final

463. World Bank, *Ease of Doing Business Rankings*, available at https://archive.doingbusiness.org/en/rankings accessed on 29 September 2020.
464. Open Ownership, *Beneficial Ownership in Law: Definitions and Thresholds*, p. 16, available at https://www.openownership.org/en/publications/beneficial-ownership-in-law-definitions-and-thresholds/defining-beneficial-ownership/ accessed 2 September 2024.
465. Open Ownership, *Beneficial Ownership in Law: Definitions and Thresholds*, p. 13, available at https://www.openownership.org/en/publications/beneficial-ownership-in-law-definitions-and-thresholds/defining-beneficial-ownership/ accessed 21 August 2024.
466. Open Ownership, *Beneficial Ownership in Law: Definitions and Thresholds*, p. 11, available at https://www.openownership.org/en/publications/beneficial-ownership-in-law-definitions-and-thresholds/defining-beneficial-ownership/ accessed 21 August 2024.

BO holders. To define BO as truly effective and to cover all types of indirect ownership and control, it is also necessary to cover indirect ownership and control. Consequently, any definition of BO must focus on actual and real ownership and control, that is, de facto ownership and control, rather than legal ownership and control.[467] A natural person may exercise control over a legal entity or arrangement, without formal control or ownership.[468] For instance, the spouse or relative of the shareholder may exert influence over shareholders' voting due to their close personal relationships. Family members, due to their relationships which are based on trust, shared interests and loyalty, may exert influence over the shareholders by leveraging their relationships. This aspect is crucial, as the focus of the definitions of BO is primarily on the direct and indirect aspects of control and ownership. The non-inclusion of such an informal nature in the definition of BO has been problematic in many countries.[469] For instance, an evaluation of the Chinese definition of control in BO revealed that it covered shareholders with voting rights and did not account for informal relationships with family and close relatives to control legal persons. This created opportunities for control without identification as the beneficial owner.

Individuals may exert control over their legal owners and remain beneficial owners. Therefore, defining control and ownership separately while defining BO is necessary.[470] Based on its advantages, the 'control' element for inclusion in the BO definition is assessed 'positively'. Furthermore, it is recommended that the definition of indirect ownership and control should be widened to encompass informal control to include those persons that do not have 15 % but that nevertheless exercise control, for instance, together with others (family members, nominees, proxies), indirectly (through a chain of legal entities), through other means, etc.

4.7.4 Element 4: Broad Definition

A broad definition of BO is beneficial, as it facilitates the investigation of law enforcement agencies.[471] This allows for a comprehensive investigation without legal barriers that may exist in a narrow, legal, and formalistic definition of BO. A broad definition of BO provides clarity and assistance to the parties involved in creating,

467. Open Ownership, *Beneficial Ownership in Law: Definitions and Thresholds*, p. 6, available at https://www.openownership.org/en/publications/beneficial-ownership-in-law-definitions-and-thresholds/defining-beneficial-ownership/ accessed 21 August 2024.
468. R. Berkhout and F. Fernando (eds), *Unmasking Control: A Guide to Beneficial Ownership Transparency*, International Monetary Fund, Washington, D.C. (2022), available at https://www.imf.org/en/Publications/Books/Issues/2022/10/06/Unmasking-Control-A-Guide-to-Beneficial-Ownership-Transparency-517096 accessed 21 August 2024.
469. Transparency International, *China Beneficial Ownership Transparency* (2015), available at https://www.transparency.org/files/content/publication/2015_BOCountryReport_China.pdf accessed on 29 September 2020.
470. Open Ownership, *Beneficial Ownership in Law: Definitions and Thresholds*, p. 4, available at https://www.openownership.org/en/publications/beneficial-ownership-in-law-definitions-and-thresholds/defining-beneficial-ownership/ accessed 21 August 2024.
471. Open Ownership, *Beneficial Ownership in Law: Definitions and Thresholds*, p. 8, available at https://www.openownership.org/en/publications/beneficial-ownership-in-law-definitions-and-thresholds/defining-beneficial-ownership/ accessed 2 September 2024.

administering, or dissolving legal persons or arrangements.[472] This includes determining the control and ownership instances that must be identified and reported as BO. A formalistic and legal definition may require amendments and updates to keep pace with the techniques employed by individuals who intend to hide their BO. However, such an approach may not be feasible, as in many countries, amending laws necessitates parliament's approval. In addition, drafting a strict legal and formalistic definition of BO and creating a comprehensive list of all forms of ownership, control, and relevant examples are challenging.[473] The complexity of this task is further compounded by the need for more harmonization between national legal systems and definitions, which makes identifying legal persons and arrangements with cross-border ownership and control, and multiple interposed legal persons and legal arrangements challenging. Therefore, the BO definition must be drafted broadly to capture the several types of formal and informal ownership and control.[474] However, a broad definition may inadvertently include cases that do not represent significant BO or control, resulting in excessive information that may not help identify actual beneficial owners. Therefore, the characteristic of a 'broad BO definition' is assessed 'positively'.

4.8 INTERIM CONCLUSION

This chapter discusses the importance of defining BO to prevent tax avoidance, aggressive tax planning and tax evasion. The definition varies between countries, depending on the type of legal system and other domestic factors. A normative framework provides a structured approach to evaluating the definition of BO. Based on the international standards on BO, the following elements emerge from international standards.

The legal definition of BO must clearly define BO, including specific details of the types and extent of BO and control that could qualify a natural person as the beneficial owner. Furthermore, the definition must clearly state that the beneficial owner is a natural person, as there is always a natural person at the end of the ownership chain, even when companies are owned by companies. Open ownership has already highlighted this in its recommendations to define BO. This is essential as it was found in its 2019 review that some countries do not explicitly state that a natural person is beneficial in their definition of BO.[475]

The definition must specify that it focuses not only on cases of direct ownership and control but also on cases of indirect ownership and control. Formal measures of

472. Open Ownership, *Beneficial Ownership in Law: Definitions and Thresholds*, p. 20, available at https://www.openownership.org/en/publications/beneficial-ownership-in-law-definitions-and-thresholds/defining-beneficial-ownership/ accessed 2 September 2024.
473. Open Ownership, *Beneficial Ownership in Law: Definitions and Thresholds*, p. 8, available at https://www.openownership.org/en/publications/beneficial-ownership-in-law-definitions-and-thresholds/defining-beneficial-ownership/ accessed 2 September 2024.
474. *Ibid.*
475. Open Ownership, *Beneficial Ownership in Law: Definitions and Thresholds*, p. 6, available at https://www.openownership.org/en/publications/beneficial-ownership-in-law-definitions-and-thresholds/defining-beneficial-ownership/ accessed 21 August 2024.

control, such as holding a certain percentage of shares or voting rights or the right to appoint board members, and informal measures of control, such as influence through family members, nominees, proxies, indirectly through a chain of legal entities and through any other possible scenarios, must be provided explicitly in the definition. Such a comprehensive way of defining control is necessary, as some jurisdictions have a limited scope of control in their definition that extends only to shareholders who have voting rights. In addition to defining formal and informal measures of control, the definition must also specify how cases of cumulative ownership or control are treated under the definition, especially in cases where multiple parties' own shares that if considered collectively exceed the threshold. Further, it would be recommended to use a relatively low threshold of 15% that would make the scope of the definition broader and would help mitigate some of the drawbacks of having no threshold.

The definition must also clearly specify exemptions or exceptions, such as non-applicability to publicly listed or government-owned companies and provide detailed justifications for these exemptions and exceptions.

A definition must be drafted to cover all instances where BO can be held. This definition could be supplemented by a list of examples that provide diverse ways for BO to be held. A broad definition helps investigators investigate and seek information to determine whether specific individuals are beneficial owners of the legal entity or legal arrangement. Supplementing this with a list of examples also assists reportable persons in reporting BO with confidence and legal stability.

Inclusion of these elements while drafting the BO provides a solid basis for justifying the criteria for assessing the legal definition of BO. They emphasize the importance of a clear definition, inclusiveness, and adaptability of the legal definition to identify ownership and control, leading to the accurate identification of BO.

Lastly, in case no natural person is identified under the criteria, the definition must specifically identify a senior managing official as BO.[476]

Based on the analysis in this chapter, the following definition of BO as a good practice is recommended:

> Beneficial owner refers to the natural person(s) who ultimately owns or controls a legal person or legal arrangements individually or cumulatively with other persons. This includes natural person(s) who (a) directly or indirectly hold at least 15% of the shares or interest in a company or limited liability partnership; or (b) directly or indirectly hold at least 15% of the voting rights in a company or limited liability partnership; or (c) directly or indirectly hold the right to appoint or remove a majority of the directors or partners in a company or limited liability partnership; or (d) otherwise having the right to exercise or exercising significant influence or control over a company or limited liability partnership or (e) having the right to exercise, or exercising significant influence or control over the activities of a trust or firm. Where no natural person is identified under (a) or (e) above, the identity of the relevant natural person who holds the position of senior managing official must be identified as beneficial owner. Significant influence or control includes

476. FATF, *FATF Recommendations: International Standards on Combating Money Laundering and the Financing of Terrorism & Proliferation* (FATF 2023), Paris, France, p. 44, available at www.fatf-gafi.org/en/publications/Fatfrecommendations/Fatf-recommendations.html accessed 21 August 2024.

exercising influence through family members or close associates or using nominees or proxies for acting on behalf. Indirect control includes controlling through chain of legal persons or legal arrangements or through financial instruments or contractual arrangements or any other form of informal control.[477]

477. The definition has been adapted from the FATF definition as well as section 868 of the Beneficial Ownership definition in the Companies and Allied Matters Act, 2020 of Nigeria.

CHAPTER 5

Comparative Analysis of the Definition of Beneficial Ownership in Kenya, Nigeria and South Africa

5.1 INTRODUCTION

The previous chapter provided a normative framework for defining BO. It analysed the definition of BO under various international frameworks such as FATF, UNCAC, the World Bank, Tax Treaties, the Global Forum and other international initiatives such as the EITI, the G20 principles on BO, the 5th AMLD, and the Open Ownership Initiative. It positively assessed elements such as the use of the term natural person, control including informal control, use of thresholds at 15%, and a broad definition for an ideal definition of BO. This chapter aims to assess the current legal framework for the definition of BO in Kenya, Nigeria, and South Africa with these elements for any inconsistencies and to provide practical advice on how they could address inconsistencies in their domestic legal frameworks in this respect. For that purpose, this chapter will review the definitions of BO under the legal framework in the context of companies' legislation and money laundering in Kenya (section 5.2), Nigeria (section 5.3), and South Africa (section 5.4), along with a summary of observations in the last peer reviews by the FATF and mutual evaluations of the Global Forum. It should be noted that the tax laws in these countries do not address the issue of BO for the purposes of preventing IFFs resulting from tax avoidance. Therefore, tax laws of these countries are not subject to the analysis made in this chapter.

5.2 KENYA

5.2.1 Beneficial Ownership Definition in the Companies Act 2015

The Companies Act of 2015 is the primary legislation governing the establishment of companies and other legal arrangements in Kenya.[478] Section 93 and 93A provide a legal framework that requires collection of BO information.[479]

The term 'beneficial owners' used in section 93A has been defined as: 'The natural person who ultimately owns or controls a legal person or arrangements or the natural person on whose behalf a transaction is conducted and includes those persons who exercise effective control over a legal person or arrangement.'[480] In addition, the term 'ultimately owns or controls' is defined as 'a situation in which ownership is exercised through a chain of ownership or by means of control other than direct control'.[481]

This definition of BO is identical to the old definition of the FATF. The updated definition by the FATF includes additional wording: 'Only a natural person can be the ultimate beneficial owner, and more than one natural person can be the ultimate beneficial owner of a given legal person or arrangement.'[482] Inclusion of 'natural person' in the BO definition fulfils the 'good practice' definition of BO.

The Companies (BO Information) (Amendment) Regulations of 2023 provide detailed rules for implementing section 93A, 93 B and 93C.[483] Regulation 2 provides criteria for identifying BO. A natural person who holds at least 10% of issued shares or voting rights or holds the right to appoint or remove directors or exercises 'significant

---

478. Kenya Gazette Supplement Acts (2015), Nairobi, 15 September 2015, available at https://gazettes.africa/akn/ke/officialGazette/government-gazette-supplement/2015-09-15/155/eng@2015-09-15 accessed 21 August 2024.
479. G. Chege and S.K. Kirika, Effect of Macroeconomic Factors on Trading Volumes of Manufacturing and Allied Companies Listed in Nairobi Securities Exchange, *International Journal of Finance and Accounting* 6, no. 1, 32-52, available at https://iprjb.org/journals/index.php/IJFA/article/view/1337 accessed on 1 August 2024.
480. Section 3 on Interpretation of provisions under Part 1 of Preliminary defines Beneficial ownership, available at http://kenyalaw.org:8181/exist/kenyalex/actview.xql?actid=CAP.%20486 accessed on 1 August 2024.
481. OECD, *Global Forum on Transparency and Exchange of Information for Tax Purposes: Kenya 2024 (Second Round, Combined Review): Peer Review Report on the Exchange of Information on Request*, Global Forum on Transparency and Exchange of Information for Tax Purposes (OECD Publishing 2024), Paris, para. 113, available at https://doi.org/10.1787/348052b1-en accessed on 22 August 2024.
482. Financial Action Task Force (FATF), *Guidance on Beneficial Ownership for Legal Persons*, FATF Guidance (2023), p. 15, available at http://www.fatf-gafi.org/publications/FATFrecommendations/guidance-beneficial-ownership-legalpersons.html accessed on 22 April 2024.
483. The Companies (Beneficial Ownership Information) (Amendment) Regulations of 2023, available at https://brs.go.ke/wp-content/uploads/2023/11/L.-N.-162-Companies-Beneficial-Ownership-Information-Amendment-Regulations-2023.pdf accessed on 1 August 2024. Also Grant Thornton Kenya, *Beneficial Ownership*, available at https://www.grantthornton.co.ke/insights/beneficial-ownership/ accessed on 6 Sept 2024; EY, *Kenya Publishes Additional Regulations on Beneficial Ownership*, available at https://globaltaxnews.ey.com/news/2022-5432-kenya-publishes-additional-regulations-on-beneficial-ownership accessed on 6 September 2024.

influence' or 'significant control' over the company is considered a beneficial owner.[484] Inclusion of 10% threshold in the BO definition is relatively low as against the 15% proposed in the 'good practice' definition of BO.

In addition, Regulation 2A addresses the identification of BO in the case of a company that is limited by guarantee, which does not have shareholders in the traditional sense. The criteria for identification of such a company include the same thresholds as prescribed in Regulation 2, but focus on voting rights, significant influence, the right to appoint a board of directors, control over assets, and liquidation rights. An explicit inclusion of liquidation rights as a criterion indicates that the power to wind up can also be considered a significant form of control.

The term 'significant control' has been defined to include situations of indirect control exercised through financial arrangements, strategic positions or close personal relationships.[485] This term ensures that even indirect control is recognized as BO and allows for closing loopholes through which control can be exercised over a company.

The term 'significant influence' has been defined as 'the power to participate in a company's operating and financial policies without necessarily having full control over them' This definition implies that an individual does not need direct control over a company to be considered a beneficial owner. If a natural person can influence the critical decisions of the company without having any formal control (e.g., holding a percentage of shares or voting rights), they should be considered beneficial owners for the purpose of the act. Such situations may include influences that allow the company to make strategic decisions, informal influences of the company through close relationships with family members and influences through financial arrangements or agreements that allow for the ability to take part in critical decisions of the company. The term 'significant influence' allows for capturing indirect or informal control situations, ensuring that the actual beneficial owners are identified.

484. Regulation 2, The Companies (Beneficial Ownership Information) (Amendment) Regulations of 2023, available at https://brs.go.ke/wp-content/uploads/2023/11/L.-N.-162-Companies-Beneficial-Ownership-Information-Amendment-Regulations-2023.pdf accessed on 1 August 2024.

485. The Companies (Beneficial Ownership Information) (Amendment) Regulations of 2023, p. 846, available at https://brs.go.ke/wp-content/uploads/2023/11/L.-N.-162-Companies-Beneficial-Ownership-Information-Amendment-Regulations-2023.pdf accessed on 1 August 2024. 'Significant control includes control that can be exercised through –

(a) debt instruments or other financial arrangements such as where a lender or creditor controls a legal person via the provisions of the lending agreement which provides that debt is convertible into voting equity, or where a third party.
influences a shareholder by means of a financial or other relationship but does not include instances where a bank provides financing to a legal person;

(b) positions held within a legal person such as being responsible for the strategic decisions that affect business practices or general direction of the legal person including senior managing officials.

(c) informal means such as through close personal connections to family or associates including informal nominee arrangements or when an individual is using, enjoying or benefiting from the assets owned by the legal person, or

(d) differential voting rights that give certain shareholders more control than others in this case, even a shareholding that falls well below a specified threshold may in fact give a minority shareholder control over the company; and'.

Notably, the regulations also define 'family' as 'the beneficial owner's spouse, a child or stepchild of the beneficial owner, a child or stepchild of the beneficial owner's spouse who lives with the beneficial owner and is under 18 years old, a parent of the beneficial owner, A brother or sister of the beneficial owner. A brother or sister of the spouse of the beneficial owner, A grandchild of the beneficial owner, A spouse of any relatives as mentioned earlier (e.g., in-laws)'. Family members may indirectly exert control over a company because of their relationships with beneficial owners. For example, a parent may exert influence over a company, which is held in the child's name. In such cases, both parents and children would be considered beneficial owners because of their informal relationships.

Further, when multiple family members collectively own shares or voting rights that cross the threshold, their holdings may be combined to determine whether they collectively exert control over the company. This ensures that even when the individual members of the family do not cross the threshold for identification of BO, their combined influence is recognized for identifying control under the definition of 'significant influence'. Including criteria such as 'significant influence' and 'significant control' ensures that individuals who might not hold direct control or who informally control the company are identified as beneficial owners. Inclusion of 'significant control' and 'significant influence' fulfils the 'control including informal control' criteria which is according to the 'good practice' definition of BO. Furthermore, the definition is also broad which fulfils the 'good practice' definition of BO.

In addition, Regulation 4A requires nominee shareholders or directors to disclose their status and provide details of nominees who hold shares in their names.[486] It is of particular importance, as it addresses the issue of nominee arrangements where a nominee can be used to obscure the true beneficial owner who controls the company. By requiring compulsory disclosure of such nominee shareholders or directors, the regulations ensure the transparency of nominee arrangements and prevent the risk of their misuse for illicit purposes.

Kenya's business registration service offers illustrations of various direct and indirect holding situations, as well as instances of significant influence and control.[487]

486. Regulation 4A, The Companies (Beneficial Ownership Information) (Amendment) Regulations of 2023, available at https://brs.go.ke/wp-content/uploads/2023/11/L.-N.-162-Companies-Beneficial-Ownership-Information-Amendment-Regulations-2023.pdf accessed on 1 August 2024.

487. Guide on Beneficial Ownership Information Requirements, *Kenya Business Registration Services*, pp. 11-12, available at https://brs.go.ke/wp-content/uploads/2023/03/Guide-on-Disclosure-of-Beneficial-Ownership-Information.pdf accessed 1 August 2024.

Table 5.1 Adapted and Summarized from Scenarios Provided in Guide from BO Info, Kenya Business Registration, Pages 28-34

Situation	*Description*	*Identification of BO*
Direct Ownership	Company A is owned by Mr P (90%) and Company B (10%). Company B is held by Ms. Q (50%) and Mr R (50%)	Mr P is the Main BO Ms Q and Mr R also BO as they own Company B, which has a stake in Company A
Direct Ownership *(Complex)*	Company A is owned by five companies (C, D, E, F, G)	Individuals who control over 10% of shares through stakes in 4 companies are identified as BO.
Direct and Indirect Ownership	Company A is held by Ms L (56%), Mr M (41%), and Nominees of Mr M (3%)	Ms L and Mr M, identified as BO
Control by influence	Mr N owns the voting shares of, and Mr O controls the operations of Company C.	Both N and O are identified as BO
Joint Shareholding	Mr. S and Mrs. T hold more than 10% jointly with Ms. U in Company A	Mr. S, Mrs. T and Ms. U identified as BO
Joint Voting Agreement	Mr. A, Mrs B, Ms. C, Mr D control over 10% of company E through a voting agreement	All four individuals are identified as BO
Holdings through nominee	Mr A holds 10% in Company P via Mr B (nominee)	Mr A is identified as BO
Holdings through nominee (complex)	Mr A holds 10% in Company P via Mr E, who is a nominee for Company X	Mr A is identified as BO
Trusts and other legal arrangements	Trust W owns shares in Company P	The settlor, Trustee, protector, beneficiaries, and any controlling persons of Trust W are identified as BO.
Trusts and other legal persons	Trust W owns shares in Company P, with the Trustee of Trust W being a legal person.	The settlor, protector, beneficiaries, and any controlling persons of Trust W and beneficial owner of Trustee, a legal person, is identified as BO.
Trusts and other legal persons (complex)	Trust W owns shares in Company P, with the Trustee of Trust W being a legal person. Beneficiaries of Trust W are individuals.	The settlor, protector, beneficiaries and any controlling persons of Trust W and beneficial owner of Trustee, a legal person, is identified as BO.

In the case of Limited Liability Partnerships, section 31B of the Limited Liability Partnership Act 2012 requires LLPs to maintain a register of beneficial owners similar to companies. However, in its peer review, the Global Forum highlighted the need for continuous updates and filing of such information, which poses a risk to BO transparency.[488] Furthermore, such a risk has also been highlighted in the case of general partnerships.

5.2.2 Beneficial Ownership Definition in the Proceeds of Crime and Anti-money Laundering Act, 2009 (Amended 2022)

The Anti-money laundering legislation in Kenya is established through the proceeds of the Crime and Anti-Money Laundering Act of 2009, which was amended in 2022 (PCAMLA). The Act was implemented through the proceeds of the Crime and Anti-Money Laundering Regulations of 2023.

Regulation 14 of the PCAMLA requires reportable institutions (Banks, Insurance companies, Forex Institutions, Cooperative financial banks, and other designated financial businesses and professions such as casinos, real estate agents, accounting firms, law firms, and non-governmental organizations) to undertake customer due diligence to identify the BO of their customers. This regulation emphasizes the need for transparency and the identification of beneficial owners of legal persons or arrangements that go beyond merely identifying their customers. It aligns with 'FATF standards to prevent the misuse of legal persons and legal arrangements for illicit purposes.'[489]

In addition, Regulation 14(3)(b) requires the reporting institutions to take 'reasonable measures' to 'identify beneficial owners during customer due diligence, ensuring that the ownership and control structure of the client is verified'.[490] The requirement to take 'reasonable measures' means that financial institutions must make genuine efforts to identify BO, which may involve tracing complex ownership and control structures.

488. OECD, *Global Forum on Transparency and Exchange of Information for Tax Purposes: Kenya 2024 (Second Round, Combined Review): Peer Review Report on the Exchange of Information on Request*, Global Forum on Transparency and Exchange of Information for Tax Purposes (OECD Publishing 2024), Paris, para. 152, available at https://doi.org/10.1787/348052b1-en accessed on 22 August 2024.
489. OECD, *Global Forum on Transparency and Exchange of Information for Tax Purposes: Kenya 2024 (Second Round, Combined Review): Peer Review Report on the Exchange of Information on Request*, Global Forum on Transparency and Exchange of Information for Tax Purposes (OECD Publishing 2024), Paris, para. 90, available at https://doi.org/10.1787/348052b1-en accessed on 22 August 2024.
490. Regulation 14, it states that:

> (1) A reporting institution shall undertake customer due diligence measures.
> (2) In carrying out the obligation under sub-regulation (1), a reporting institution shall –
> (a) …
> (b) identify the beneficial owner and take reasonable measures to verify the beneficial owner's identity, such that the reporting institution is satisfied that it knows who the beneficial owner is and understands the ownership and control structure of the customer in case of legal persons and arrangements.

Regulation 2 of the PCAMLA defines beneficial owners as 'a natural person who ultimately owns or controls a customer or the natural person on whose behalf a transaction is being conducted and includes any natural person who ultimately exercises effective control over a legal person or arrangement'.[491] Prior to the amendment of this definition, the term 'persons' was used instead of 'natural person'.[492] Regulation 14(1)(d) of the 2013 regulations clarified that the term signifies a natural person. Inclusion of 'natural person' in the BO definition fulfils the 'good practice' definition of BO.

This broad definition covers direct and indirect ownership and control in its scope, ensuring that individuals who use the complex ownership structures of legal persons and legal arrangements to disguise their ownership and control are still identified under the regulations. Including the term 'ultimately owns and controls' ensures that individuals who influence the decision-making process and control without having any formal recognition are identified as beneficial owners. The meaning of the term 'ultimately' used for identifying BO has not been provided in the regulation. Therefore, there may be questions about whether the term 'ultimately' is to be interpreted to mean any natural person in control of ownership either directly or indirectly, individually, or jointly with any other individual. This doubt in interpreting the term raised the concerns that customer due diligence would not 'consistently identify beneficial ownership information of foreign and domestic companies registered in Kenya'.[493]

The PCAML regulations do not provide a threshold for identifying beneficial owners. The absence of a threshold requires all individuals who are beneficial owners or who exert significant control over the legal person or legal arrangements through means other than ownership to be identified as beneficial owners. It also requires the identification of beneficial owners, managing companies, corporations, and other legal persons. Exclusion of 'threshold' in the BO definition as against the 15% proposed in the 'good practice' definition of BO does not fulfil the 'good practice' definition of BO.

Regulation 22(1) and (2) of PCAML mandates that reportable institutions identify the beneficial owners of legal persons and legal arrangements, and for these purposes, they need to understand their ownership and control structure. This regulation reinforces the need to identify beneficial owners by understanding control and ownership, which may be absent in complex ownership and control structures.

491. Regulation 2 of PCAMLA, available at https://www.treasury.go.ke/wp-content/uploads/2023/09/POCAMLA-REGULATIONS.pdf accessed on 1 August 2024.
492. OECD, *Global Forum on Transparency and Exchange of Information for Tax Purposes: Kenya 2024 (Second Round, Combined Review): Peer Review Report on the Exchange of Information on Request*, Global Forum on Transparency and Exchange of Information for Tax Purposes (OECD Publishing 2024), Paris, para. 94, available at https://doi.org/10.1787/348052b1-en accessed on 22 August 2024.
493. OECD, *Global Forum on Transparency and Exchange of Information for Tax Purposes: Kenya 2024 (Second Round, Combined Review): Peer Review Report on the Exchange of Information on Request*, Global Forum on Transparency and Exchange of Information for Tax Purposes (OECD Publishing 2024), Paris, para. 96, available at https://doi.org/10.1787/348052b1-en accessed on 22 August 2024.

Regulation 16 of the PCAML supplements Regulation 22 to identify the beneficial owners of legal persons. It provides a three-step cascading approach for identifying beneficial owners. The first step is to identify the natural person who owns or controls the company due to ownership. In case of doubts in control by the natural person with ownership, or if no single person is identified as a beneficial owner, then the natural person who controls the company through management, influence, or other means is identified as a beneficial owner. If there are doubts about this, the senior management official holding the top management position in the company is identified as the beneficial owner.[494] The identification of the BO of partnerships is dealt with in a similar manner.[495] In the case of trusts, the identities of trustees, beneficiaries, settlors, protectors, or any other person with control must be identified to identify beneficial owners.[496] The definition of BO and regulations for its identification align with FATF standards on BO.[497] Inclusion of 'control including informal control' in the BO definition fulfils the 'good practice' definition of BO.

In its peer review report, the Global Forum notes that PCAML is the primary source of information on BO in the case of general partnerships, LLPs and Trusts. Supervision through other legislation needs to be higher for general partnerships, LLPs, and trusts. Therefore, PCAML cannot be considered a reliable source for obtaining BO information in the case of such arrangements.[498]

5.2.3 FATF and Global Forum Evaluations

As discussed earlier in this chapter, the legal framework for BO in Kenya is primarily addressed by the Companies Act 2015, the Companies (BO Information) Regulation 2023, and the Proceeds of Crime and Anti-money Laundering Regulations 2023. The FATF conducted its second round of mutual evaluation of Kenya and issued a report in

494. OECD, *Global Forum on Transparency and Exchange of Information for Tax Purposes: Kenya 2024 (Second Round, Combined Review): Peer Review Report on the Exchange of Information on Request*, Global Forum on Transparency and Exchange of Information for Tax Purposes (OECD Publishing 2024), Paris, para. 97, available at https://doi.org/10.1787/348052b1-en accessed on 22 August 2024.
495. Regulation 17 of PCAMLA, available at https://www.treasury.go.ke/wp-content/uploads/2023/09/POCAMLA-REGULATIONS.pdf accessed on 1 August 2024.
496. Regulation 18 of PCAMLA, available at https://www.treasury.go.ke/wp-content/uploads/2023/09/POCAMLA-REGULATIONS.pdf accessed on 1 August 2024.
497. OECD, *Global Forum on Transparency and Exchange of Information for Tax Purposes: Kenya 2024 (Second Round, Combined Review): Peer Review Report on the Exchange of Information on Request*, Global Forum on Transparency and Exchange of Information for Tax Purposes (OECD Publishing 2024), Paris, para. 99, available at https://doi.org/10.1787/348052b1-en accessed on 22 August 2024.
498. OECD, *Global Forum on Transparency and Exchange of Information for Tax Purposes: Kenya 2024 (Second Round, Combined Review): Peer Review Report on the Exchange of Information on Request*, Global Forum on Transparency and Exchange of Information for Tax Purposes (OECD Publishing 2024), Paris, para. 43, available at https://doi.org/10.1787/348052b1-en accessed on 22 August 2024.

September 2022.[499] The mutual evaluation report highlighted concerns regarding the transparency of BO. Subsequently, the Global Forum issued its peer review report in March 2024. The following table highlights the gaps in evaluation and current developments in BO based on these reports.

Table 5.2 Kenya: FATF And Global Forum Evaluations (Recommendation 24 on Legal Persons)

Criteria	*Description*	*2022 FATF Evaluation*	*2024 Global Forum Review*
24.1	Assessment of ML/TF Risks of misuse of legal persons	Lacked a comprehensive assessment.	No changes were found.
24.2	Mechanism to prevent misuse	Some mechanisms exist, but improvement is needed.	Improvements were noted in the supervision of financial institutions by the Central Bank of Kenya, but gaps still exist in the supervision of Non-Financial Institutions
24.3	Company Registry	Inconsistent compliance and enforcement	Amendments to the Companies Act and new regulations were introduced in 2023, but evidence of their effectiveness remains to be demonstrated.
24.4	Accuracy of BO Information	The mechanism for verifying and updating information was found to be weak	Legislative improvements were noticed, and concern about the accuracy of the information as well as enforcement
24.5	Verification of BO Information	Limited verification process with primary reliance on self-reporting	No changes were found
24.12	Disclosure by Nominees	Disclosure to tax authorities, but not to other relevant authorities	Legislative changes were introduced to evidence its effectiveness

499. ESAAMLG, *Anti-money Laundering and Counter-Terrorist Financing Measures: Kenya, Second Round Mutual Evaluation Report*, ESAAMLG (2022), Dar es Salaam, available at https://www.esaamlg.org/reports/MER%20of%20Kenya-%20September%202022.pdf accessed on 22 August 2024.

Table 5.3 Kenya: FATF and Global Forum Evaluations (Recommendation 25 on Trust and Similar Legal Arrangements)

Criteria	*Description*	*2022 FATF Evaluation*	*2024 Global Forum Review*
25.1	Assessment of ML/TF Risks of misuse of trusts and similar legal arrangements	No dedicated risk assessment for trusts and similar legal arrangements	No changes were found
25.2	Mechanism to prevent misuse	Measures exist but rely primarily on the AML Framework	No changes, with limited improvements
25.3	Obligations of Trustee to maintain BO Information	No clear Obligation	Legislative amendments made changes in the obligations of the Trustee.
25.4	Accuracy of BO Information	Concerns about the accuracy and availability of BO information on Trust and other similar arrangements	No changes were found
25.5	Verification of Trustee Information	Limited verification process with primary reliance on self-reporting	No changes were found
25.12	Disclosure by Nominees of Trustees	No requirement for such disclosure	*No update*

The 2022 mutual evaluation found Kenya 'partially compliant' with recommendations 24 and 25. The Global Forum 2024 peer review acknowledged Kenya's efforts to align with FATF standards by improving its legal framework and enforcement mechanism concerning BO. However, some gaps still exist in fully complying with the FATF standards. In its June 2024 review, FATF classified Kenya in its 'grey list' of countries that required increased monitoring.[500] Kenya has committed to improving collection of BO information and regulations of Trusts for the purpose of identification of BO.

5.2.4 Conclusion and Summary

The definition of BO in the Companies Act of 2015 is in alignment with the elements of the 'good practice' definition of BO, except that it uses a 'threshold' of 10% in the definition which is against the 'good practice' definition of BO which proposes a relatively low threshold of 15%. The definition of BO in PCAMLA does not provide for

500. FATF, *High-Risk and Other Monitored Jurisdictions: Increased Monitoring June 2024* (2024), available at https://www.fatf-gafi.org/en/publications/High-risk-and-other-monitored-jurisdictions/increased-monitoring-june-2024.html accessed on 13 August 2024.

'threshold' as against the 15% proposed in the 'good practice' definition of BO. Therefore, it is recommended that Kenya increase the threshold to 15% in the definition of BO in the Companies Act of 2015 and include the threshold in the PCAMLA.

5.3 NIGERIA

5.3.1 Beneficial Ownership Definition in the Companies and Allied Matters Act, 2020

The Companies and Allied Matters Act, 2020 (CAMA) is the primary legislation governing the establishment of companies and other legal arrangements in Nigeria.[501] The Companies and Allied Matters Act, 2020 uses the term 'Person with significant control' to define BO. Section 868, which defines the meaning of various terms used in the Act, defines the term 'person of significant control' as:

> any person (a) directly or indirectly holding at least 5% of the shares or interest in a company or limited liability partnership; (b) directly or indirectly holding at least 5% of the voting rights in a company or limited liability partnership; (c) directly or indirectly holding the right to appoint or remove a majority of the directors or partners in a company or limited liability partnership; (d) otherwise having the right to exercise or exercising significant influence or control over a company or limited liability partnership or (e) having the right to exercise, or exercising significant influence or control over the activities of a trust or firm whether or not it is a legal entity but would satisfy any of the first four conditions if it were an individual.

Furthermore, the term 'person' used in this section has been defined under section 868 as 'includes an individual, company, or other entity with legal rights and is subject to obligations'.

This definition covers the concept of BO through ownership and control, including direct and indirect ownership and control. It not only applies to companies but also to limited liability partnerships. This definition provided in CAMA addresses direct as well as indirect ownership and control. Such ownership and control are determined by using a threshold of 5% of shares or voting rights.

The term control has been considered the 'right to appoint or remove a majority of the directors or partners in a company or limited liability partnership' or 'right to exercise or exercising significant influence or control over a company, limited liability partnership, the activities of a trust or firm whether or not it is a legal entity'. The term 'significant influence' has not been defined in the act. However, the Global Forum in its review, indicated that the term can be interpreted in a broad manner and could be

501. Kenya: Companies and Allied Matters Act (2020), available at https://www.cac.gov.ng/wp-content/uploads/2020/12/CAMA-NOTE-BOOK-FULL-VERSION.pdf accessed on 1 August 2024.

interpreted to cover cases of control without ownership.[502] The criteria for identification of BO specified paragraphs (a) to (d) of the definition are to be applied cumulatively, therefore, the 'notion of control has been used even when a natural person can be identified under the criteria of ownership'.[503] This is in alignment with the FATF standards. The definition specifically does not address the 'informal control' through family members which is crucial for the 'good practice' definition of BO.

A notable difference in the definition of BO in Nigeria is the threshold used to identify BO. Nigeria uses 5% (FATF prescribes a threshold of 25%)[504] as a threshold in its definition to identify BO. Inclusion of 5% threshold in the BO definition is relatively low as against the 15% proposed in the 'good practice' definition of BO.

The definition of BO specified in section 868 does not align with the definition provided by the FATF fully for several reasons.[505] First, the definition does not include the term 'natural person', which is crucial to the FATF definition. Second, this definition does not consider situations in which multiple individuals jointly exercise control.[506] Compared to the definition of BO in Kenya, the definition of a person of significant interest in Nigeria does not include the identification of senior management officials of the company where no beneficial owner has been identified under the ownership or control criteria provided in section 868.[507] Furthermore, the definition of BO focuses more on legal ownership than on BO, which requires separating legal ownership from natural ownership and control.[508] This lack of focus on BO leads to noncompliance with FATF standards on BO. Exclusion of 'natural persons' in the BO definition is against the 'good practice' definition of BO.

502. OECD, *Global Forum on Transparency and Exchange of Information for Tax Purposes: Nigeria 2023 (Second Round): Peer Review Report on the Exchange of Information on Request,* Global Forum on Transparency and Exchange of Information for Tax Purposes (OECD Publishing 2023), Paris, para. 117, available at https://doi.org/10.1787/90bade22-en accessed on 1 August 2024.
503. *Ibid.*
504. FATF, *FATF Recommendations, International Standards on Combating Money Laundering and the Financing of Terrorism & Proliferation* (FATF 2023), Paris, France, Footnote 37, p. 67, available at www.fatf-gafi.org/en/publications/Fatfrecommendations/Fatf-recommendations.html accessed on 1 August 2024.
505. OECD, *Global Forum on Transparency and Exchange of Information for Tax Purposes: Nigeria 2023 (Second Round): Peer Review Report on the Exchange of Information on Request,* Global Forum on Transparency and Exchange of Information for Tax Purposes (OECD Publishing 2023), Paris, para. 118, available at https://doi.org/10.1787/90bade22-en accessed on 1 August 2024.
506. *Ibid.*
507. OECD, *Global Forum on Transparency and Exchange of Information for Tax Purposes: Nigeria 2023 (Second Round): Peer Review Report on the Exchange of Information on Request,* Global Forum on Transparency and Exchange of Information for Tax Purposes (OECD Publishing 2023), Paris, para. 17, available at https://doi.org/10.1787/90bade22-en accessed on 1 August 2024.
508. Nigeria Extractive Industry Transparency Initiative, *The Need to Know Who Owns What in Nigeria's Extractive Sector,* Policy Brief, Issue 1 (May 2016), available at https://eiti.org/sites/default/files/attachments/policy_dialogue_on_beneficial_ownership_final.pdf accessed on 1 August 2024.

Sections 119 and 791 also include references to the term 'person with significant control'[509] and provide for disclosure of capacity by the shareholders in the case of companies and of significant control in the case of limited liability partnerships. Section 119 requires any shareholder to disclose the capacity in which the shares are being held.[510] This includes whether the shares are held beneficially or on behalf of someone else. It imposes onus on reporting BO to the individuals themselves.[511] Similarly, section 791 requires disclosure by a person with significant control over liability partnerships. By shifting the burden to provide BO information on the individuals themselves, it requires clarity whether the shareholder is the owner or holding the shares on behalf of someone else.

Section 120 obliges disclosure by substantial shareholders of a public company of their BO which includes indirect interest. A person is identified as a 'substantial shareholder' if the individual can exercise 5% or more of the voting rights of a public company held by him or through his nominees. Therefore, nominees would have to be reported under section 120 as 'substantial shareholder' if they hold 5% or more of the voting rights of the public company. This section ensures that shareholders or their nominees who hold substantial shareholding in the company are transparent about their ownership which includes BO. However, section 120 also has a few drawbacks. First, it is ineffective if the shareholding is less than the threshold of 5%.[512] Second, it also does not cover private companies in its scope.[513] Therefore, nominees of private companies do not have to disclose their ownership interests. This issue was identified by the Global Forum in its 2023 peer review, wherein it recommended that Nigeria 'ensure that accurate identity information on nominators and BO information behind nominee shareholders is available in line with the standard'.[514]

509. Central Bank of Nigeria, *Guidance on Ultimate Beneficial Owners of Legal Persons and Legal Arrangements,* Persons with Significant Control Regulations (2022), available at https://www.cbn.gov.ng/Out/2023/FPRD/Circular%20on%20Guidance%20Ultimate%20Beneficial%20Ownership%20of%20Legal%20Persons%20and%20Legal%20Arrangements.pdf accessed on 1 August 2024.
510. 'Notwithstanding the provisions of section 120, every person with significant control over a company shall, within seven days of becoming such a person, indicate to the company in writing the particulars of such control.'
511. C. Nwapi, C. Ezeigbo and O. Oke, Developments in Beneficial Ownership Disclosure in the Extractive Industries in Nigeria, *The Extractive Industries and Society,* 8 (2021), 443-456 https://doi.org/10.1016/j.exis.2020.12.012 accessed 3 September 2025.
512. OECD, *Global Forum on Transparency and Exchange of Information for Tax Purposes: Nigeria 2023 (Second Round): Peer Review Report on the Exchange of Information on Request,* Global Forum on Transparency and Exchange of Information for Tax Purposes (OECD Publishing 2023), Paris, para. 147, available at https://doi.org/10.1787/90bade22-en accessed on 1 August 2024.
513. *Ibid.*
514. *Ibid.*

5.3.2 Beneficial Ownership Definition in the Money Laundering (Prevention and Prohibition) Act 2022

Anti-money laundering legislation in Nigeria is established through the Money Laundering (Prevention and Prohibition) Act 2022 (MLA). Section 4 of the MLA requires 'financial institutions and designated non-financial businesses and professions to identify the BO of their customers'. The institutions are required to identify beneficial owners using 'reliable, independent source document or data' while ensuring the identification of beneficial owners with due verification. The section ensures that the financial institution conducts a thorough due diligence when identifying and verifying BO information.

Section 30 of the MLA defines the term beneficial owner as follows: 'Beneficial owner' refers to '(a) the natural person who ultimately owns or controls a customer, (b) the natural person on whose behalf a transaction is being conducted, and (c) the person who exercises effective control over a legal person or arrangement.' This definition is crucial as it provides a key legal framework for identification of individuals who may not be legal owners but may significantly control or benefit from the ownership. This definition is aligned with the FATF standards on BO as it addresses direct and indirect cases of ownership and control.[515] Inclusion of 'natural person' in the BO definition fulfils the 'good practice' definition of BO.

The meaning of 'control' has been enumerated in the guidelines issued by the Central Bank of Nigeria.[516] These guidelines recognize that BO can extend beyond straightforward ownership of a certain percentage of shares and may include situations where control is exerted in a complex and diversified manner. Such situations include scenarios where individuals may act alone or jointly with other individuals exercising control over a legal entity. This guidance emphasizes the importance of understanding several ways through which control can be exercised, which may not be clear from direct ownership alone.[517] The guidelines provide a three-step cascading approach for identifying BO. In the first step, the identity of natural persons with a controlling interest in the legal person is verified. 'In case of doubts about the natural person identified in the first step through ownership interests or if no person is found to exercise control through ownership, then the natural person who controls the legal person through other means is required to be identified as beneficial owner.'[518] In case no natural person is identified in the first two steps, then senior managing officials

515. OECD, *Global Forum on Transparency and Exchange of Information for Tax Purposes: Nigeria 2023 (Second Round): Peer Review Report on the Exchange of Information on Request*, Global Forum on Transparency and Exchange of Information for Tax Purposes (OECD Publishing 2023), Paris, para. 129, available at https://doi.org/10.1787/90bade22-en accessed on 1 August 2024.
516. Central Bank of Nigeria, *Guidance on Ultimate Beneficial Owners of Legal Persons and Legal Arrangements*, Persons with Significant Control Regulations (2022), available at https://www.cbn.gov.ng/Out/2023/FPRD/Circular%20on%20Guidance%20Ultimate%20Beneficial%20Ownership%20of%20Legal%20Persons%20and%20Legal%20Arrangements.pdf accessed on 1 August 2024.
517. *Ibid.*
518. *Ibid.*

should be identified as beneficial owners by taking reasonable measures. The third step offers the option of a backstop leading to identification of beneficial owners.[519] The rationale behind the cascading approach is to ensure that all possible scenarios are evaluated to identify beneficial owners who are ultimately in control of a legal entity. This approach ensures that complex and opaque structures are not misused for concealing BO. This definition aligns with the FATF standards.[520] The definition does not specifically provide for the informal control as provided in the 'good practice' definition of BO.

In case of Trusts and cooperative societies, MLA is the only source of BO information. However, no specific frequency has been provided in the act or regulations for carrying out customer due diligence or for updating the information.[521] In case of cooperative societies, there are 'no obligations to engage anti-money laundering obliged persons' which may entail the beneficial information concerning cooperative societies not being available.[522]

5.3.3 FATF and Global Forum Evaluations

As discussed earlier in this chapter, the legal framework for BO in Nigeria is primarily addressed by the Companies and Allied Matters Act, 2020 (CAMA) and Money Laundering (Prevention and Prohibition) Act 2022 (MLA). The FATF conducted its second round of mutual evaluation of Nigeria and issued its second follow-up report in November 2023.[523] The mutual evaluation report highlighted concerns regarding the transparency of BO. Subsequently, the Global Forum issued its peer review report in March 2023. The following table highlights the gaps in evaluation and current developments in BO based on those reports.

519. OECD, *Global Forum on Transparency and Exchange of Information for Tax Purposes: Nigeria 2023 (Second Round): Peer Review Report on the Exchange of Information on Request,* Global Forum on Transparency and Exchange of Information for Tax Purposes (OECD Publishing 2023), Paris, para. 129, available at https://doi.org/10.1787/90bade22-en accessed on 1 August 2024.
520. *Ibid.*
521. OECD, *Global Forum on Transparency and Exchange of Information for Tax Purposes: Nigeria 2023 (Second Round): Peer Review Report on the Exchange of Information on Request,* Global Forum on Transparency and Exchange of Information for Tax Purposes (OECD Publishing 2023), Paris, p. 18, available at https://doi.org/10.1787/90bade22-en accessed on 1 August 2024.
522. *Ibid.*
523. GIABA, *Anti-Money Laundering and Counter-Terrorist Financing Measures – Nigeria, Second Enhanced Follow-Up Report and Technical Compliance Re-Rating,* GIABA (2023), Dakar, available at https://www.fatf-gafi.org/content/dam/fatf-gafi/fsrb-fur/Nigeria-GIABA-Follow-Up-Report-ENG-2024.pdf accessed on 1 August 2024.

Table 5.4 Nigeria: FATF and Global Forum Evaluations (Recommendation 24 on Legal Persons)

Criteria	*Description*	*Global Forum Review (March 2023)*	*FATF Evaluation (November 2023)*
24.1	Assessment of ML/TF Risks of misuse of legal persons	Lacked a comprehensive assessment, particularly for legal persons like LLPs and entities in free trade zones.	Progress noted, but the risk of entities in free trade zones still exists.
24.2	Mechanism to prevent misuse	Some mechanisms exist, but enforcement was weak, especially concerning LLPs and general partnerships.	Improvements were noted, but gaps still exist in the enforcement of entities in free trade zones.
24.3	Company Registry	Inconsistent registration process and enforcement	Inconsistent registration process and enforcement in case of entities in free trade zones.
24.4	Accuracy of BO Information	The mechanism for verifying and updating information was found to be weak, especially for LLPs and general partnerships.	Noted the same concerns
24.5	Verification of BO Information	Limited verification process with primary reliance on self-reporting	No changes were found
24.12	Disclosure by Nominees	Disclosure requirement inconsistently applied.	Improvement noted, but effective enforcement still an issue

Table 5.5 Nigeria: FATF and Global Forum Evaluations (Recommendation 25 on Trust and Similar Legal Arrangements)

Criteria	*Description*	*2022 FATF Evaluation*	*2024 Global Forum Review*
25.1	Assessment of ML/TF Risks of misuse of trusts and similar legal arrangements	No dedicated risk assessment for trusts and similar legal arrangements	No changes were found
25.2	Mechanism to prevent misuse	Measures exist but rely primarily on the AML Framework, with limited focus on trusts and partnerships	Limited improvements were found with no improvements in Trusts.

Criteria	*Description*	*2022 FATF Evaluation*	*2024 Global Forum Review*
25.3	Obligations of Trustee to maintain BO Information	No clear Obligation	Some Legislative amendments but concerns remain.
25.4	Accuracy of BO Information	Concerns about the accuracy and availability of BO information on Trust and other similar arrangements	No changes were found
25.5	Verification of Trustee Information	Limited verification process with primary reliance on self-reporting	No changes were found
25.12	Disclosure by Nominees of Trustees	No requirement for such disclosure	*No update*

The 2022 mutual evaluation found Nigeria 'partially compliant' with recommendations 24 and 25.[524] The Global Forum 2023 peer review acknowledges Nigeria's efforts to align with FATF standards by improving its legal framework and enforcement mechanism concerning BO. However, some gaps still exist in fully complying with the FATF standards. In its June 2024 review, FATF classified Nigeria in its 'grey list' of countries that required increased monitoring.[525] Nigeria has committed to ensuring access to up-to-date and accurate BO information.

5.3.4 Conclusion and Summary

The definition of BO in section 868 of the Companies and Allied Matters Act is not in alignment with the elements of the 'good practice' definition of BO. It does not use the term 'natural persons' in the definition, which is against the 'good practice' definition of BO. Furthermore, the definition specifically does not address the 'informal control' through family members which is crucial for the 'good practice' definition of BO. Inclusion of 5% threshold in the BO definition is relatively low as against the 15% proposed in the 'good practice' definition of BO. It is therefore recommended that Nigeria should in future include 'natural persons' while broadening the scope to include informal control through family members in the definition of BO in the Companies and Allied Matters Act. Further, it should increase the threshold to 15% in the definition of BO in the Companies and Allied Matters Act.

524. GIABA (2023), *Anti-Money Laundering and Counter-Terrorist Financing Measures – Nigeria, Second Enhanced Follow-Up Report and Technical Compliance Re-Rating* GIABA (2023), para. 133, Dakar, available at https://www.fatf-gafi.org/content/dam/fatf-gafi/fsrb-fur/Nigeria-GIABA-Follow-Up-Report-ENG-2024.pdf accessed on 1 August 2024.

525. FATF, *High-Risk and Other Monitored Jurisdictions: Increased Monitoring June 2024* (2024), available at https://www.fatf-gafi.org/en/publications/High-risk-and-other-monitored-jurisdictions/increased-monitoring-june-2024.html accessed on 13 August 2024.

The definition of BO in the Money Laundering (Prevention and Prohibition) Act 2022 includes the term 'natural person' in the definition. However, the definition does not specifically provide for the informal control as provided in the 'good practice' definition of BO. It is therefore recommended that Nigeria should in future include informal control through family members in the definition of BO in the MLA.

5.4 SOUTH AFRICA

5.4.1 Beneficial Ownership Definition in the Companies Act, 2008

The Companies Act 2008 is amended by the General Laws (Anti-Money Laundering and Combating Terrorism Financing) Amendment Act 2022.

Section 1 of the Companies Act defines a beneficial owner as: 'in respect of a company, means an individual who, directly or indirectly, ultimately owns that company or exercises effective control of that company, including through (a) the holding of beneficial interests in the securities of that company (b) the exercise of, or control of the exercise of the voting rights associated with securities of that company (c) the exercise of, or control of the exercise of the right to appoint or remove members of the board of directors of that company (d) the holding of beneficial interests in the securities, or the ability to exercise control including through a chain of ownership or control, of a holding company of that company (e) the ability to exercise control, including through a chain of ownership or control, of (i) a juristic person other than a holding company of that company (ii) a body of persons, corporate or unincorporated (iii) a person acting on behalf of a partnership (iv) a person acting in pursuance of the provisions of a trust agreement or (f) the ability to otherwise materially influence the management of that company'.

The term 'beneficial owner' defined in the Companies Act is broad, capturing both direct and indirect forms of ownership and control. This broad definition is essential to ensure that all relevant forms of control over a company are subject to regulatory scrutiny. Including individuals who control voting rights or have the power to appoint or remove directors aligns with the concept of 'effective control' which is critical for identifying BO. Subsection (d) explicitly addresses situations in which control is exercised by holding companies. This is common in corporate structures where ownership is layered, and the beneficial owner may be disguised. By including holding companies, this section ensures BO disclosure throughout the entire chain of ownership. Subsection (e) includes control exercised through juristic persons, corporate bodies, partnerships, or trusts. This is crucial in cases where control is exercised not through ownership of shares by legal agreements, partnerships, or trusts. It captures scenarios in which individuals may exert control through indirect means, thus ensuring that such arrangements are not used to evade regulatory scrutiny. Subsection (f) introduces 'material influence' on the management of the company as a criterion for identifying BO. This is a crucial addition to the definition as it recognizes that influence can be exercised without formal agreements or positions. This ensures that individuals who may not own shares of the company or do not fulfil any criteria of control can still be identified as beneficial owners if they have a significant influence on the operations or critical decisions of the company. This is particularly important when informal controls such as close family relationships are used to influence control. This 'comprehensive definition of BO aligns with FATF standards for BO'.

Inclusion of 'natural person' and 'control including informal control' in the BO definition fulfils the 'good practice' definition of BO. Furthermore, this definition is also 'broad'.

In addition, an essential feature of the Companies Act 2008 is that it differentiates BO requirements based on whether the company falls in the category of 'affected company'. Affected companies refer to companies with complex ownership structures, those involved in high-risk sectors, publicly traded companies, or large private companies.[526]

5.4.2 Beneficial Ownership Definition in the Financial Intelligence Centre Act, 2001

The anti-money laundering legislation in South Africa was established through the Financial Intelligence Centre Act (FICA) in 2001.

Section 21 B of the FICA requires financial institutions, designated non-financial businesses, and professionals to identify the BO of their customers by undertaking customer due diligence. This section ensures that financial institutions conduct thorough due diligence when identifying and verifying BO information.

Section 1 of the FICA defines that the term beneficial owner 'means a natural person who directly or indirectly (i) ultimately owns or exercises effective control of (aa) a client of an accountable institution or (bb) a legal person, partnership or trust that owns or exercises effective control of as the case may be, a client of an accountable institution or (ii) exercises control of a client of an accountable institution on whose behalf a transaction is being conducted and (b) includes (i) in respect of legal persons, each natural person contemplated in section 21B(2)(a) (ii) in respect of a partnership each natural person contemplated in section 21B(3)(b) and (iii) in respect of a trust, each natural person contemplated in section 21B(4)(c), (d) and (e)'.

This definition of BO under FICA is comprehensive and includes individuals who exert indirect control, such as ownership in holding companies or through complex ownership structures. This ensures that all individuals who influence the legal person or transaction are identified. Further, the focus on the 'natural person' aids in piercing the veil of legal persons that might otherwise obscure real beneficial owners. Inclusion of 'natural person' in the BO definition fulfils the 'good practice' definition of BO.

In the context of due diligence, section 21B(2) provides a three-step cascading approach for identifying the BO of legal persons. First, the identity of a natural person with a controlling interest in a legal person is verified. In the case of doubts about the natural person identified in the first step through an ownership interest, or if no person

526. Affected company means a regulated company as set out in section 117(1)(i) and a private company that is controlled by or a subsidiary of a regulated company as a result of any circumstances contemplated in section 2(2)(a) or 3(1)(a).

is found to exercise control through ownership, the natural person who controls the legal person through other means is required to be identified as the beneficial owner. If no natural person is identified in the first two steps, senior management officials are required to be identified as beneficial owners by taking appropriate measures. This third step offers a backstop option for identifying the beneficial owners.[527] The rationale behind the cascading approach is to ensure that all possible scenarios are evaluated in order to identify beneficial owners who ultimately control a legal entity. This approach ensures that complex and opaque structures are not misused to conceal the BO.

This definition aligns with FATF standards.[528] Inclusion of 'control including informal control' in the BO definition fulfils the 'good practice' definition of BO.

Additionally, in the case of partnerships, section 21B(3) provides a legal basis for identifying beneficial owners. This requires all reportable institutions to identify all the partners in a partnership. This is in addition to the general information on identity and business relationships provided in section 21 and 21A of the FICA.

Section 22 of the FICA requires reportable institutions to maintain a record of the identity of the clients and beneficial owners, as well as how such BO was identified, and any additional information concerning the transactions conducted.

5.4.3 FATF and Global Forum Evaluations

As discussed earlier, the legal framework for BO in South Africa is primarily addressed by the Companies Act of 2008 and the Financial Intelligence Centre Act (FICA) 2001. The Global Forum issued its peer review report in October 2022. The FATF conducted its follow-up report in South Africa and issued its report in November 2023.[529] The mutual evaluation report highlights concern regarding the transparency of BO. Based on these reports, the following table highlights the gaps in evaluation and current developments in BO in South Africa.

527. OECD, *Global Forum on Transparency and Exchange of Information for Tax Purposes: Nigeria 2023 (Second Round): Peer Review Report on the Exchange of Information on Request*, Global Forum on Transparency and Exchange of Information for Tax Purposes (OECD Publishing 2023), Paris, para. 129, available at https://doi.org/10.1787/90bade22-en accessed on 1 August 2024.
528. OECD, *Peer Review Report: Second Round, Combined Review – South Africa*, Global Forum on Transparency and Exchange of Information for Tax Purposes (OECD Publishing 2022), Paris, p. 47, available at https://www.oecd.org/en/publications/global-forum-on-transparency-and-exchange-of-information-for-tax-purposes-south-africa-2022-second-round-combined-review_0cb5c667-en.html accessed on 1 August 2024.
529. FATF, *Anti-Money Laundering and Counter-Terrorist Financing Measures: South Africa, 2nd Enhanced Follow-Up Report* (FATF 2023), Paris, available at https://www.fatf-gafi.org/content/fatf-gafi/en/publications/Mutualevaluations/south-africa-fur-2023.html accessed on 1 August 2024.

Table 5.6 South Africa: FATF and Global Forum Evaluations (Recommendation 24 on Legal Persons)

Criteria	*Description*	*Global Forum Review (October 2022)*	*FATF Evaluation (November 2023)*
24.1	Assessment of ML/TF Risks of misuse of legal persons	Lacked a comprehensive assessment.	Progress was noted.
24.2	Mechanism to prevent misuse	Some mechanisms exist, but they could be more robust, especially in the case of non-financial sectors.	Improvements were noted, but gaps exist in non-financial sectors.
24.3	Company Registry	The accuracy of information and enforcement were inconsistent.	Similar concerns
24.4	Accuracy of BO Information	The mechanism for verifying and updating information needed to be stronger, especially for LLPs and general partnerships.	Noted the same concerns
24.5	Verification of BO Information	Limited verification process and outdated information	No changes were found
24.12	Disclosure by Nominees	Disclosure requirements are inadequate and poorly enforced.	Improvement was noted, but effective enforcement is still an issue.

Table 5.7 South Africa: FATF and Global Forum Evaluations (Recommendation 25 on Trust and Similar Legal Arrangements)

Criteria	*Description*	*Global Forum Review (October 2022)*	*FATF Evaluation (November 2023)*
25.1	Assessment of ML/TF Risks of misuse of trusts and similar legal arrangements	No dedicated risk assessment for trusts and similar legal arrangements	No changes were found
25.2	Mechanism to prevent misuse	Measures exist but rely primarily on the AML Framework, with a limited focus on trusts and partnerships	Limited improvements were found with no improvements in Trusts.
25.3	Obligations of Trustee to maintain BO Information	No clear Obligation	There are some Legislative amendments, but concerns remain.

Criteria	*Description*	*Global Forum Review (October 2022)*	*FATF Evaluation (November 2023)*
25.4	Accuracy of BO Information	Concerns about the accuracy and availability of BO information on Trust and other similar arrangements	No changes were found
25.5	Verification of Trustee Information	Limited verification process with primary reliance on self-reporting	No changes were found
25.12	Disclosure by Nominees of Trustees	No requirement for such disclosure	*No update*

The 2023 mutual evaluation found that South Africa is 'largely compliant'[530] for recommendations 24 and 25. The Global Forum 2023 peer review acknowledges South Africa's efforts to align with FATF standards by improving its legal framework and enforcement mechanism concerning BO. It is rated as 'largely compliant' with EOIR standards.[531] However, some gaps still exist in fully complying with the FATF standards. In its June 2024 review, FATF classified South Africa in its 'grey list' of countries that required increased monitoring.[532] South Africa has committed to ensuring timely access to up-to-date and accurate BO information, along with imposing sanctions for any non-compliance.

5.4.4 Conclusion and Summary

The definition of BO in The Companies Act 2008 and the Financial Intelligence Centre Act (FICA) of 2001 in South Africa are in alignment with the elements of the 'good practice' definition of BO except it does not use any 'threshold' in the definition which is against the 'good practice' definition of BO which proposes a relatively low threshold of 15%. The definition of BO in FICA also does not provide for a 'threshold' as against the 15% proposed in the 'good practice' definition of BO. Therefore, it is recommended that South Africa include the threshold to 15% in the definition of BO in the Companies Act of 2015 and FICA.

530. FATF, *Anti-Money Laundering and Counter-Terrorist Financing Measures – South Africa, 2nd Enhanced Follow-Up Report* (FATF 2023), Paris, p. 31, available at https://www.fatf-gafi.org/content/fatf-gafi/en/publications/Mutualevaluations/south-africa-fur-2023.html accessed on 1 August 2024.
531. OECD, *Global Forum on Transparency and Exchange of Information for Tax Purposes: South Africa 2022 (Second Round, Combined Review): Peer Review Report on the Exchange of Information on Request*, Global Forum on Transparency and Exchange of Information for Tax Purposes (OECD Publishing 2022), Paris, p. 11, available at https://doi.org/10.1787/0cb5c667-en accessed on 1 August 2024.
532. FATF, *High-Risk and Other Monitored Jurisdictions: Increased Monitoring June 2024* (2024), available at https://www.fatf-gafi.org/en/publications/High-risk-and-other-monitored-jurisdictions/increased-monitoring-june-2024.html accessed on 13 August 2024.

5.5 INTERIM CONCLUSION

The following recommendations have been proposed to the focus countries based on the analysis of the legal framework on BO for aligning the definition with the elements of the 'good practice' definition of BO:

Kenya: It is recommended that Kenya increase the threshold to 15% in the definition of BO in the Companies Act of 2015 and include the threshold in the PCAMLA.
Nigeria: It is recommended that Nigeria include the term 'natural person' in its definition of BO in section 868 of the Companies and Allied Matters Act, while broadening the scope to include informal control through family members. MLA should also broaden the scope to include informal control through family members. Also, it is recommended that Nigeria increase the threshold to 15% in the definition of BO in the Companies and Allied Matters Act.
South Africa: The existing definition of BO in South Africa is in alignment with the elements of 'good practice' definition of BO, except for the threshold. It is recommended that South Africa increase the threshold to 15% in the definition of BO in the Companies Act 2008 and FICA.

Chapter 6
Outcomes and Conclusion

6.1 OUTCOMES

The main objective of this research was to compare the legal definition of BO, in relation to legal persons and legal arrangements in Kenya, Nigeria and South Africa, with the 'good practice' BO definition. The objective was carried out to formulate recommendations for these countries on how they can strengthen their legal definition of BO to prevent tax evasion and avoidance in relation to IFFs.

6.1.1 Key Findings Against Research Questions

(a) What Fundamental Elements Emerge from Existing International Standards for Defining BO?

Based on the definition of BO provided by FATF, UNCAC, the World Bank, the EITI Initiative, the Open Ownership Initiative, and the 5th AMLD, some key elements emerge for defining BO. First, a beneficial owner is always a 'natural person(s)' who is behind the legal person or legal arrangement.[533] It is imperative that at the end of the ownership chain, a natural person will always own or control the legal person or arrangement. Therefore, it is essential to include the term 'natural person(s)' in the definition of BO. Second, the threshold approach for identification of BO, which is used by several countries[534] and also advocated by FATF at 25%, is a good criterion for

533. FATF, *Transparency and Beneficial Ownership*, FATF Guidance (2014) (as amended in November 2023) available at http://www.fatf-gafi.org/media/fatf/documents/reports/Guidance-transparency-beneficial-ownership.pdf accessed on 29 September 2020.

534. Extractive Industries Transparency Initiative, *Legal Approaches to Beneficial Ownership Transparency in EITI Countries* (June 2019), p. 5, available at https://eiti.org/files/documents/legal_approaches_to_beneficial_ownership_transparency_in_eiti_countries.pdf accessed on 29 September 2020.

identifying BO. Open ownership indicates a threshold between 5% and 15%, as a good range for setting the threshold.[535] A relatively low threshold, such as 5%, would be prone to disadvantages such as a higher cost of compliance and affecting ease of doing business. In contrast, a higher threshold of 25% would be at risk of manipulation. Therefore, a relatively balanced threshold of 15% would help mitigate some of the drawbacks of having no threshold or a higher threshold and would make the scope of the definition broader. Third, ownership can be held directly or indirectly by controlling the legal person or legal arrangement. An effective definition of BO should cover all direct and indirect types of ownership and control. Furthermore, informal control through family members, nominees, proxies, indirectly through a chain of legal entities or through other means, etc., should be recognized in the definition to include those persons that do not have 15% but that nevertheless exercise control, for instance, together with others. Lastly, the broad definition that captures in its scope not only direct and indirect ownership but also cases of indirect and informal control facilitate the identification of various types of BO.

(b) To What Extent Is the Current Legal Framework for the Definition of BO in Kenya, Nigeria and South Africa Inconsistent with These Elements?

Kenya

- Section 93A of the Companies Act 2015 includes all the elements of the 'good practice' definition on BO, except that it uses a 'threshold' of 10% in the definition which is against the 'good practice' definition of BO which proposes a relatively low threshold of 15%.[536]
- Regulation 2 of The Proceeds of Crime and Anti-Money Laundering Act (PCAMLA) does not provide for a 'threshold' as against the 15% proposed in the 'good practice' definition of BO.

Nigeria

- Section 868 of the Companies and Allied Matters Act 2020 does not include the term 'natural person' for identifying BO in its definition, which is inconsistent with the good practice definition of BO. The definition also does not specifically address 'informal control' through family members which is essential for an effective definition of BO. It provides for 5% threshold in the BO definition which is relatively lower as against the 15% proposed in the 'good practice' definition of BO.

535. Open Ownership, *Beneficial Ownership in Law: Definitions and Thresholds*, p. 11, available at https://www.openownership.org/en/publications/beneficial-ownership-in-law-definitions-and-thresholds/defining-beneficial-ownership/ accessed 21 August 2024.
536. Kenya, *Regulation 2 of The Companies (Beneficial Ownership Information) (Amendment) Regulations of 2023*, available at https://brs.go.ke/regulations/ accessed on 24 August 2024.

- Section 30 of the Money Laundering (Prevention and Prohibition) Act 2022 does not specifically provide for the informal control as provided in the 'good practice' definition of BO.

South Africa

- The recently amended[537] Companies Act 2008 and the Financial Intelligence Centre Act (FICA) 2001 include all elements of the good practice definition of BO, except that it does not include any 'threshold' in the definition which is against the 'good practice' definition of BO which proposes a relative low threshold of 15%.

(c) What Measures Could Be Taken to Better Align the Legal Framework for Defining BO in Kenya, Nigeria, and South Africa with Such Principles?

- Kenya should increase the threshold to 15% in the definition of BO in the Companies Act of 2015 as a criterion in Regulation 2 of The Companies (BO Information) (Amendment) Regulations of 2023 and in PCAMLA for identifying control for identification of BO.
- Nigeria should include the term 'natural person' in section 868 on BO definition of Companies and Allied Matters Act 2020. The scope of the definition should be broadened to include informal control through family members in the definition of BO in the Companies and Allied Matters Act 2020 and in the Money Laundering Act. Further, it should increase the threshold to 15% in the definition of BO in the Companies and Allied Matters Act.
- South Africa should increase the threshold to 15% in the definition of BO in the Companies Act of 2018 and in FICA for identifying control for identification of BO.

6.2 CONCLUSION

This research addressed the critical issue of strengthening the legal definition of BO to prevent tax evasion and tax avoidance related to IFFs in Kenya, Nigeria and South Africa. It aimed to identify inconsistencies in the legal framework and formulate policy advice to address them based on the model good-practice definition of BO. This research found that all three target countries are trying to improve their legislation on identifying the BO of legal persons and legal arrangements. However, some issues still need to be addressed regarding the legal definition of BO in Kenya and Nigeria. The

537. South Africa, *General Laws (Anti-money Laundering and Combating Terrorism Financing) Amendment Act 2022*, available at https://www.gov.za/documents/acts/general-laws-anti-money-laundering-and-combating-terrorism-financing-amendment-act accessed on 24 August 2024.

legal definition of BO in South Africa except threshold aligns with the elements of the good practice definition of BO.

6.3 AREAS FOR FUTURE RESEARCH

The decision of the Court of Justice of the European Union in November 2022, wherein the court concluded that fundamental rights in respect of personal and private life, as well as personal data protection enshrined under Articles 7 and 8 of the Charter of Fundamental Rights of the European Union, are violated by the provision of public access to BO information, highlighted the issue of the impact of BO transparency on privacy and data protection.[538] While giving its verdict, the court answered the question of 'the interference with the fundamental rights guaranteed in Articles 7 and 8 of the Charter, resulting from the general public's access to information on BO' in the affirmative, whereas it held Article 1(15)(c) of Directive (EU) 2018/843, which allows public access to BO information, as invalid. This ruling not only has implications for the EU and but also for other countries following similar jurisprudence. The court's decision emphasized the importance of upholding the right to privacy while balancing public interest when allowing public access to BO information.

In the literature, Johana Hey points out the strengths and weaknesses of public disclosure.[539] She notes that disclosing tax-related information to the public acts as an 'instrument for tax enforcement' and considers the 'public eye an effective means of control'. However, this view conflicts with the guarantees provided in the constitutions, such as the right to privacy and confidentiality. Privacy rights are considered fundamental human rights worldwide and have been incorporated into numerous international legal instruments. Several countries' constitutions also recognize these rights as fundamental human rights granted to their citizens under their constitutions. Internationally, such rights to privacy and confidentiality are provided in international legislation, which provides a legal basis for enforcing such rights.[540] To implement the right to privacy enshrined in their respective constitutions, many countries have incorporated data protection legislation to prevent unauthorized disclosure of information.

538. Court of Justice of the European Union (CJEU), *Case C-100/21, FN*, Judgment of the Court (First Chamber) of 23 November 2022, ECLI:EU:C:2022:924, available at https://curia.europa.eu/juris/document/document.jsf?docid=268059&mode=req&pageIndex=1&dir=&occ=first&part=1&text=&doclang=EN&cid=9481 accessed on 24 August 2024.

539. J. Hey, Chapter 7: General Report – Transparency and Publicity in Tax Transparency, in F. Başaran Yavaşlar and J. Hey (eds), *Tax Transparency*, IBFD, 2020, section 7.3.2.1, Books IBFD https://www.ibfd.org/sites/default/files/2021-04/19_018_tax_transparency_final_web.pdf accessed 3 September 2025.

540. For example, Art. 8 of the *European Convention on Human Rights (ECHR)*; Art. 17 of the *International Covenant on Civil and Political Rights (ICCPR)*; Art. 1 of the *Convention for the Protection of Individuals with regard to Automatic Processing of Personal Data*; Art. 12 of the *Universal Declaration of Human Rights (UDHR)*; Arts 7 and 8 of the *Charter of Fundamental Rights of the European Union*; Art. 16(1) of the *Consolidated Version of the Treaty on the Functioning of the European Union (TFEU)*; and the *EU General Data Protection Regulation (GDPR), Regulation (EU) 2016/679.*

However, in the literature, differing views exist on the right to privacy and the right to data protection of taxpayers. Ivaniševic notes from the ECtHR's Montenegro case that the right to data protection encompasses the right to privacy and involves all information handled, including the private information of individuals.[541] The EU regulation on the protection of natural persons concerning the processing of personal data and the free movement of such data distinguishes that data protection is only allowed for natural persons. By contrast, the right to privacy includes legal persons.[542] Privacy involves (Article 8 of ECHR) the 'right to respect private and family life, home and correspondence', while data protection only focuses on personal information.

The term 'private life' is fundamental to the right to privacy and has not been defined. There is also no definition of it in tax law. The ECtHR states that it is a broad concept and includes 'aspects relating to one's identity (such as a person's name, photograph, financial status or physical and moral integrity), covers the physical and psychological integrity of a person and embraces multiple aspects of the person's physical and social identity'.[543] In addition, protecting personal data is essential for protecting the right to privacy granted under Article 8 of the ECHR.[544] Article 8 provides a legal basis for determining the disclosure of data that may affect the privacy of individuals.

In contrast, Baker states that 'privacy and data protection overlay the entire field of transparency'.[545] Gilbert suggests a distinction between 'privacy' and 'data protection' based on the legal system of the country as well as language.[546] Therefore, BO

541. B. Ivaniševic, Distinction Between Privacy and Data Protection in ECtHR's Montenegro Case, *Lexology* (13 February 2018), available at https://www.lexology.com/library/detail.aspx?g=24bf666f-b092-495b-b12a-afe1c0d47598 accessed 24 August 2024; European Court of Human Rights (ECtHR): DE: *Niemietz v. Germany*, 16 December 1992, Case no. 13710/88, para. 29; FR: *Couderc and Hachette Filipacchi Associés v. France*, 10 November 2015, Case no. 40454/07, para. 83; RO: *Bărbulescu v. Romania*, 5 September 2017, Case no. 61496/08, para. 70; UA: *Denisov v. Ukraine*, 25 September 2018, Case no. 76639/11, para. 95; CH: *G.S.B. v. Switzerland*, 22 December 2015, Case no. 28601/11, para. 51.

542. Regulation (EU) 2016/679 of the European Parliament and of the Council of 27 April 2016 on the protection of natural persons with regard to the processing of personal data and on the free movement of such data, and repealing Directive 95/46/EC (General Data Protection Regulation), available at https://eur-lex.europa.eu/eli/reg/2016/679/oj accessed on 22 August 2024.

543. F. Başaran Yavaşlar, Chapter 11: General Report – Limitations of Transparency and Protection of the Taxpayer in Tax Transparency, in F. Başaran Yavaşlar and J. Hey (eds), *Tax Transparency*, IBFD, 2020, Footnote 1, Books IBFD, https://www.ibfd.org/sites/default/files/2021-04/19_018_tax_transparency_final_web.pdf accessed 3 September 2025.

544. European Court of Human Rights (ECtHR): FI: *Satakunnan Markkinapörssi Oy and Satamedia Oy v. Finland*, 27 June 2017, Case no. 931/13, para. 137; UK: *S. and Marper v. The United Kingdom*, 4 December 2008, Case no. 30562/04, para. 103.

545. P. Baker, *Right to Privacy*, 2018 EATLP Congress in Zürich (*online link not accessible in the original literature where it was referenced*) in F. Başaran Yavaşlar, Chapter 11: General Report – Limitations of Transparency and Protection of the Taxpayer in Tax Transparency, in F. Başaran Yavaşlar and J. Hey (eds), *Tax Transparency*, IBFD, 2020, Footnote 7, Books IBFD, https://www.ibfd.org/sites/default/files/2021-04/19_018_tax_transparency_final_web.pdf accessed 3 September 2025.

546. F. Gilbert, *Privacy v. Data Protection: What Is the Difference?* (1 October 2014), available at https://www.francoisegilbert.com/?p=937 accessed on 24 August 2024.

transparency, which deals with the public disclosure of information about individuals, needs proper legal analysis considering these privacy rights, as these rights have far-reaching impacts.

Bibliography

African Union Agenda 2063: The Africa We Want. https://au.int/en/agenda2063/overview (accessed 11 September 2024).

African Union Commission. (2015). Report on Illicit Financial Flows from Africa. https://au.int/en/documents/20210708/report-high-level-panel-illicit-financial-flows-africa (accessed 11 September 2024).

African Union Commission. (2019). Domestic Resource Mobilisation: Fighting Against Corruption and Illicit Financial Flows. AUC Publishing. https://au.int/sites/default/files/documents/37326-doc-k-15353_au_advocacy_brief_brochure_dev v3.pdf (accessed 11 September 2024).

Aliprandi, G., Busschots, T. and Oliveira, C. (2023). Mapping the Global Geography of Shell Companies. Tax Observatory. https://www.taxobservatory.eu/publication/mapping-the-global-geography-of-shell-companies/ (accessed 11 September 2024).

Alstadsæter, A., Johannesen, N. and Zucman, G. (2019). Tax Evasion and Inequality. American Economic Review, 109(6), 2073-2103.

Avi-Yonah, R. (2000). Globalisation, Tax Competition, and the Fiscal Crisis of the Welfare State. Harvard Law Review, 113, 1578.

Barreix, A., Roca, J. and Velayos, F. (2016). A Brief History of Tax Transparency. Inter-American Development Bank. https://publications.iadb.org/publications/english/document/A-Brief-History-of-Tax-Transparency.pdf (accessed 11 September 2024).

Başaran Yavaşlar, F. and Hey, J. (eds) (2020). Tax Transparency, IBFD, https://www.ibfd.org/sites/default/files/2021-04/19_018_tax_transparency_final_web.pdf (accessed 11 September 2024).

Beer, S., Coelho, M. and Leduc, S. (2019). Hidden Treasures: The Impact of Automatic Exchange of Information on Cross-Border Tax Evasion. IMF Working Paper WP/19/286. https://www.imf.org/en/Publications/WP/Issues/2019/12/20/Hidden-Treasure-The-Impact-of-Automatic-Exchange-of-Information-on-Cross-Border-Tax-Evasion-48781 (accessed 11 September 2024).

Berkhout, R. and Fernando, F. (eds). (2022). Unmasking Control: A Guide to Beneficial Ownership Transparency. International Monetary Fund. https://www.imf.org/

en/Publications/Books/Issues/2022/10/06/Unmasking-Control-A-Guide-to-Beneficial-Ownership-Transparency-517096 (accessed 11 September 2024).

Blum, J.A. et al. (1998). Financial Havens, Banking Secrecy and Money Laundering. United Nations Office for Drug Control and Crime Prevention. https://gfintegrity.org/wp-content/uploads/2022/06/UN-FINANCIAL-HAVENS-laundering.pdf (accessed 11 September 2024).

Central Bank of Nigeria. (2023). Guidance on Ultimate Beneficial Owners of Legal Persons and Legal Arrangements, Persons with Significant Control Regulations. https://www.cbn.gov.ng/Out/2023/FPRD/Circular%20on%20Guidance%20Ultimate%20Beneficial%20Ownership%20of%20Legal%20Persons%20and%20Legal%20Arrangements.pdf (accessed 11 September 2024).

Chhina, R. (2022). Beneficial Ownership Transparency in Asia and the Pacific. Asian Development Bank. https://www.adb.org/publications/beneficial-ownership-transparency-asia-pacific (accessed 11 September 2024).

Chowla, P. and Falcao, T. (2016). Illicit Financial Flows: Concepts and Scope. Interagency Task Force. https://www.un.org/esa/ffd/wp-content/uploads/2017/02/Illicit-financial-flows-conceptual-paper_FfDO-working-paper.pdf (accessed 11 September 2024).

Christensen, J. (2011). The Looting Continues: Tax Havens and Corruption. Critical Perspectives on International Business, 7(2), 177-196. https://doi.org/10.1108/17422041111128249 (accessed 11 September 2024).

Cobham, A. (2016). Breaking the Vicious Circles of Illicit Financial Flows, Conflict and Insecurity. Great Insights Magazine. https://ecdpm.org/work/prosperity-for-peace-volume-5-issue-1-february-2016/breaking-the-vicious-circles-of-illicit-financial-flows-conflict-and-insecurity (accessed 11 September 2024).

Cobham, A. (2017). The Significance and Subversion of SDG 16.4: Multinational Tax Avoidance as IFF. Tax Justice Network. https://www.un.org/esa/ffd/ffdforum/wp-content/uploads/sites/3/2017/05/ED1-Cobham.pdf (accessed 11 September 2024).

Cobham, A. and Janský, P. (2017). Global Distribution of Revenue Loss from Tax Avoidance: Re-estimation and Country Results. WIDER Working Paper Series wp-2017-55. World Institute for Development Economic Research (UNU-WIDER). https://www.wider.unu.edu/publication/global-distribution-revenue-loss-tax-avoidance (accessed 11 September 2024).

Cobham, A. and Janský, P. (2017). Measurement of Illicit Financial Flows: Background Paper Prepared for UNCTAD. UNODC-UNCTAD Expert Consultation on the SDG Indicator on Illicit Financial Flows. https://www.unodc.org/documents/data-and-analysis/statistics/IFF/Background_paper_B_Measurement_of_Illicit_Financial_Flows_UNCTAD_web.pdf (accessed 11 September 2024).

Cockfield, A.J. (2016). Big Data and Tax Haven Secrecy. Florida Tax Review, 18(8), 483-539.

Council of the European Union. (2016). ECOFIN Council, Criteria 1.4. https://data.consilium.europa.eu/doc/document/ST-9295-2022-INIT/en/pdf (accessed 11 September 2024).

Court of Justice of the European Union. (2022). Luxembourg Business Registers ('LBR'), WM and Luxembourg Business Registers ('LBR') (Case C-37/20). https://curia.europa.eu/juris/document/document.jsf?docid=268059&mode=req&p.Index=1&dir=&occ=first&part=1&text=&doclang=EN&cid=9481 (accessed 11 September 2024).

Deutsche Welle. (2021). Chasing Africa's Tax Dodgers, available at https://www.dw.com/en/africas-problem-with-tax-avoidance/a-48401574 (accessed 13 August 2024).

Department for Business Innovation and Skills, HMRC. (2016). Beneficial Ownership Transparency: Enhancing the Transparency of Beneficial Ownership Information of Foreign Companies Undertaking Certain Economic Activities in the U.K. https://assets.publishing.service.gov.uk/government/uploads/system/uploads/attachment_data/file/512333/bis-16-161-beneficial-ownership-transparency.pdf (accessed 11 September 2024).

Duri, J. (2018). Combating Corruption-Related Illicit Financial Flows from Africa: Legal Approaches and Challenges. African Human Rights Yearbook, 2, 321-346. https://www.ahry.up.ac.za/duri-j (accessed 11 September 2024).

Dun & Bradstreet. (2016). Beneficial Ownership, Why the Devil Really Is in the Detail, https://www.dnb.co.uk/content/dam/english/business-trends/db-4981-beneficial-ownership-whitepaper.pdf (accessed 29 September 2020).

Elliffe, C. (2011). The Thickness of a Prison Wall: When Does Tax Avoidance Become a Criminal Offence? New Zealand Business Law Quarterly, 17(4), 441-466. https://papers.ssrn.com/sol3/papers.cfm?abstract_id=1992652 (accessed 11 September 2024).

Etter-Phoya, R., Danzi, E. and Jalipa, R. (2020). Beneficial Ownership Transparency in Africa: The State of Play in 2020. SSRN Electronic Journal. https://papers.ssrn.com/sol3/papers.cfm?abstract_id=3640402 (accessed 11 September 2024).

Etter-Phoya, R. et al. (2023). Beneficial Ownership Transparency in Africa in 2022. SSRN Electronic Journal. https://papers.ssrn.com/sol3/papers.cfm?abstract_id=4395017 (accessed 11 September 2024).

European Commission. (1996). Taxation in the European Union: Discussion Paper for the Informal Meeting of the ECOFIN Council. SEC (96) 487 final. https://www.verginet.net/UserFiles/File/Avrupa_Birligi/Taxation/General_Information/taxation_sec(1996)487_en%204%20Ek%203.pdf (accessed 11 September 2024).

European Commission. (2006). Taxation Papers: A History of the Tax Package: The Principles and Issues Underlying the Community Approach. https://taxation-customs.ec.europa.eu/document/download/e969dff0-d4f8-4bb2-98f5-eeecd327b31a_en?filename=taxation_paper_10_history_en.pdf (accessed 11 September 2024).

European Commission. (2012). Recommendation of 6 December 2012 on Aggressive Tax Planning. C(2012) 8806 final. https://taxation-customs.ec.europa.eu/document/download/995ded83-3321-4935-8b38-db8a2d675e9f_en?filename=c_2012_8806_en.pdf (accessed 11 September 2024).

European Parliament. (2015). Report on Tax Avoidance and Tax Evasion as Challenges for Governance, Social Protection and Development in Developing Countries.

https://www.europarl.europa.eu/doceo/document/A-8-2015-0184_EN.html (accessed 11 September 2024).

European Parliament and Council. (2015). Directive (EU) 2015/849 on the prevention of the use of the financial system for the purposes of money laundering or terrorist financing. https://eur-lex.europa.eu/legal-content/EN/TXT/?uri=CELEX%3A32015L0849 (accessed 11 September 2024).

European Parliament and Council. (2018). Directive (EU) 2018/843 amending Directive (EU) 2015/849 on the prevention of the use of the financial system for money laundering or terrorist financing. https://eur-lex.europa.eu/legal-content/EN/TXT/?uri=CELEX:32018L0843 (accessed 11 September 2024).

Extractive Industries Transparency Initiative. (2019). Legal Approaches to Beneficial Ownership Transparency in EITI Countries. https://eiti.org/sites/default/files/attachments/legal_approaches_to_beneficial_ownership_transparency_in_eiti_countries.pdf (accessed 11 September 2024).

Extractive Industries Transparency Initiative & Open Ownership. (2023). Technical Guidance: Defining and Capturing Data on the Ownership and Control of State-Owned Enterprises. https://eiti.org/guidance-notes/defining-and-capturing-data-ownership-and-control-state-owned-enterprises (accessed 11 September 2024).

Farny, O. et al. (eds). (2015). Tax Avoidance, Tax Evasion and Tax Heavens. Arbeit Kammer Wien. https://www.arbeiterkammer.at/infopool/wien/Studie_tax_avoidance.pdf (accessed 11 September 2024).

Financial Action Task Force. (1990). The Forty Recommendations of the Financial Action Task Force on Money Laundering. https://www.fatf-gafi.org/media/fatf/documents/recommendations/pdfs/FATF%20Recommendations%201990.pdf (accessed 11 September 2024).

Financial Action Task Force. (2000). Review to Identify Non-cooperative Countries or Territories: Increasing the Worldwide Effectiveness of Anti-money Laundering Measures. https://www.fatf-gafi.org/content/dam/fatf-gafi/annual-reports/1999%202000%20NCCT%20ENG.pdf (accessed 11 September 2024).

Financial Action Task Force. (2006). The Misuse of Corporate Vehicles, Including Trust and Company Service Providers. https://www.fatf-gafi.org/content/dam/fatf-gafi/reports/Misuse%20of%20Corporate%20Vehicles%20including%20Trusts%20and%20Company%20Services%20Providers.pdf.coredownload.inline.pdf (accessed 11 September 2024).

Financial Action Task Force. (2014, as amended in November 2023). Guidance on Transparency and Beneficial Ownership. http://www.fatf-gafi.org/media/fatf/documents/reports/Guidance-transparency-beneficial-ownership.pdf (accessed 11 September 2024).

Financial Action Task Force. (2018). Professional Money Laundering. https://www.fatf-gafi.org/en/publications/Methodsandtrends/Professional-money-laundering.html (accessed 11 September 2024).

Financial Action Task Force. (2023). FATF Recommendations: International Standards on Combating Money Laundering and the Financing of Terrorism & Proliferation.

www.fatf-gafi.org/en/publications/Fatfrecommendations/Fatf-recommendations.html (accessed 11 September 2024).

Financial Action Task Force. (2023). Methodology for Assessing Compliance with the FATF Recommendations and the Effectiveness of AML/CFT Systems. https://www.fatf-gafi.org/en/publications/Mutualevaluations/Fatf-methodology.html (accessed 11 September 2024).

Financial Action Task Force. (2023). Guidance to Beneficial Ownership of Legal Persons (Recommendation 24). https://www.fatf-gafi.org/en/publications/Fatfrecommendations/Guidance-Beneficial-Ownership-Legal-Persons.html (accessed 11 September 2024).

Financial Action Task Force. (2024). High-Risk and Other Monitored Jurisdictions: Increased Monitoring June 2024. https://www.fatf-gafi.org/en/publications/High-risk-and-other-monitored-jurisdictions/increased-monitoring-june-2024.html (accessed 11 September 2024).

Financial Action Task Force: Egmont Group. (2018). Concealment of Beneficial Ownership. https://www.fatf-gafi.org/en/publications/Methodsandtrends/Concealment-beneficial-ownership.html (accessed 11 September 2024).

Financial Crimes Enforcement Network. FinCEN Reminds Financial Institutions CDD Rule Becomes Effective Today. https://www.fincen.gov/news/news-releases/fincen-reminds-financial-institutions-cdd-rule-becomes-effective-today (accessed 11 September 2024).

Financial Stability Forum. (2000). Report of the Working Group on Offshore Centres. http://www.fsb.org/wp-content/uploads/r_0004b.pdf (accessed 11 September 2024).

Forstater, M. (2018). Illicit Financial Flows, Trade Misinvoicing, and Multinational Tax Avoidance: The Same or Different? Center for Global Development Policy Paper No. 123. https://www.cgdev.org/sites/default/files/illicit-financial-flows-trade-misinvoicing-and-multinational-tax-avoidance.pdf (accessed 11 September 2024).

G20. (2009). Leaders' Statement, The Pittsburgh Summit. https://home.treasury.gov/system/files/206/pittsburgh_summit_leaders_statement_250909.pdf (accessed 11 September 2024).

G20. (2013). Leaders Declaration. https://www.bundesfinanzministerium.de/Content/EN/Standardartikel/Topics/world/G7-G20/G20-Documents/2013-Russia-Leaders-Declaration.pdf?__blob=publicationFile&v=1 (accessed 11 September 2024).

G20. (2014). High-Level Principles on Beneficial Ownership Transparency. https://star.worldbank.org/publications/g20-high-level-principles-beneficial-ownership-transparency (accessed 11 September 2024).

G7. (1989). 1989 Paris Summit, Economic Declaration. http://www.g8.utoronto.ca/summit/1989paris/communique/index.html (accessed 11 September 2024).

G7. (1996). 1996 Lyon Summit, Economic Communique: Making a Success of Globalisation for the Benefit of All. http://www.g8.utoronto.ca/summit/1996lyon/communique.html (accessed 11 September 2024).

Garcia-Bernardo, J. and Jánský, P. (2021). Profit Shifting of Multinational Corporations Worldwide. https://doi.org/10.19088/ictd.2021.005 (accessed 11 September 2024).

German Federal Government. G8 Lough Erne German Action Plan, Germany's Action Plan to Prevent the Misuse of Legal Persons and Legal Arrangements. https://www.bundesregierung.de/resource/blob/974430/388980/9bc2bd31db6d65025 4f566e957385037/g8-lough-erne-deutscher-aktionsplan-data.pdf?download=1 (accessed 11 September 2024).

GIABA. (2023). Anti-money Laundering and Counter-Terrorist Financing Measures: Nigeria, Second Enhanced Follow-Up Report and Technical Compliance Re-Rating. https://www.fatf-gafi.org/content/dam/fatf-gafi/fsrb-fur/Nigeria-GIAB A-Follow-Up-Report-ENG-2024.pdf (accessed 11 September 2024).

Gilmour, P. (2020). Lifting the Veil on Beneficial Ownership: Challenges of Implementing the UK's Registers of Beneficial Owners. Journal of Money Laundering Control, 23(4). https://www.emerald.com/insight/content/doi/10.1108/JMLC-02-2020-0014/full/html (accessed 11 September 2024).

Gilmour, P. (2021). Freeports: Innovative Trading Hubs or Centres for Money Laundering and Tax Evasion? Journal of Money Laundering Control, 25(1), 63-71.

Global Financial Integrity. (2015). Illicit Financial Flows and Development Indices: 2008–2012.

Global Forum on Transparency and Exchange of Information for Tax Purposes & Inter-American Development Bank. (2019). A Beneficial Ownership Implementation Toolkit. OECD Publishing. https://publications.iadb.org/en/beneficial-ownership-implementation-toolkit (accessed 11 September 2024).

Global Witness. The Great Rip-off: Anonymous Companies and their victims. http://greatripoffmap.globalwitness.org/#!/ (accessed 11 September 2024).

González-Barreda, P.H. (2020). Beneficial Ownership in Tax Law and Tax Treaties. Hart Publishing.

Gordon, P.H. Beneficial Ownership and Trusts: A Critical Analysis of a Central FATF Definition and Its Failure to Meet Policy Objective [Master's thesis]. University of Sydney. https://ses.library.usyd.edu.au/handle/2123/29387 (accessed 11 September 2024).

Government of Jersey. Annotated Versions Jersey CRS Guidance Notes. https://www.gov.je/sitecollectiondocuments/tax%20and%20your%20money/id%20annotat ed%20versions%20jersey%20crs%20guidance%20notes%2010272017%20vp.pdf (accessed 11 September 2024).

Harrington, B. (2016). Capital Without Borders. Harvard University Press. https://www.hup.harvard.edu/books/9780674244771 (accessed 11 September 2024).

Hebous, S. and Johannesen, N. (2021). At Your Service! The Role of Tax Havens in International Trade with Services. European Economic Review, 135(C). https://ideas.repec.org/a/eee/eecrev/v135y2021ics0014292121000908.html (accessed 11 September 2024).

Henry, J.S. (2012). The Price of Offshore Revisited: New Estimates for Missing Global Private Wealth, Income, Inequality, and Lost Taxes. Tax Justice Network.

https://taxjustice.net/cms/upload/pdf/Price_of_Offshore_Revisited_120722.pdf (accessed 11 September 2024).

Hook, G.P. (2022), Beneficial Ownership and Trusts: A Critical Analysis of a Central FATF Definition and Its Failure to Meet Policy Objective [Master's thesis]. University of Sydney. https://ses.library.usyd.edu.au/handle/2123/29387 (accessed 11 September 2024).

International Consortium of Investigative Journalists. (2016). Giant Leak of Offshore Financial Records Exposes Global Array of Crime and Corruption. https://www.icij.org/investigations/panama-papers/20160403-panama-papers-global-overview/ (accessed 11 September 2024).

International Monetary Fund. (2014). Spillovers in International Corporate Taxation. IMF Policy Paper. https://www.imf.org/external/np/pp/eng/2014/050914.pdf (accessed 11 September 2024).

Jánský, P. and Prats, A. (2015). International Profit-Shifting Out of Developing Countries and the Role of Tax Havens. Development Policy Review, 33(3), 271-292. https://doi.org/10.1111/dpr.12113 (accessed 11 September 2024).

Jimenez, A.M. (2006). Loopholes in the EU Savings Tax Directive. Bulletin for International Taxation, IBFD. https://papers.ssrn.com/sol3/papers.cfm?abstract_id=2471813 (accessed 11 September 2024).

Johannesen, N. (2014). Tax Evasion and Swiss Bank Deposits. Journal of Public Economics, 111, 61.

Kelly, J.F. (2017). International Tax Regulation by United States Fiat: How FATCA Represents Unsound International Tax Policy. Wisconsin International Law Journal, 34(4).

Kenya Business Registration Services (2023). Guide on Beneficial Ownership Information Requirements. https://brs.go.ke/wp-content/uploads/2023/03/Guide-on-Disclosure-of-Beneficial-Ownership-Information.pdf (accessed 11 September 2024).

Kenya Gazette Supplement Acts. (2015). Nairobi, 15 September 2015. https://gazettes.africa/akn/ke/officialGazette/government-gazette-supplement/2015-09-15/155/eng@2015-09-15 (accessed 11 September 2024).

Kenya Revenue Authority (2020-2021). Annual Revenue Performance Report. https://www.kra.go.ke/news-center/press-release/1299-annual-revenue-performance-fy-2020-2021 (accessed 11 September 2024).

Knobel, A. (2020). Beneficial Ownership Definitions: Determining 'Control' Unrelated to Ownership. Tax Justice Network. https://www.taxjustice.net/2020/07/23/beneficial-ownership-definitions-determining-control-unrelated-to-ownership/ (accessed 11 September 2024).

Kruger, D. and Broomberg, W. (2003). Broomberg on Tax Strategy (4th ed.). LexisNexis Butterworths.

Lejour, A. and van't Riet, M. (2023). Disentangling Business- and Tax-Motivated Bilateral Royalty Flows. CPB Discussion Paper. https://ideas.repec.org/p/cpb/discus/450.html (accessed 11 September 2024).

Lemaitre, S. (2021). Beneficial Ownership Disclosure at the U.N. General Assembly Against Corruption. CMI – Anti-Corruption Resource Centre. https://medium.

com/u4-anti-corruption-resource-centre/beneficial-ownership-disclosure-at-ungass-2021-d1b3439f8f36 (accessed 21 August 2024).

Martini, M., Technical Guide: Implementing the G20 Beneficial Ownership Principles. Transparency International. https://knowledgehub.transparency.org/product/implementing-the-g20-beneficial-ownership-principles-a-technical-guide (accessed 11 September 2024).

Migai, C., Illicit Financial Flows, and the Extractive Industries in Africa: A Focus on Transparency and Exchange of Information for Tax Purposes [Doctoral dissertation].

Muchhala, B. (2018). The Right to Development and Illicit Financial Flows: Realizing the Sustainable Development Goals and Financing for Development. Human Rights Council, Working Group on the Right to Development. https://www.ohchr.org/sites/default/files/Documents/Issues/Development/Session19/A_HRC_WG.2_19_CRP_3.docx (accessed 11 September 2024).

Ndikumana, L. and Boyce, J.K. (2018). Capital Flight from Africa: Updated Methodology and New Estimates. PERI Research Report. https://peri.umass.edu/images/CapFlightAfrica-5-28-21.pdf (accessed 11 September 2024).

Neve, L.E.C. (2017). The Peer Review Process of the Global Forum on Transparency and Exchange of Information for Tax Purposes. Erasmus Law Review, 2, 89-105. https://www.elevenjournals.com/tijdschrift/ELR/2017/2/ELR_2017_010_003 (accessed 11 September 2024).

Nigeria Extractive Industry Transparency Initiative. (2016). The Need to Know Who Owns What in Nigeria's Extractive Sector. Policy Brief, Issue 1. https://eiti.org/sites/default/files/attachments/policy_dialogue_on_beneficial_ownership_final.pdf (accessed 11 September 2024).

Nwapi, C., Ezeigbo, C. and Oke, O. (2021). Developments in Beneficial Ownership Disclosure in the Extractive Industries in Nigeria. The Extractive Industries and Society, 8, 443-456.

OECD. (1998). Harmful Tax Competition: An Emerging Global Issue. https://www.oecd-ilibrary.org/taxation/harmful-tax-competition_9789264162945-en (accessed 11 September 2024).

OECD. (2000). Improving Access to Bank Information for Tax Purposes. https://www.oecd-ilibrary.org/taxation/improving-access-to-bank-information-for-tax-purposes_9789264181267-en (accessed 11 September 2024).

OECD. (2001). Behind the Corporate Veil: Using Corporate Entities for Illicit Purposes. https://www.oecd-ilibrary.org/finance-and-investment/behind-the-corporate-veil_9789264195608-en (accessed 11 September 2024).

OECD. (2006). Council at Ministerial Level, Communiqué. https://one.oecd.org/document/PAC/COM/NEWS(2006)13/en/pdf (accessed 11 September 2024).

OECD. (2008). Study into the Role of Tax Intermediaries. https://www.oecd-ilibrary.org/taxation/study-into-the-role-of-tax-intermediaries_9789264041813-en (accessed 11 September 2024).

OECD. (2010). The Global Forum on Transparency and Exchange of Information for Tax Purposes: A Background Information Brief.

OECD. (2011). Implementing the Tax Transparency Standards: A Handbook for Assessors and Jurisdictions (2nd ed.). https://www.oecd-ilibrary.org/taxation/implementing-the-tax-transparency-standards_9789264110496-en (accessed 11 September 2024).

OECD. (2013). Addressing Base Erosion and Profit Shifting. https://www.oecd.org/en/publications/addressing-base-erosion-and-profit-shifting_9789264192744-en.html (accessed 11 September 2024).

OECD. (2014). Illicit Financial Flows from Developing Countries. https://www.oecd.org/en/publications/measuring-oecd-responses-to-illicit-financial-flows-from-developing-countries_9789264203501-en.html (accessed 11 September 2024).

OECD. (2014). Standard for Automatic Exchange of Financial Account Information in Tax Matters. https://read.oecd-ilibrary.org/taxation/standard-for-automatic-exchange-of-financial-account-information-for-tax-matters_9789264216525-en#p.1 (accessed 11 September 2024).

OECD. (2015). Action 6: Preventing the Granting of Treaty Benefits in Inappropriate Circumstances, OECD/G20 Base Erosion and Profit Shifting Project 2015 (final report). https://www.oecd-ilibrary.org/taxation/preventing-the-granting-of-treaty-benefits-in-inappropriate-circumstances-action-6-2015-final-report_9789264241695-en (accessed 11 September 2024).

OECD. (2015). Global Forum, Tax Transparency 2015: Report on Progress. https://www.oecd.org/tax/transparency/global-forum-annual-report-2015.pdf (accessed 11 September 2024).

OECD. (2017). Model Tax Convention on Income and on Capital: Condensed Version 2017. https://www.oecd.org/ctp/treaties/model-tax-convention-on-income-and-on-capital-condensed-version-20745419.htm (accessed 11 September 2024).

OECD. (2017). Standard for Automatic Exchange of Financial Account Information in Tax Matters (2nd ed.). http://dx.doi.org/10.1787/9789264267992-en (accessed 11 September 2024).

OECD. (2022). Global Forum on Transparency and Exchange of Information for Tax Purposes: South Africa 2022 (Second Round, Combined Review) – Peer Review Report on the Exchange of Information on Request. https://doi.org/10.1787/0cb5c667-en (accessed 11 September 2024).

OECD. (2023). Global Forum on Transparency and Exchange of Information for Tax Purposes: Nigeria 2023 (Second Round): Peer Review Report on the Exchange of Information on Request. https://doi.org/10.1787/90bade22-en (accessed 11 September 2024).

OECD. (2023). Handbook for Peer Reviews on Transparency and Exchange of Information on Request: Second Round. https://www.oecd.org/tax/transparency/documents/handbook-for-peer-reviews-on-transparency-and-exchange-of-information-on-request.pdf (accessed 11 September 2024).

OECD. (2024). Beneficial Ownership and Tax Transparency: Implementation and Remaining Challenges – OECD and Global Forum Report to G20 Finance Ministers and Central Bank Governors. https://doi.org/10.1787/f95790b1-en (accessed 11 September 2024).

OECD & Inter-American Development Bank. (2024). Building Effective Beneficial Ownership Frameworks: A Joint Global Forum and IDB Toolkit – Second Edition. www.oecd.org/tax/transparency/documents/effective-beneficial-ownership-frameworks-toolkit-second-edition-2024.pdf (accessed 11 September 2024).

OECD Global Forum. (2018). Tax Transparency in Africa 2018: Africa Initiative Progress Report. https://www.oecd.org/tax/transparency/documents/africa-initiative-report-2018.pdf (accessed 11 September 2024).

OECD Global Forum. (2022). Tax Transparency in Africa 2022: Africa Initiative Progress Report. https://www.oecd.org/tax/transparency/documents/tax-transparency-in-africa-2022.htm (accessed 11 September 2024).

OECD Global Forum. (2023). Tax Transparency in Africa 2023: Africa Initiative Progress Report. https://web-archive.oecd.org/temp/2023-07-21/659894-tax-transparency-in-africa-2023.htm (accessed 11 September 2024).

OECD Global Forum. (2024). Tax Transparency in Africa 2024: Africa Initiative Progress Report. https://web-archive.oecd.org/tax/transparency/documents/tax-transparency-in-africa-2024.htm (accessed 11 September 2024).

Oguttu, A., Curbing Offshore Tax Avoidance: The Case of South African Companies and Trusts. University of South Africa. https://uir.unisa.ac.za/handle/10500/1929 (accessed 11 September 2024).

Open Ownership. (2020). Beneficial Ownership in Law: Definitions and Thresholds. https://www.openownership.org/en/publications/beneficial-ownership-in-law-definitions-and-thresholds/defining-beneficial-ownership/ (accessed 11 September 2024).

Organization for Economic Cooperation and Development. (2019). Tax Transparency in Africa 2021: Africa Initiative Progress Report. https://www.oecd.org/tax/transparency/documents/Tax-Transparency-in-Africa-2021.pdf (accessed 11 September 2024).

Piccioto, S. (2018). Illicit Financial Flows and Tax Haven and Offshore Secrecy System. Tax Justice Network. https://www.taxjustice.net/2018/02/08/illicit-financial-flows-tax-haven-offshore-secrecy-system/ (accessed 11 September 2024).

Ribadu, N., The Impact of Panama Papers on Africa. https://www.europarl.europa.eu/cmsdata/116489/5%20-%2003%20Ribadu_%20statement.pdf (accessed 11 September 2024).

Signé, L., Sow, M. and Madden, P. (2020). Illicit Financial flows in Africa. Africa Growth Initiative, Policy Brief, Brookings Institute for Africa. https://www.brookings.edu/wp-content/uploads/2020/02/Illicit-financial-flows-in-Africa.pdf (accessed 11 September 2024).

Somare, M., Automatic Exchange of Financial Account Information for Tax Purposes in the Light of Preventive Measures under the 4th Anti-Money Laundering Directive [Doctoral dissertation].

South African Revenue Service. (2005). Discussion Paper on Tax Avoidance and Section 103 of the Income Tax Act, 1962 (Act No. 58 of 1962). https://www.sars.gov.za/wp-content/uploads/Legal/DiscPapers/LAPD-LPrep-DP-2005-01-Discussion-Paper-Tax-Avoidance-Section-103-of-Income-Tax-Act-1962.pdf (accessed 11 September 2024).

Steenkamp, L. (2012). Combating Impermissible Tax Avoidance Through Efficient Administrative Approaches: What SARS Can Learn from Its Canadian Counterpart. The Comparative and International Law Journal of Southern Africa, 45(2), 227-257. https://unisapressjournals.co.za/index.php/CILSA/article/view/11379 (accessed 11 September 2024).

Stolen Asset Recovery Initiative, The Puppet Masters: How the Corrupt Use Legal Structures to Hide Stolen Assets and What to Do about It. World Bank. https://openknowledge.worldbank.org/entities/publication/ec364fd2-92f8-58a0-bd4e-155ac0f644d6 (accessed 11 September 2024).

Tax Justice Network. (2012). Tax Us If You Can (2nd ed.). www.taxjustice.net/cms/upload/pdf/TUIYC_2012_FINAL.pdf (accessed 11 September 2024).

Tax Justice Network. (2020). Argentina Finally Has a Beneficial Ownership Register. https://www.taxjustice.net/2020/04/20/argentina-finally-has-a-beneficial-ownership-register-now-it-should-make-it-public/ (accessed 11 September 2024).

The Economist. (27 August 2020). Bribery Pays If You Don't Get Caught. https://www.economist.com/business/2020/08/27/bribery-pays-if-you-dont-get-caught (accessed 11 September 2024).

The World Bank. (2016). The World Bank Group's Response to Illicit Financial Flows: A Stocktaking. http://documents.worldbank.org/curated/en/502341468179035132/The-World-Bank-Group-s-response-to-illicit-financial-flows-a-stocktaking (accessed 11 September 2024).

Transparency International. (2015). Implementation of the G20 Beneficial Ownership Principles. https://knowledgehub.transparency.org/assets/uploads/kproducts/2015_ImplementationG20BOPrinciples_EN.pdf (accessed 11 September 2024).

U.S. Government, U.S. Action Plan to Implement G-20 High-Level Principles on Beneficial Ownership. https://obamawhitehouse.archives.gov/blog/2015/10/16/us-action-plan-implement-g-20-high-level-principles-beneficial-ownership (accessed 11 September 2024).

UNCTAD. (2014). Trade and Development Report. https://unctad.org/publication/trade-and-development-report-2014 (accessed 11 September 2024).

UNCTAD. (2020). Economic Development in Africa Report 2020: Tackling Illicit Financial Flows for Sustainable Development in Africa. https://unctad.org/system/files/official-document/aldcafrica2020_en.pdf (accessed 11 September 2024).

UNCTAD. (2020). Africa Could Gain $89 Billion Annually by Curbing Illicit Financial Flows. https://unctad.org/press-material/africa-could-gain-89-billion-annually-curbing-illicit-financial-flows-un-says (accessed 11 September 2024).

UNCTAD. (2023). Statistical Measurement of Tax and Commercial Illicit Financial Flows: Pilot Testing Methodologies for SDG Indicator 16.4.1. https://unctad.org/system/files/official-document/stat2023d1_en.pdf (accessed 11 September 2024).

UNCTAD & UNODC. (2020). Conceptual Framework for the Statistical Measurement of Illicit Financial Flows. https://www.unodc.org/documents/data-and-analysis/

statistics/IFF/IFF_Conceptual_Framework_for_publication_15Oct.pdf (accessed 11 September 2024).
UNECA. (2015). Illicit Financial Flows: Report of the High-Level Panel on Illicit Financial Flows from Africa. https://repository.uneca.org/handle/10855/22695 (accessed 11 September 2024).
UNECA. (2017). Economic Report on Africa. https://www.uneca.org/economic-report-africa-2017 (accessed on 21 August 2024).
UNECA. (2018). A Study on the Global Governance Architecture for Combating Illicit Financial Flows. https://repository.uneca.org/handle/10855/24320 (accessed 11 September 2024).
UNECA. (2018). Base Erosion and Profit Shifting in Africa: Reforms to Facilitate Improved Taxation of Multinational Enterprises. https://repository.uneca.org/handle/10855/24382 (accessed 11 September 2024).
UNECA. (2019). Economic Report on Africa 2019: Fiscal Policy for Sustainable Development in Africa. https://www.uneca.org/economic-report-africa-2019 (accessed 11 September 2024).
United Nations. (2017). Model Double Taxation Convention Between Developed and Developing Countries, 2017 Update. https://www.un.org/esa/ffd/wp-content/uploads/2018/05/MDT_2017.pdf (accessed 11 September 2024).
United Nations. (2024). Promotion of Inclusive and Effective International Tax Cooperation at the United Nations. https://financing.desa.un.org/document/promotion-inclusive-and-effective-international-tax-cooperation-united-nations-a78235 (accessed 11 September 2024).
United Nations Environment Programme, Our Work in Africa. https://www.unep.org/regions/africa/our-work-africa (accessed 11 September 2024).
United Nations Office on Drugs and Crime. (2011). Estimating Illicit Financial Flows Resulting from Drug Trafficking and Other Transnational Organized Crimes. https://www.unodc.org/documents/data-and-analysis/Studies/Illicit_financial_flows_2011_web.pdf (accessed 11 September 2024).
United Nations Office on Drugs and Crime. (2016). Guidance to Filling in the Revised Draft Self-Assessment Checklist on the Implementation of Chapters II (Preventive Measures) and V (Asset Recovery) of the United Nations Convention Against Corruption. https://www.unodc.org/documents/treaties/UNCAC/WorkingGroups/ImplementationReviewGroup/20-24June2016/V1603598e.pdf (accessed 11 September 2024).
United Nations Office on Drugs and Crime. (2023). Enhancing Beneficial Ownership Transparency: A Study of Beneficial Ownership Registration Systems. https://www.unodc.org/documents/treaties/UNCAC/COSP/session10/CAC-COSP-2023-CRP.5.pdf (accessed 11 September 2024).
United Nations Office on Drugs and Crime. (2024). Implementation of Beneficial Ownership Transparency in ASEAN Member States and Timor-Leste. https://www.unodc.org/roseap/uploads/documents/Publications/2024/Implementation_of_Beneficial_Ownership_Transparency_in_ASEAN_Member_States_and_Timor-Leste.pdf (accessed 11 September 2024).

United Nations Secretariat, Thematic Report: Implementation of Provisions of a Cross-Cutting Nature in Chapters II and V of the United Nations Convention Against Corruption. https://www.unodc.org/documents/treaties/UNCAC/WorkingGroups/ImplementationReviewGroup/7-11Nov2022/CAC-COSP-IRG-2022-8/2211181E.pdf (accessed 11 September 2024).

United States Government Accountability Office. (2006). Report on Company Formations: Minimal Ownership Information Is Collected and Available. https://www.gao.gov/assets/gao-06-376.pdf (accessed 11 September 2024).

United States Money Laundering Threat Assessment Working Group. (2005). U.S. Money Laundering Threat Assessment. U.S. Department of the Treasury.

United States Treasury Department, Report on the Problem of Corporate Tax Shelters.

van der Does de Willebois, E. et al. (2011). The Puppet Masters: How the Corrupt Use Legal Structures to Hide Stolen Assets and What to Do about It. World Bank. https://star.worldbank.org/sites/star/files/puppetmastersv1.pdf (accessed 11 September 2024).

van Thiel, S. (2012). European Union Action Against Tax Avoidance and Evasion. CESifo Forum, 2. https://www.ifo.de/DocDL/forum2-12-focus2.pdf (accessed 11 September 2024).

van Thiel, S. (2022). Chapter 23, Harmful Tax Competition, and the Code of Conduct for Business Taxation. In P.J. Wattel, O. Marres, H. Vermeulen and D.M. Weber (eds), European Tax Law, Volume I (Full Edition) (8th ed., pp. 801-802).

Vogel, K. (2022). Klaus Vogel on Double Taxation Conventions (5th ed.).

World Bank. (2020). Chapter 9: Beneficial Ownership Transparency. In Enhancing Government Effectiveness and Transparency: The Fight Against Corruption. https://www.worldbank.org/en/topic/governance/publication/enhancing-government-effectiveness-and-transparency-the-fight-against-corruption (accessed 11 September 2024).

World Bank. (2013). Building on Progress to Implement the EITI Standard Extractive Industries Transparency Initiative: Multi-Donor Trust Fund (EITI MDTF), Annual Report 2013. https://www.worldbank.org/content/dam/Worldbank/document/Extractives/EITI-MDTF%20Annual%20Report%202013.pdf (accessed 11 September 2024).

World Bank, Ease of Doing Business Rankings. https://archive.doingbusiness.org/en/rankings (accessed 11 September 2024).

World Bank, Illicit Financial Flows (IFFs). https://www.worldbank.org/en/topic/financialsector/brief/illicit-financial-flows-iffs (accessed 11 September 2024).

WU Global Tax Policy Center, Tax Transparency and Corruption (2019-2023). Vienna University of Economics and Business. www.wu.ac.at/en/taxlaw/institute/gtpc/current-projects/tax-transparency-and-corruption (accessed 11 September 2024).

Table of Cases

ES: Audiencia Nacional (AN), 18 July 2006, JUR\2006\204307, JUR\2007\8915 and JUR\2007\16549
ES: Audiencia Nacional (AN), 10 November 2006, JUR\2006\284679
ES: Audiencia Nacional (AN), 13 November 2006, JUR\2006\284618
ES: Audiencia Nacional (AN), 26 March 2007, JUR\2007\101877

United Kingdom

UK: *Levene v. Inland Revenue* [1928] UKHL AC 21, 16
UK: *ICR v. Duke of Westminster* [1936] 51 TIR 467, 16, 20
UK: *Indofood International Finance Ltd*, 8 ITLR 653

Table of Legislation

International

European Union

Kenya

Nigeria

South Africa

United States

SERIES ON INTERNATIONAL TAXATION

1. Alberto Xavier, *The Taxation of Foreign Investment in Brazil,* 1980 (ISBN 90-200-0582-0).
2. Hugh J. Ault & Albert J. Rädler, *The German Corporation Tax Law with 1980 Amendments,* 1981 (ISBN 90-200-0642-8).
3. Paul R. McDaniel & Hugh J. Ault, *Introduction to United States International Taxation,* 1981 (ISBN 90-6544-004-6).
4. Albert J. Rädler, *German Transfer Pricing/Prix de Transfer en Allemagne,* 1984 (ISBN 90-6544-143-3).
5. Paul R. McDaniel & Stanley S. Surrey, *International Aspects of Tax Expenditures:* A *Comparative Study,* 1985 (ISBN 90-654-4163-8).
6. Kees van Raad, *Nondiscrimination in International Tax Law,* 1986 (ISBN 90-6544-266-9).
7. Sijbren Cnossen (ed.), *Tax Coordination in the European Community,* 1987 (ISBN 90-6544-272-3).
8. Ben Terra, *Sales Taxation. The Case of Value Added Tax in the European Community,* 1989 (ISBN 90-6544-381-9).
9. Rutsel S.J. Martha, *The Jurisdiction to Tax in International Law: Theory and Practice of Legislative Fiscal Jurisdiction,* 1989 (ISBN 90-654-4416-5).
10. Paul R. McDaniel & Hugh J. Ault, *Introduction to United States International Taxation* (3rd revised edition), 1989 (ISBN 90-6544-423-8).
11. Manuel Pires, *International Juridicial Double Taxation of Income,* 1989 (ISBN 90-6544-426-2).
12. A.H.M. Daniels, *Issues in International Partnership Taxation,* 1991 (ISBN 90-654-4577-3).
13. Arvid A. Skaar, *Permanent Establishment: Erosion of a Tax Treaty Principle,* 1992 (ISBN 90-6544-594-3).
14. Cyrille David & Geerten M.M. Michielse (eds), *Tax Treatment of Financial Instruments,* 1996 (ISBN 90-654-4666-4).
15. Herbert H. Alpert & Kees van Raad (eds), *Essays on International Taxation,* 1993 (ISBN 90-654-4781-4).
16. Wolfgang Gassner, Michael Lang & Eduard Lechner (eds), *Tax Treaties and EC Law,* 1997 (ISBN 90-411-0680-4).
17. Glória Teixeira, *Taxing Corporate Profits in the EU,* 1997 (ISBN 90-411-0703-7).
18. Michael Lang et al. (eds), *Multilateral Tax Treaties,* 1998 (ISBN 90-411-0704-5).
19. Stef van Weeghel, *The Improper Use of Tax Treaties,* 1998 (ISBN 90-411-0737-1).

20. Klaus Vogel (ed.), *Interpretation of Tax Law and Treaties and Transfer Pricing in Japan and Germany,* 1998 (ISBN 90-411-9655-2).
21. Bertil Wiman (ed.), *International Studies in Taxation: Law and Economics; Liber Amicorum Leif Mutén,* 1999 (ISBN 90-411-9692-7).
22. Alfonso J. Martín Jiménez, *Towards Corporate Tax Harmonization in the European Community,* 1999 (ISBN 90-411-9690-0).
23. Ramon J. Jeffery, *The Impact of State Sovereignty on Global Trade and International Taxation,* 1999 (ISBN 90-411-9703-6).
24. A.J. Easson, *Taxation of Foreign Direct Investment,* 1999 (ISBN 90-411-9741-9).
25. Marjaana Helminen, *The Dividend Concept in International Tax Law: Dividend Payments Between Corporate Entities,* 1999 (ISBN 90-411-9765-6).
26. Paul Kirchhof, Moris Lehner, Kees van Raad, Arndt Raupach & Michael-Rodi (eds), *International and Comparative Taxation: Essays in Honour of Klaus Vogel,* 2002 (ISBN 90-411-9841-5).
27. Krister Andersson, Peter Melz & Christer Silfverberg (eds), *Liber Amicorum Sven-Olof Lodin,* 2001 (ISBN 90-411-9850-4).
28. Juan Martín Jovanovich, *Customs Valuation and Transfer Pricing: Is It Possible to Harmonize Customs and Tax Rules?,* Second Edition, 2018 (ISBN 978-90-411-6134-5).
29. Stefano Simontacchi, *Taxation of Capital Gains under the OECD Model Convention: With Special Regard to Immovable Property,* 2007 (ISBN 978-90-411-2549-1).
30. Michael Lang, Josef Schuch, & Claus Staringer (eds), *Tax Treaty Law and EC Law,* 2007 (ISBN 978-90-411-2629-0).
31. Duncan Bentley, *Taxpayers' Rights: Theory Origin and Implementation,* 2007 (ISBN 978-90-411-2650-4).
32. Sergio André Rocha, *Interpretation of Double Taxation Conventions: General Theory and Brazilian Perspective,* 2008 (ISBN 978-90-411-2822-5).
33. Robert F. van Brederode, *Systems of General Sales Taxation: Theory, Policy and Practice,* 2009 (ISBN 978-90-411-2832-4).
34. John G. Head & Richard Krever (eds), *Tax Reform in the 21st Century: A Volume in Memory of Richard Musgrave,* 2009 (ISBN 978-90-411-2829-4).
35. Jens Wittendorff, *Transfer Pricing and the Arm's Length Principle in International Tax Law,* 2010 (ISBN 978-90-411-3270-3).
36. Marjaana Helminen, *The International Tax Law Concept of Dividend,* Second Edition, 2017 (ISBN 978-90-411-8394-1).
37. Robert F. van Brederode (ed.), *Immovable Property under VAT: A Comparative Global Analysis,* 2011 (ISBN 978-90-411-3126-3).
38. Dennis Weber & Stef van Weeghel, *The 2010 OECD Updates: Model Tax Convention & Transfer Pricing Guidelines - A Critical Review,* 2011 (ISBN 978-90-411-3812-5).
39. Yariv Brauner & Martin James McMahon, Jr. (eds), *The Proper Tax Base: Structural Fairness from an International and Comparative Perspective— Essays in Honour of Paul McDaniel,* 2012 (ISBN 978-90-411-3286-4).
40. Robert F. van Brederode (ed.), *Science, Technology and Taxation,* 2012 (ISBN 978-90-411-3125-6).

41. Oskar Henkow, *The VAT/GST Treatment of Public Bodies*, 2013 (ISBN 978-90-411-4663-2).
42. Jean Schaffner, *How Fixed Is a Permanent Establishment?*, 2013 (ISBN 978-90-411-4662-5).
43. Miguel Correia, *Taxation of Corporate Groups*, 2013 (ISBN 978-90-411-4841-4).
44. Veronika Daurer, *Tax Treaties and Developing Countries*, 2014 (ISBN 978-90-411-4982-4).
45. Claire Micheau, *State Aid, Subsidy and Tax Incentives under EU and WTO Law*, 2014 (ISBN 978-90-411-4555-0).
46. Robert F. van Brederode & Richard Krever (eds), *Legal Interpretation of Tax Law*, 2014 (ISBN 978-90-411-4945-9).
47. Radhakishan Rawal, *Taxation of Cross-border Services*, 2014 (ISBN 978-90-411-4947-3).
48. João Dácio Rolim, *Proportionality and Fair Taxation*, 2014 (ISBN 978-90-411-5838-3).
49. Paulo Rosenblatt, *General Anti-avoidance Rules for Major Developing Countries*, 2015 (ISBN 978-90-411-5839-0).
50. Gaspar Lopes Dias V.S., *Tax Arbitrage through Cross-Border Financial Engineering*, 2015 (ISBN 978-90-411-5875-8).
51. Geerten M.M. Michielse & Victor Thuronyi (eds), *Tax Design Issues Worldwide*, 2015 (ISBN 978-90-411-5610-5).
52. Oktavia Weidmann, *Taxation of Derivatives and Cryptoassets*, Second Edition, 2024 (ISBN 978-94-035-2383-5).
53. Chris Evans, Richard Krever & Peter Mellor (eds), *Tax Simplification*, 2015 (ISBN 978-90-411-5976-2).
54. Reuven Avi-Yonah & Joel Slemrod (eds), *Taxation and Migration*, 2015 (ISBN 978-90-411-6136-9).
55. Alexander Bosman, *Other Income under Tax Treaties: An Analysis of Article 21 of the OECD Model Convention*, 2015 (ISBN 978-90-411-6610-4).
56. John Abrahamson, *International Taxation of Manufacturing and Distribution*, 2016 (ISBN 978-90-411-6664-7).
57. Frederik Boulogne, *Shortcomings in the EU Merger Directive*, 2016 (ISBN 978-90-411-6713-2).
58. Angelika Meindl-Ringler, *Beneficial Ownership in International Tax Law*, 2016 (ISBN 978-90-411-6833-7).
59. Andreas Waltrich, *Cross-Border Taxation of Permanent Establishments: An International Comparison*, 2016 (ISBN 978-90-411-6832-0).
60. Sergio André Rocha & Allison Christians (eds), *Tax Sovereignty in the BEPS Era*, 2017 (ISBN 978-90-411-6707-1).
61. Peter Antony Wilson, *BRICS and International Tax Law*, 2018 (ISBN 978-90-411-9435-0).
62. Louise Otis, Brigitte Alepin & Blanca Moreno-Dodson (eds), *Winning the Tax Wars: Tax Competition and Cooperation*, 2018 (ISBN 978-90-411-9460-2).

63. Marta Castelon, *International Taxation of Income from Services under Double Taxation Conventions: Development, Practice and Policy*, 2018 (ISBN 978-90-411-9594-4).
64. D.M. Broekhuijsen, *A Multilateral Tax Treaty: Designing an Instrument to Modernise International Tax Law*, 2018 (ISBN 978-90-411-9872-3).
65. John Abrahamson, *International Taxation of Energy Production and Distribution*, 2018 (ISBN 978-90-411-9101-4).
66. Leopoldo Parada, *Double Non-taxation and the Use of Hybrid Entities*, Second Edition, 2024 (ISBN 978-94-035-4666-7).
67. Richard Snoeij, *International Tax Aspects of Sovereign Wealth Investors: A Source State Perspective*, 2018 (ISBN 978-90-411-9431-2).
68. Aleksandra Bal, *Taxation, Virtual Currency and Blockchain*, 2019 (ISBN 978-94-035-0103-1).
69. Werner Haslehner, Georg Kofler, Katerina Pantazatou & Alexander Rust (eds), *Tax and the Digital Economy: Challenges and Proposals for Reform*, 2019 (ISBN 978-94-035-0361-5).
70. Eva Escribano, *Jurisdiction to Tax Corporate Income Pursuant to the Presumptive Benefit Principle: A Critical Analysis of Structural Paradigms Underlying Corporate Income Taxation and Proposals for Reform*, 2019 (ISBN 978-94-035-0640-1).
71. Jérôme Monsenego & Jan Bjuvberg (eds), *International Taxation in a Changing Landscape: Liber Amicorum in Honour of Bertil Wiman*, 2019 (ISBN 978-90-411-9234-9).
72. Kasper Dziurdź, *Non-discrimination in Tax Treaty Law and World Trade Law: The Impact of Formal, Substantive and Subjective Approaches*, 2019 (ISBN 978-94-035-0904-4).
73. Félix Daniel Martínez Laguna, *Hybrid Financial Instruments, Double Nontaxation and Linking Rules*, 2019 (ISBN 978-94-035-1074-3).
74. Jan Gooijer, *Tax Treaty Residence of Entities*, 2019 (ISBN 978-94-035-1301-0).
75. John Abrahamson, *International Taxation of Banking*, 2020 (ISBN 978-94-035-1094-1).
76. Richard Krever & François Vaillancourt (eds), *The Allocation of Multinational Business Income: Reassessing the Formulary Apportionment Option*, 2020 (ISBN 978-94-035-0614-2).
77. Ajit Kumar Singh, *Exploring the Nexus Doctrine in International Tax Law*, 2021 (ISBN 978-94-035-3363-6).
78. Galya Savir, *Regulation and Tax in Space*, 2021 (ISBN 978-94-035-3393-3).
79. Rita Julien, *Credit Method Compatibility and Constraints under EU Law: An Analysis of the Case Law of the CJEU*, 2022 (ISBN 978-94-035-2363-7).
80. Sergio André Rocha & Allison Christians (eds), *A Multilateral Convention for Tax: From Theory to Implementation*, 2022 (ISBN 978-90-411-9428-2).
81. Brigitte Alepin, Lyne Latulippe & Louise Otis (eds), *Coordination and Cooperation: Tax Policy in the 21st Century*, 2022 (ISBN 978-94-035-3740-5).
82. Chunyang Zhang, *The Role of Tax Law in Mergers and Acquisitions: A Chinese Perspective*, 2022 (ISBN 978-94-035-3741-2).

83. Florian Navisotschnigg, *Substance in International Tax Law: DEMPE Approach, Substantial Activity Requirement and Beneficial Ownership*, 2022 (ISBN 978-94-035-4895-1).
84. Mees Vergouwen, *The Effect of Directives Within the Area of Direct Taxation on the Interpretation and Application of Tax Treaties*, 2023 (ISBN 978-94-035-0907-5).
85. Rachna Matabudul, *Tax Treaty Dispute Resolution: Lessons from the Law of the Sea*, 2023 (ISBN 978-94-035-3407-7).
86. David Orzechowski-Zölzer, *The Taxation of Fees for Technical Services on the Basis of Article 12A UN Model Convention*, 2024 (ISBN 978-94-035-4297-3).
87. David Rüll, *The Resolution of International Tax Disputes: From the Established Mechanisms Towards an Institutionalised International Instrument*, 2024 (ISBN 978-94-035-2088-9).
88. Savvas Kostikidis, *Residence and Economic Substance of Subsidiary Corporations in International and European Tax Law*, 2024 (ISBN 978-94-035-3858-7).
89. Céline Braumann, *Customary International Law and Tax Jurisdiction*, 2025 (ISBN 9789-40-353-888-4).
90. Sophia Piotrowski, *Fiscal State Aid Schemes: Selectivity and Limits to Enforcement*, 2025 (ISBN 978-94-035-0389-9).
91. Benjamín Sevilla Bernabéu, *General Anti-Avoidance Rules: A Comparative, International and European Perspective*, 2025 (ISBN 978-94-035-2489-4).
92. Jie Wang, *Reconsidering Formulary Apportionment in the Post-BEPS Era*, 2025 (ISBN 978-94-035-2729-1).
93. Siddhesh Rao, *Defining Beneficial Ownership: Implications for Preventing Tax Avoidance and Tax Evasion-Related IFFs in Africa*, 2026 (ISBN 978-94-035-4559-2).

www.ingramcontent.com/pod-product-compliance
Ingram Content Group UK Ltd.
Pitfield, Milton Keynes, MK11 3LW, UK
UKHW020820290926
15470UKWH00003B/1283

9 789403 545592